IN DARKNESS, A
Light STILL SHINES

52 Stories of Hope
Gleaned from the Homeless, Poor, and those who Care for Them

BARRY F. FEAKER
WITH
TAMI R. FEAKER & JESSICA S. HOSMAN

IN DARKNESS, A LIGHT STILL SHINES

Cover design by James Kresge (pixelfixgraphics.com)
Cover photo by Jim Sovanski (sovanskiphoto.com)
In cover photo: Enrique Acuna
Text reviewed by Tami Feaker, Jackie Fraenza, Terry Hund, Debi Smith, Kevin Swift and Monica Urban

ISBN-13: 978-0615730646 (Topeka Rescue Mission)
ISBN-10: 0615730647
Printed in the United States of America.

Table of Contents

Acknowledgements – *Giving Thanks* v

Purpose – *The "Why" Behind the Story* vii

Introduction – *Finding Purpose* xi

Chapters ....

   Chapter 1 - A Drunk in the Street 1

   Chapter 2 - Scary Guy with the Big Heart...........................7

   Chapter 3 - An Angelic Encounter? 13

   Chapter 4 - The Beginnings of Rescue 19

   Chapter 5 - The Best Christmas 23

   Chapter 6 - Cooking with Umbrellas....................................29

   Chapter 7 - The 600-Year-Old Man 33

   Chapter 8 - Learning to Love Those Who Are Different....43

   Chapter 9 - The Beauty and the Beast.................................49

   Chapter 10 - Learning to Skate...57

   Chapter 11 - When I'm Tempted to Run 63

   Chapter 12 -Ground Beef...69

   Chapter 13 - Eggs, Milk and Butter 73

   Chapter 14 - Shredded Lettuce 77

   Chapter 15 -Homeless in Chicago 81

   Chapter 16 -The Worst Disease...89

   Chapter 17 -The Intruder 97

   Chapter 18 -One Vet's Story..103

Table of Contents - Continued

Chapter 19 – Desperation 109

Chapter 20 – The Freezer 119

Chapter 21 – The Lure of Compromise 123

Chapter 22 – The Man with the Gun...........................127

Chapter 23 – From Awkward to Amazing.........................133

Chapter 24 – The Kiss...139

Chapter 25 – Laying Down Their Lives..........................145

Chapter 26 – Standing in the Midst of Falling.................151

Chapter 27 – Acquiring the Impossible 155

Chapter 28 – The Praying Man 161

Chapter 29 – Underground Fuel Tanks 167

Chapter 30 – Finding Rest – The Story of George 171

Chapter 31 – Kitty - An Unlikely Messenger 177

Chapter 32 – Hope in the Storm 183

Chapter 33 – Something to Give 189

Chapter 34 – What Have I Done? 195

Chapter 35 – Walking in His Steps.............................201

Chapter 36 – A Love Story.....................................207

Chapter 37 – The Gift 213

Chapter 38 – One Man's Chapter 219

Chapter 39 – Searching for Love...............................227

Table of Contents - Continued

Chapter 40 – Should We Let Him Die? 235

Chapter 41 – The Look 241

Chapter 42 – The Impact and Sacrifice of One 247

Chapter 43 – Miracle in Topeka, Kansas 255

Chapter 44 – Daddy, Make Me a Promise........................263

Chapter 45 – The Darkest of Nights.............................267

Chapter 46 – The Long Bus Ride 275

Chapter 47 – Listening to the Still Small Voice................285

Chapter 48 – Becoming Barry....................................291

Chapter 49 – The Fish with a Coin 295

Chapter 50 – Thank You for Keeping Me........................301

Chapter 51 – Pray God Will Kill Me.............................307

Chapter 52 – Mending a Broken Heart..........................315

Conclusion – *It's Never Too Late* 325

Appendix 329

Appendix One -   About the Author – Barry Feaker 329

Appendix Two -   On the Cover – Tami Feaker 331

Appendix Three -   On the Cover – Jessica Hosman 333

Appendix Four -   About the Topeka Rescue Mission 335

Appendix Five -   Subject Index............................. 337

ACKNOWLEDGEMENTS

Giving Thanks

*"I thank my God, making mention of
thee always in my prayers."*
Philemon 1:4

My deepest thanks and appreciation to a very patient, loving, merciful God who, for reasons that are still mysterious to me, called me to this work of rescue; as well as an incredible Savior that I have come to know and love more with each passing day.

I am grateful to my mother and father who gave me life and ingrained into me a lifestyle of service, which helped to lay a foundation for the work I do today.

Special thanks to my wife, Tami, for stepping out in faith to follow Christ by reaching out to those who suffer even in the midst of her own daily health challenges. *Thank you for enduring long nights and long days, living sacrificially, and encouraging me to hang in there when at times I felt like giving up. Thank you for being a partner in our pioneering efforts to help those in need and make our community a better place to live. Thank you for living these stories with me.*

To my little buddies, my daughters now grown, Rebecca and Elizabeth, who have sacrificed and shared in the growth of this ministry. *Your love and support for Dad has meant more than you can know. I could not have moved forward apart from your support.*

Thank you to the Topeka Rescue Mission Board of Directors, volunteers, contributors, prayer partners and the many staff who have sacrificed their financial security and worked long, hard hours with very little recognition. You truly exemplify "faith with its sleeves rolled up."

Appreciation to Tami Feaker, Jackie Fraenza, Terry Hund, Debi Smith, Kevin Swift and Monica Urban for taking the time to read and review the text of this book and for providing feedback and insight. As well as James Kresge, Jim Sovanski and Enrique Acuna for contributing to the excellent cover design.

Many thanks to Jessica Hosman for translating these stories and their applications from my thoughts to the pages in this book.

Great appreciation and thanks for the key people in my life who have helped to prop me up in times of darkness when I have been weak... you know who you are.

Also, I want to especially thank those who have helped me to truly see the love of God and taught me some of the most invaluable lessons in my life... those who are and have been homeless, poor and broken. Your lives matter in this world more than you possibly know. Thank you for making a tremendous difference in mine.

The "Why" Behind the Story

"And the Lord answered me,
and said, 'Write the vision,
and make it plain upon tables,
that he may run that readeth it."
Habakkuk 2:2

The stories found in this book have not always been enjoyable ones to experience. While each one is purposed to bring encouragement and hope, it has often been through darkness and discouragement that the inspiration and lessons for each one has come. It is through these experiences I have learned and realized that even in darkness, a light still shines...

For over twenty-five years, I have served at the Topeka Rescue Mission. During this time, I have faced challenges more immense than I ever imagined possible. Many times, the struggles amidst the lives of the broken individuals who have come through the doors of the Mission experiencing homelessness, addiction and illness have been more overwhelming than I can adequately describe. Yet today, I am witnessing the same levels of hopelessness and despair emerging through all walks of life to a staggering degree. Broken relationships, financial uncertainties, and seemingly impossible situations are plaguing multitudes, tempting them to give up on life. That is the reason for this book. My prayer in sharing these writings is that you would be encouraged and reminded that, whatever you face in life, there is always hope for a brighter tomorrow.

While the stories shared provide a snapshot into some of the events that have occurred in my life since arriving at the Mission, the real purpose in writing them is to record some of the lessons I have learned and truths that have been revealed in some of my darkest and most challenging moments.

When the Israelites had finally been released from the grips of Pharaoh, they quickly encountered another challenge. The vastness of the Red Sea was before them. The situation looked impossible and there seemed to be no way to continue walking forward without tasting death. In their fear and uncertainty God spoke, "Don't be afraid... be still... and move forward" (Exodus 14:13).

My life and the experiences I have faced have been a lot like the Israelites. I have been challenged, gained victory, and then almost immediately faced another impossible circumstance which prevented me from moving forward. I have been left numerous times with the same question as they, "What can I do when I have nowhere to turn?" I have been unable to go backwards, yet seemingly blocked from moving ahead. It has been in those times when I have been reminded that, regardless of what is before or behind me, I can trust God with my life and still find the strength to go on.

I am not, and will never claim to be, a perfected man of faith. While I have tried to pursue such a life, I have been guilty of faltering when faced with life's challenges. While others might view my faith to be great, it is really through the faith of others that I have learned to be strong.

There are numerous lives I have had the privilege of encountering through the years which have been invaluable in my growth and walk with God. Through their struggles, sacrifice, dedication and love for God, my eyes have been opened and my horizons widened. Whether it has been a homeless individual coming to the Mission for shelter, a donor giving a timely gift, or an unexpected word of encouragement from someone I knew, each encounter has left a significant imprint on my life and been used by God to strengthen my resolve and help me to continue pressing forward, even when times have been rough.

While it would be impossible to capture the fullness of what has been revealed to me over these years, this book is my attempt to give an inside view of how each of us can learn, grow and experience more out of each and every day. It is divided into 52 short chapters and can serve as a weekly devotional to last throughout the year, or can be used as a method of inspiration when a breath of encouragement is needed. While the stories are recorded chronologically, they do not have to be read in any particular order. For your convenience, a subject index is listed at the back of this book.

Each story begins with a scripture and ends with an application and prayer. The prayers are short and simplistic for the purpose of guiding your conversations with God. While they touch on key components of the story and application read, they are not meant to serve as the sole communication between you and the Lord, but rather a catalyst for deeper prayer and conversation once the story ends.

You will notice that this book is not a literary work of excellence. While sentences may seem unstructured or lacking in technique, I pray that you will be able to see past the imperfections and into my heart. My aim was to share as though you and I were conversing, rather than focusing on formal grammatical detail.

Even though some of the names throughout this book have been changed to protect the privacy of persons involved, all stories are true records of factual events that have occurred in my life as I remember them. The challenges surrounding each one have been immense; yet, I still stand amazed at the way God can bring treasure and light out of the darkness faced. As I share excerpts from various encounters, I pray that you too can see the hope of light for the path you face. While your life is unique and it sometimes feels as though there is no way out from overwhelming circumstances you face, there really is always hope. There is not one situation you can experience that will ever be too difficult for God. As His Word says, the darkness can never fully extinguish the light that eternally shines (John 1:5, paraphrased).

Whether you are a Christian or not, if you have ever faced discouragement, hopelessness or fear, I pray this book helps you. It is not an attempt to convert you into a particular religion; it is an attempt to offer you hope for your future and purpose for your life. May you find that and more as you embark on the journey before you.

My prayer for you as you begin…

Dear Lord,

You know every detail of the person's life that holds this book in their hands. You know the trials and discouragement they face, and the answers they seek. I pray as they read through the pages before them that they will experience their true hope and purpose for living. May all hopelessness flee as they open up their hearts to receive from You.

In Jesus' Name. Amen.

Finding Purpose

*"...I am come that they might have
life, and that they might have it
more abundantly."*
John 10:10

*Before becoming the Executive Director of the Topeka
Rescue Mission, there were many stepping stones and struggles I
had to overcome along the way. For many years, I went through
the motions of life without much sense of fulfillment or joy. I was
hungering for more of God and more out of life but, in time, I
realized it was in all of the wrong places that I sought...*

When I was twelve years old, I attended a Billy
Graham Crusade. Touched by the message and impact I felt,
I went to the altar and accepted Jesus Christ into my heart.
While it was a powerful moment, my life didn't begin to
really change until over a decade later.

I was working at the Menninger Psychiatric Hospital
and had finally arrived at a place in my career where I was
satisfied and content. I had been married for a couple of
years and finally started attending church with my wife,
Tami. Though I had made the commitment for Christ many
years prior, I had never really pursued a relationship with
Him.

During the summer of 1980, a friend introduced me to
an evangelist by the name of Jerry Boaz who was hosting a
week-long revival in Topeka, Kansas. After we chatted for a

few minutes, Jerry handed me his Bible and had me read from Romans 1:22: *Professing themselves to be wise, they became fools.* I looked up at him with bewilderment and unbelief as he began to insinuate the passage was pertaining to me. I was highly offended. I felt like I had finally arrived and attained what I had gone to school for and strived at for many years. Now, a man I did not know was mocking me? I walked away from him angry and insulted.

As the days progressed, my curiosity got the best of me and I decided I had to see what kind of message this man could possibly be sharing with others. I went to a meeting and was shocked to hear the evangelist, who had irritated me so, speaking with a great sense of passion and conviction. The longer he spoke, the more the Holy Spirit began penetrating my heart. I could now see that my life was not fully surrendered to the Lord. I went to church on Sundays, but that was where the relationship stopped. No other depth was present in my walk.

The more I listened to the words being spoken, the more I realized that my entire life was to be about Christ... not just a portion of it. I began sensing God was going to send me somewhere that I would serve Him full-time. Though I didn't understand, I accepted what I believed God was speaking.

While I had once been satisfied and proud of the accomplishments I had achieved, the passion quickly began to fade. My quest for more began and, by August of that same year, Tami and I packed up our belongings and moved to Kansas City where we began attending Bible School.

Years of equipping, challenges and further growth of my faith swiftly passed as I found work in various ministries. While I felt I should have been happy, with each new Christian endeavor I began, I was left questioning my faith and desiring more out of life and my relationship with

God. Through profession I was serving Him full-time, but I felt fruitless and empty inside. Over and over again I thought that surely there was more to the Christian walk than what I was experiencing.

A few years passed and the dryness of my life seemed to increase with each passing day. I was miserable. It felt like God had put me on the shelf and nothing I put my hands to would bear fruit. I was grieving the death of my dad and continually stressing out about our meager finances. Because money was needed to support my family and I was not faring well in ministry, I eventually went back to the familiar field of mental health where I had worked prior. When I returned, the only position available was a significant demotion from when I had left. I dreaded getting up every morning, and my attitude was horrible. It wasn't until a friend and fellow colleague of mine asked me a question that I truly realized how bad it was.

"What are you doing here?" my friend asked one day. "Have you been called to serve in ministry?" he proceeded to ask. Honestly, I wasn't sure about anything at that point in my life. I had no idea what God expected of me, or what it was that I was supposed to be doing. I was still doing some part-time ministry with youth, but the time I was devoting to the Lord's work through ministry was sparse in comparison to the hours I was working at Topeka State Hospital.

My friend reminded me there was a possibility that I was supposed to be serving the Lord full-time through the State Hospital, but then he opened my eyes further. Boldly, he told me that even if I was where God wanted me to be, my attitude was so bad He couldn't use me. He suggested I get right with God... now. Through those words the conviction came. I knew I needed to find my contentment in Him, regardless of where He placed me in life. I repented to the Lord and earnestly told Him that, from that point forward, I would do whatever He wanted me to do, wherever He wanted me to do it. Even so, my heart's cry still remained: *Would You please put me somewhere where You are actively working in the world today?* I had heard about the ways in which He moved so mightily in foreign lands and was desperate to see the same in my life.

I decided to further my training and became ordained in ministry. I had always thought the ultimate service God wanted for my life was to become a pastor; maybe then I would finally experience the abundant life Jesus spoke of in His Word. When a church contacted me with this exact request, I was hopeful and thought everything was finally falling into place. It made sense for me to take the position. It was what I had given my life for, and it was what I believed God would want. But each time I prayed, I kept sensing He was instead telling me, "No." *What was I missing? Was I not to become a full-time pastor after all?* Obediently, I turned down the position and was left feeling confused and distressed once again.

Not long after, I received a surprise phone call from my insurance agent. He was serving on the Board of Directors at the Topeka Rescue Mission and, to my astonishment, was calling me about a ministry opportunity that was available. I was not interested in the slightest and immediately turned him down.

I had not given the conversation a second thought when, days later, I was approached by a deacon in the church I attended. He also served on the Mission's Board and came to me with the same scenario. Again, not interested, I tried to make my posture known. This member, however, was a bit more persistent in his pursuit. Out of frustration and an attempt to get him off of my back more than anything else, I scribbled down my work history onto a piece of paper and earnestly hoped I would not hear back from him on the subject ever again.

It was months later when I received an invitation from that same Board member asking me to meet him in the old Mission building for coffee. Thinking this was just an old friend who wanted to get together to chat, I naively agreed. When I arrived at the Mission, I was shocked to find four Board members sitting around a table waiting for me... none of which included my friend who had given the invitation.

Wasting no time Leonard Johnson, the Board treasurer since 1959 who still serves faithfully today, turned to me and asked, "Why do you want the job at the Mission?" I was shocked. I didn't want the job and had no idea what he was talking about! Trying not to make my absent friend look too terribly bad, I began stammering over my words and stalling as I wondered about the best way to respond. Before I knew it, it was as if the Lord took a hold of my tongue and words I could have never come up with on my own began flowing from my mouth. I didn't even know what the Mission currently consisted of so I was flabbergasted when the Lord spoke through me of what it could one day be!

The men sat and listened with intrigue. Then the next question came, "Can you do the job?" I still didn't know what the job was, so I immediately answered, "No." As I paused, however, God took control once again and had me continue, "but with God, all things are possible."

I went home that night and shared the details of the bizarre events with Tami. As I did, she immediately confirmed what was stirring in my heart. She too thought I was supposed to be directing the Topeka Rescue Mission. Within a few days, I received a call from the Board president asking me to come in for a second interview with the entire twenty-four member Board for the position of Executive Director.

When I arrived for the interview, I was extremely embarrassed to see copies of my make-shift resume being passed around the table. I sat down and was acutely aware of what the Board members were whispering to one another. Some looked at the resume and murmured of my lack of professionalism and rescue mission experience. Others shook their head at my age saying that twenty-nine was entirely too young for such a huge endeavor. I felt my face becoming flushed and inwardly prayed for the Lord to have His way. The interview lasted for two intense hours and as it concluded, the Board made a point to let me know there were ten other applicants they were considering, and each had a wealth of experience in the field.

Though it looked impossible and unlikely in the natural, I left the interview filled with excitement, peace and a knowing that God was at work. I felt assured that in time I would be offered the position. Within hours, the call I was anticipating arrived, but the offer came with just one tiny glitch. The Mission was struggling financially and was only prepared to offer me a part-time salary. I had a wife, two small children, and a home. The Board was aware of this and knew the type of salary they were presenting would not work. They asked me to pray about a figure which I could afford, and said that they would be doing the same.

Tami and I prayed and asked the Lord for clarification on what my new salary should be. As we did, I saw a figure flash before my mind. Though it was still substantially less than what we could afford, we both believed that if the Lord had revealed it, then He would provide for all of our needs and bless our decision.

A follow-up meeting with four members of the Executive Board was scheduled for two days later, and I went with the figure in hand. Before I could say a word, Leonard told me that the Board had been praying and he pulled an index card from out of his coat. As he laid it on the table I looked at the card and immediately recognized the figure... it was the exact amount God had shown me just days before. He asked if it would be acceptable and I just smiled. God had let me know beyond a shadow of a doubt that His hand was on the decision and I accepted the position. For more than twenty-five years I have remained and experienced more of God through those who are homeless, addicted, poor and broken, than I ever thought possible.

There was a season that lasted for years when I was discontent, unhappy and felt like I was just going through the motions of life. Nothing I put my hands to excited me, and I felt as though I was just taking up space on this earth. I knew there was more, but I didn't know how to get there. What I realized in hindsight was that there was nothing God was requiring me to do other than fully surrender to Him. Once I did, He took the reins and orchestrated the details of my life to ensure I was placed exactly where He wanted me to be. It was then the passions in my life were able to blossom and bloom into the fullness of what I desired and God had intended all along.

God has placed individual and unique passions inside each one of us. What is it that stirs your heart and really makes you excited about life?

For me, I was so busy focusing on what I thought I should be doing that I lost sight of what I was created to be doing. In turn, I was chronically weary and discontent. It wasn't until I opened myself up to the idea of something new that the Lord was able to put me into the place *He desired,* so that I could experience the abundance of life *I desired.*

Are you one who is tired and weary, spinning in circles or desiring more of God? It starts with a pursuit. A turning to God and openness to embrace what He's already placed within. The passions inside of you are there for a reason. And the reason is not so they would stay buried and unclaimed. Jesus said, "I came to give *you* life, more and better than you ever dreamed of!" (John 10:10, the Message). How many of us can say we're experiencing that? Often the reason we are not is because we're busy doing what we think we have to do, versus being the person God designed us to be.

Let this be the time you start dreaming again. Start by asking yourself what the passions are that lie deep inside. Then ask the Lord to draw them up and put you into the place where you can fully be the person He created you to be. Don't settle for less. You're far too precious and important to this world.

Dear Lord,

May I not settle for less than who it is You say I am. Let me see who it is that You have created me to be. Reveal the passions You've given that have been buried within. Stir them up in my heart. Use them and use me to bring life to others in this world. Open the doors and guide my steps so that I might fully embrace the abundance of life Your Son has to give.

In Jesus' Name. Amen.

CHAPTER ONE

A Drunk in the Street

*"... the Lord seeth not as man seeth;
for a man looketh on the outward
appearance, but the Lord
looketh on the heart."*
1 Samuel 16:7

The judgments of man can bring destruction and pain, but the love of God will bring healing and peace. On my first day at the Mission, I was faced with an opportunity to choose between the two. It was through my encounter with an elderly stranger that the Lord showed me there is always more that lies within, beyond what my natural eyes can see...

It was April 21, 1986. My first day as new Executive Director at the Topeka Rescue Mission.

I had no idea what to expect. I walked through the doors and was greeted by a guest of the Mission who was working behind the front desk. He was tiny, no more than seventy-pounds, and was practically swallowed up by the big taped up leather chair in which he sat. Enthusiastically, I introduced myself and then hinted for a guidance of sorts. Without looking at me, he pointed around the corner and casually said with a cigar hanging loosely from his mouth, "You should probably go to your office."

I walked down the hall and into my new office as my eyes surveyed the surroundings. I gazed upon the dreary brown paneling that covered the four walls. Resting inside sat an old beat-up desk and worn leather chair held together by nothing but dirty and frayed duct tape. I sat down and exhaled slowly. I was the only staff member and I had no idea what to do.

The day went by fairly uneventfully as I tried to acclimate to my surroundings while curious guests popped in and out of my office.

It was around two o'clock when my phone rang for the first time. On the other line was a nearby business owner whom I had never met. I could tell he was eager to speak to someone in charge and he abruptly asked if I was the new director. When I confirmed I was, he told me there was "a drunk" walking down the middle of the street towards the Mission with his pants pulled down. He was clearly disgusted and told me I needed to do something about it quickly. I thanked him for the information and promptly rushed outside. Ten inquisitive men, who were already suspicious of me invading their territory, followed closely behind eager to see what I was going to do.

I looked north and immediately spotted a man who was slowly shuffling down the street in our direction with his trousers dropped down around his ankles. He appeared elderly, his body was thin and his skin extremely weathered. His clothes were dirty and tattered. The closer he came I was able to realize he was not intoxicated at all, but instead worn and aged beyond his years.

The man stuck out his hand in a gesture for help up to the sidewalk where I stood. I helped him up the curb and with his head down he timidly asked if I had a belt. I was not sure if I heard him correctly. "A belt," he softly continued. "I need a belt to keep my pants up." I awkwardly looked at the watchful onlookers who had followed me outside and asked if we had an extra belt. One of the men thought he could find one and ran inside to check.

As we waited, I asked the man if he needed a place to stay or something to eat. He declined them both but when I asked if he was thirsty, his eyes lit up and he immediately said, "Yes." A couple of the men brought him some water from inside and he eagerly guzzled down five large glasses as we waited for the belt to be obtained.

Within a few minutes, a man from inside the Mission returned with a makeshift belt he had managed to find. I handed it to the man but, when I did, he paused and bashfully looked into my eyes. "I am so sorry," he humbly began, "but I broke my back years ago in a construction accident and I can't pull my pants up. Will you pull my pants up for me?"

At first my heart sank and then started pounding as I froze for a brief moment wondering how to respond. Here I was, the new director of the Rescue Mission, standing on the sidewalk with half of the Mission's population watching me with crossed arms just waiting to see what I was going to do. I felt pressured and knew I couldn't mess this up. *Was it appropriate for me to do this, or should I ask someone else?* Looking back into the man's desperate eyes, I quickly made the decision. I reached down, pulled up his trousers and laced the belt around his tiny waist. He was literally skin and bones.

I asked if I could help with anything else, but he declined. He stuck out his hand once again to grab onto mine. He squeezed my hand hard and looking deep into my eyes said with all sincerity, "Thank you... God bless you." He then turned and walked away. The guests quickly disbursed as I watched the man slowly disappear back down the street. I never saw him again.

When I first received the phone call about the allegedly drunken man, I envisioned just that. But, while the man from a distance appeared to be drunk and staggering, in reality he was injured and elderly. The story I supposed to be true was completely different from what was actually taking place.

When Jesus's original disciples walked the earth, many people examined them with criticism, skepticism and mockery. One particular day when they were observing the disciples they reasoned they must have been drunk. They didn't understand their behaviors and could come up with no other explanation. But Peter stood up and boldly defended them by declaring, "They are not drunk as you suppose..." (Acts 2:15).

Perhaps you have experienced a situation similar to the disciples or the man with the pants. While you walked through the streets of life, others may have wrongly judged you or failed to see past the outside characteristics displayed. Such misperceptions can cause pain and hurt deep within our hearts. But, just as Peter was willing to stand up and defend the men he knew, God offers that same defense to us.

Regardless of what others may say, it is God's Word that stands true. He knows you... He knows the plans He has for you which are good and not evil (Jeremiah 29:11). He says you are accepted and assures that you are eternally loved (Ephesians 1:6, Jeremiah 31:3). While the words of people can hurt, He is more than able to soothe the pain and erase the scars.

God looks within. He sees the dirt and blemishes, but He also sees the treasure buried deep underneath. He doesn't judge us based on what the world sees; He loves us based on the heart He knows. This is true for us... and others. Every life is a gift. None is perfect, but none is either wasted. Within each one is a gold that shines pure and bright. May our eyes be open to see that gift in ourselves and the countless others who cross our paths every day.

Dear Lord,

I want to see through Your eyes. Help me to cast all judgments and hurts aside as I go through my days. When I look in the mirror, help me to see gold. May that same treasure be found when I look into the eyes of others I see.

In Jesus' Name. Amen.

CHAPTER TWO

The Scary Guy with the Big Heart

*"For I reckon that the sufferings of
this present time are not worthy to be
compared with the glory which shall
be revealed in us."*
Romans 8:18

*There have been times in my life when I have become so
consumed with what was wrong that I failed to see all that was
good. Through Terrance, God showed me that as long as I have
breath in my body, there is always hope for a brighter tomorrow.
May his story encourage your heart in the same way it has mine...*

A smile still forms on my face today when I think of
Terrance. He had arrived at the Mission just a week after me
and though our ages paralleled, our experiences did not. We
were both thirty-years-old, but our lives up to that point had
told entirely different tales.

Terrance was an extremely large African-American
man who had experienced discrimination on multiple levels
throughout his entire life. Because of his huge muscular
stature he was feared, even though in reality he was one of
the kindest people I have ever met. He spent his childhood
in group homes and foster care. In time, he developed
problems with drugs and alcohol and spent portions of his
life in jail. Now, he was homeless and suffering from a
severe case of schizophrenia.

I saw Terrance for the first time when I walked into the Mission's kitchen. Because our supplies were less than adequate, he had cleverly discovered that the back of a spoon, though less timely than a peeler, could be used to skin a potato. He would spend hours peeling potatoes and, as he did, he would quietly converse with the unseen others in his mind who only he could hear.

Terrance had struggled greatly with formal education and therefore had limited reading abilities. Combining those factors with his severe mental health disorder, substance abuse and history of incarceration, his chances of ever leaving the Mission to live on his own were very slim.

In spite of his challenges, Terrance was a dedicated worker and, regardless of the task given to him, he never complained. He diligently put his all into every assignment at hand. I found out quickly that, although Terrance had been assigned and loved to work in the kitchen, the poor guy could not cook. I knew he would be with us for a while and I needed to find a better place for him to serve. The only other place at the Mission that had an opening available was the overnight shift at the front desk. I decided to give him a chance.

He was elated at the opportunity and did great for a while. He was very polite when talking with people on the phone. Additionally, his kind demeanor allowed him to utilize his gentleness without putting others in the position of fear that his stature often evoked.

He did well for a number of weeks and his mental health really seemed to stabilize. The guests liked him and his work on the phones was going great. Suddenly, signs of deterioration began and reports of Terrance talking to people who weren't really there began coming my way.

Late one night I received a call at my home from a guest of the Mission. He had snuck down the street to a payphone and called to let me know there was a huge fight going on. It was so loud that it had stirred him awake and he asked if I could get there right away. I drove as fast as I could, fully expecting the worst. As I rushed through the doors, I was shocked to find Terrance in the state I did. Calmly, he sat behind the front desk gently leafing through a magazine unaware of anything else going on.

I approached him and asked what had happened. He looked up at me confused. "The fight," I said, "Tell me what happened with the fight." Still oblivious, Terrance told me nothing eventful had taken place the entire night and that he had no idea what I was talking about. I continued to press, but his stance remained the same. According to Terrance, no fights had occurred.

I left the front desk and set out to talk with the other men who were awake. What I found out was that the fight had occurred with Terrance. When no one was around the voices in his head were so extreme they caused him to argue back. At times the yelling was so loud that the men in the dormitory were jolted awake. This was one such night and, because the shouting was so intense, they were sure something more was going on. Though I had no other place to put him, I knew I had to pull Terrance off of the desk.

After months of searching, I finally found the perfect position for Terrance. It was one that would give him value in life, but would also use his physical strength and desire to help others. Terrance became the assistant to our truck driver. In his new role, he went throughout the community lifting heavy beds, couches, dressers and large amounts of food which were donated to the Mission. He became a paid staff member and was a dependable fixture of support to the Mission for many years.

Every day without fail before Terrance left for his job, he would come into my office and, regardless of what I was doing, sit down in the chair across from my desk. He didn't knock or ask if I had the time. He would simply come in, make himself at home and then cheerfully ask how I was doing. Many mornings I was busy and irritated by his daily routine, but I never shared my frustrations with Terrance. I knew his delicate feelings would have been crushed. Instead, I gritted my teeth and did my best to pleasantly engage in our daily exchange.

I had a lot of questions for God concerning Terrance. After growing up in poverty absent from all family ties, abusing drugs, experiencing incarceration, and now suffering from severe mental illness and permanently residing in a homeless shelter... what was his purpose on earth? What was it I was supposed to be doing differently for him? As much as I asked, the answers never came.

Years into his position on the truck, an alert came out over the two-way radios we used. While picking up donations, Terrance grabbed hold of his chest, gasped for air and was now lying unconscious on the ground. I called 9-1-1 and immediately got in my car and rushed to the scene.

As Terrance lay on the ground, a doctor who was jogging across the street saw him and rushed over. He could clearly see that he had just suffered from a major heart attack and that help was needed immediately. The ambulance arrived and drove him to the hospital. I anxiously followed closely behind.

I stayed with Terrance that day and watched for the next hour and a half as the medical team did everything they could to get his heart started again. This massively strong man was now in the hands of individuals who didn't know his name, didn't know his story and didn't know the depth of his suffering.

As I sensed him slipping away, I again asked the Lord why He had allowed all of the suffering in his life, only for it to end like this. While I still didn't receive a definitive response, I began to realize that, despite his sufferings and what I had considered a wrecked life, I was watching a man travel into eternity who had done the very best he could in life with what had been given to him.

Through tears I reflected on the eight years I had known Terrance. I thought of the many days I had felt irritated when he came to check on me. He wasn't trying to be a bother; he was only trying to brighten my day. I thought of his willingness to do whatever it was I asked and giving his very best, even if it was something like cooking a meal which he knew nothing about.

As I pondered, I realized that this man had never complained about his situation in life. If ever I had seen the scripture from Philippians 2:14 lived out, it was through him. He did all things without murmuring or complaint and was more accepting of what God had given him than most people, including myself. Words can't express how devastating it was for me to realize that I was only now recognizing how truly special this man was. And I never had the chance to tell him.

Terrance found his eternal rest in the arms of the Lord that day. Suddenly all of those questions I had been asking God really didn't matter any longer. I was certain that, regardless of what he had been through in this life, he was now safe and resting in the arms of his Father.

After suffering years of persecution, imprisonment and slander, Paul encouraged us that, regardless of the pain and suffering we might go through in life, it cannot compare to the beauty and majesty that will be revealed in the end (Romans 8:18). This was a truth that Terrance clung tightly to. In spite of his sickness and other immense challenges in life, he remained faithful. He loved to study the Word of God, attend church, and show the love of Christ to those who came across his path. While in our minds his life was filled with pain, you'd never know it from the smile that always filled his face.

Through the witness of Terrance's suffering and how he responded, I was able to draw nearer to Christ. He showed me that, regardless of what we go through, we can still move forward in life with what we have left. There is no situation, sickness, sorrow or loss that can rob us of the eternal joy we will receive if we are walking with Jesus. Rather than allowing our circumstances to bring us down into the depths of despair, may we use them to rise above and be a light and example for others to see.

I don't know what you might be going through today. I don't know the sickness or tragedies that may have plagued your life for years... but I do know one thing. There is still life left in your body, which means there is still hope left for your soul. Regardless of how bad life may seem, there is always a promise of glory when we are walking with Christ. May you receive the encouragement His life has to offer you today.

Lord,

I want to see beyond my circumstances and encounter the true hope and life that You have to give. Help me to arise to each new day with a song in my heart and a smile on my face; fully aware of the goodness You still daily bring. May I never give up, but always look forward in You.

In Jesus' Name. Amen.

CHAPTER THREE

An Angelic Encounter?

*"Every good and every perfect gift is
from above, and cometh down from
the Father of lights, with whom is
no variableness, either
shadow of turning."*
James 1:17

*There can be things in life, both good and bad, that we try
to make sense of and even rationalize away. In a time when
finances were scarce, a surprise visitor came to my door with the
exact provision I needed. While some may call this a coincidence, I
know it was something more...*

When I began my ministry at the Mission, it was
obvious to both me and the Board of Directors that I lacked
proper understanding about how to operate a shelter and
work effectively with persons who were homeless. While my
years of experience working in the mental health field were
helpful, they were vastly different than the new endeavors
that were before me. At the time, the only teachers I had
were God and a few homeless individuals. They were the
ones who were educating me in the new encounters and
crises that came with each passing day.

After I had been there for just a few weeks, the Lord
placed on the hearts of our Board that I should travel to
Houston, Texas for more formal training in the area of
homelessness. The International Union of Gospel Missions
was conducting its annual training and, once approached
with the idea, I was excited to be a part of it. I was eager to

grow in my knowledge of the ministry field I had been placed and looked forward to developing a greater understanding of the needs that were before me.

As I prayed about the opportunity, I felt strongly that Tami was to attend with me. Though I didn't understand fully the reasons why, I was confident she was to be by my side. I presented the idea to the Board. They apologized but said that they just didn't have the finances. The Mission's resources remained tight and securing the funds for me to attend had been challenging enough. Sadly, they said there was no way they could afford for my wife to attend as well.

Upon hearing of our dilemma, the Mission's Ladies Auxiliary decided to help by trying to secure the funds needed for Tami to attend. Their efforts were a huge success and they were able to raise all but $100 of the necessary expense. I was blessed by their generosity, but also became concerned that the remainder of the necessary finances would not come in. The deadline to register was quickly approaching.

I sat in my office one mid-afternoon and was somewhat startled as I looked up and saw a stunningly beautiful elderly woman standing in my doorway. She stood a bit hunched over and wore glasses that magnified her sparkling eyes. Her hair was a pure glistening white and her clothes matched its glimmer from top to bottom. She politely asked if I was Barry Feaker. When I confirmed that I was, she smiled and replied, "Here... This is for you." She reached out and handed me a blank white envelope. As I took it from her hand she said, "God bless you. Have a good day." She then turned from my door and very slowly shuffled away. As I opened the envelope I was dumbfounded to find exactly five twenty-dollar bills tucked neatly inside.

While I was amazed, I wasn't fully clear of the intent of her gift. Rather than assuming it was an answer to my prayer, I wanted to clarify and thank her for her generosity. I quickly went to the front desk to ask which direction the woman had gone. As slowly as she walked, I was confident I could catch her before she left the premises.

The man working at the desk looked up at me confused and said he had been sitting there all along and had not seen any woman walk through the Mission. The way the old building was constructed, it would have been physically impossible for anyone to walk in or out of my office without walking directly past the front desk. I didn't believe he could possibly be telling the truth so I rushed outside. I looked down the street but there was no one. I came back to the front desk and again drilled the staff member. Regardless of how I tried to convince him otherwise, he held fast in confidence that no one had walked through the doors or past the desk.

Suddenly I became concerned, wondering if perhaps that woman had gone the wrong direction and gotten lost elsewhere in the building. I walked back through the shelter into the dayroom and asked each person I came in contact with if they had seen the woman in white. Not one had seen her. Confused, I went back outside one more time to look. There was still no one in sight.

I went back to my office and tried to make sense of what had just occurred. "Could it have been?" I wondered, remembering the way in which her white attire seemed to so angelically flow. While I could not be certain, the same scripture kept ringing through my mind: *Be not forgetful to entertain strangers: for thereby some have entertained angels unawares (Hebrews 13:2).* While I tried my hardest to come up with one, I realized there was no other explanation for the gift and encounter that had taken place.

I contacted the Board and explained to them about my mysterious visitor and the gift of $100. Each one I spoke with confirmed that they believed this was a direct answer to prayer and should be used to finalize the plans for my wife to join me at the training.

Tami and I went to the conference. We both grew tremendously and eventually discovered the significance of why she was supposed to be there. The Lord used this time to lay the foundation of why we were in the ministry we were. Not only did we both need to have a greater insight to the depths of the ministry of rescue, Tami needed to know and understand why her husband would be gone eighteen hours a day at times for the next several years. That is not something that would be easy for any spouse, but through the new knowledge we received and relationships that we developed during the time away, the Lord helped to make the journey more understandable for both of us.

While I was worrying early on, wondering if and how the provision for Tami to attend would come, God had it all under control. He knew it was a need and how it would be met. The inability for the Board to approve the expense due to inadequate funds, the assistance through the auxiliary, and the peculiar encounter with the lady in white were all His way of building my faith and revealing His love. While it may seem insignificant to some, for me it was huge. Through it, God was teaching me how to transition from walking by sight to walking by faith.

The ministry was, and still is, one of faith. Unlike other ministries that I had been involved with, there was no congregation to whom we could "pass the plate" and ask for money. Instead, the only one I could turn to was God Himself. Rather than just dropping the money needed in my lap, He used all of the circumstances to teach me He was paying attention, He was in control and that He would use whatever methods of provision He chose.

Now faith is the substance of things hoped for, the evidence of things not seen (Hebrews 11:1).

The Lord chose to deliver the $100 provision in an extraordinary way. I couldn't see what He was doing behind the scenes and may never know fully all of the details that surrounded my unexpected visit that day. However, I recognize now as a result that there are some areas where I don't need to know all the details. I just need to trust God and thank Him for all He is doing, even when I cannot explain or see it with my natural eyes.

To free His people out of bondage, the Lord directed Moses to stand before Pharaoh and demand "Let my people go" (Exodus 7-13). When Pharaoh's heart was hardened, God sent numerous plagues upon the land. For each miraculous sign that was performed by God, Pharaoh's magicians tried to counteract. While they were successful in producing some false signs, there came a point when they could not produce any rationale for the miracles they witnessed coming from God. Finally, they had no choice but to lay down their own understanding and declare, "This is the finger of God" (Exodus 8:19).

When I began at the Mission I was coming from a philosophical and analytical mindset... but I was hungry for God. The more I sought and drew near to Him, the more situations like the mysterious woman in white began to occur. There may be some scholars who could try to explain away this and other encounters like it. Similarly, there are situations in this world that can be rationalized and called "coincidence." It is my belief that the majority of those coincidences in life are just God's miracles in disguise. And it is by faith that I am able to see His hand at work in each one.

Because of the lessons in faith the Lord taught me early on, I am more able today to accept that which I cannot comprehend and I thank Him for His miraculous power that is still at work today. While I can be like the magicians of

Pharaoh and try to make sense of everything I witness, I have found it is more fruitful and productive to remain in awe of the One who holds the true power and thank Him for His hand at work. Every day He is still moving mightily. We just have to be willing to open up our eyes to see.

Lord,

Forgive me for the times when I have put more confidence in my intellect than in You. I want to see beyond the realm of my natural circumstances and experience Your hand at work in my life and the world around me. I hunger after the realities of You, and I choose to believe.

In Jesus' Name. Amen.

CHAPTER FOUR

The Beginnings of Rescue

"... Eye hath not seen, nor ear heard,
neither have entered into the heart of
man, the things which God hath
prepared for them that love Him."
1 Corinthians 2:9

Have you ever felt like God had given up on you and that
there was just no hope left for your life? Jerry was a man who fell
over sixty times but, regardless of his failures, he was used
mightily to change not only a community, but our nation and our
world. If God could use him, then I promise He can use you...

The miraculous provision that allowed my wife and I
to attend the Association of Gospel Rescue Missions
(AGRM) Director's Meeting in Houston left an everlasting
imprint on my heart (see chapter three). The education I
gathered and the testimonies heard forever changed my
heart and the way I viewed people in need.

One of the first speakers at the convention was the
(then current) AGRM president. In his attempt to relay the
heart and foundation of the ministry, he shared a remarkable
story. Though the facts may not be relayed word for word,
following are the details as I recall.

Jerry McAuley was well-known as a thief and an
alcoholic who lived in New York City in the late 1800s. Jerry
was an extremely hard core and rough guy. He was known
as a "river boat thief" because of his tendency to assault and
rob people as they were coming on and off of the riverboats.

He was finally caught and sentenced to many years in Sing-Sing Prison.

Jerry had been in prison for some time and was filled with much bitterness and anger. As he walked past a room filled with men, he noticed his former cellmate standing in front of the crowd speaking. Out of curiosity, he walked in and found him talking about how Jesus Christ had come into his life, saved him, helped transform his thinking, and gave him a new life. Jerry had never heard such a message before. He listened to the entire presentation. That night Jerry surrendered and humbly gave his life to Christ.

A new and remarkable change began taking place in Jerry's life. He started attending Chapel and began acting and thinking differently. Some Christians from the outside began coming into the prison and ministering to him. His behavior became so noticeably different that the person in charge of parole made the decision to release him before his sentence was up.

The people who ministered to him asked Jerry what he was going to do with his life. Though he didn't know what it would look like, he knew there were great needs and he wanted to somehow help others like himself. Perhaps he would start a shelter of some kind for men who were homeless and addicted. (Back in those days, homeless shelters and recovery services were not in place as we know them today.)

As people from the churches encouraged and prayed for him, Jerry began developing a plan to develop a homeless shelter. He had positive supports, God, a good outlook, a new life and purpose, and was doing great... all until an old tempter reappeared. Jerry picked up the bottle and, in no time, was drinking heavily once again.

Jerry's friends didn't give up. They began searching for him by going to all of the places they thought he might be. It was in a gutter in Skid Row where they finally found him. Instead of judging him, or calling him a drunk and manipulator, they reached out in compassion and showed him love. They picked him up and helped him get his life back on track.

Everything was going great for a while until Jerry again met the bottle. He started drinking and fell back into the gutter. Once more, the same people went out and looked for Jerry, helping him to clean up and start over once again.

Time and time again the same scenario occurred. More than sixty times Jerry fell, and each time he was met with the love and compassion from a people who cared. It was through their endurance and God's love that a consistent and complete change finally took place.

In 1872, at the end of his long journey of successes and failures, Jerry McAuley was used to successfully give birth to the very first rescue mission in the United States of America. Through this one life, a ministry was formed that today provides an annual average of 42 million meals, more than 15 million nights of lodging, bandages for the emotional wounds of thousands of abuse victims, and graduates 18,000-plus individuals from addiction-recovery programs.

There may be an issue you have wrestled with for years. Like Jerry, you may have had seasons when you've done great, only to fall back into the gutter once again. If this is you, know there is still hope. God has not forgotten about you and His purposes for you have not diminished.

Saul had been persecuting Christians for years. He was ruthless and cruel, even murdering and unjustly taking lives. People feared him and no one dared believe he could ever change. One day as Saul was on his way to continue his pursuit of unwarranted imprisonments towards men and women of faith, he was met with a blinding light and an encounter with Jesus took place.

At the same time, the Lord was also speaking with His servant Ananias. He told him to minister to Saul, but because of the man's reputation, Ananias was afraid. He had heard of the evil and danger of this man and was certain he had heard wrong. When the Lord repeated the directive, Ananias submissively obeyed. Through his obedience to reach out, a life was forever changed. The same man who had once murdered and imprisoned became a new creation who would soon lead multitudes to Christ (Acts 9:1-19).

To Jesus, there is not one in this world who is irrelevant or too hardcore to be reached. If there is one in your life who needs to experience His light, walk like Ananias and reach out your hand.

If you are the one who is battling, consider the lives of a hopeless drunk named Jerry and a murdering blasphemer named Saul. It was not too late for them and it's never too late for you. While we've all fallen short and done things we regret, nothing can separate us from God's love and His ability to bring change to our future.

Dear Lord,

As I read of Your goodness I'm filled with an awe. The same way You took Saul and Jerry's pasts and turned them for good, I ask You to do the same with me. Transform who I once was into the person You created me to be. May I receive Your grace and never fail to extend the same to those in my life.

In Jesus' Name. Amen.

CHAPTER FIVE

The Best Christmas

*"In every thing give thanks:
for this is the will of God in
Christ Jesus concerning you."*
1 Thessalonians 5:18

Has your life, job or ministry ever become so overwhelming and difficult that you felt like giving up? Before I began working at the Topeka Rescue Mission, I endured some great challenges that caused me to want to throw in the towel and walk away from it all. As I overcame, however, God used each one of the miracles in the midst of my trials to strengthen my faith and prepare me for what laid ahead. The following account serves as a powerful memory marker for me to recall when the responsibilities of the Mission became seemingly too immense...

When I first surrendered my life for the sake of ministering the Gospel full-time, I had a grand vision for my future. Because I walked away from everything comfortable in my life to follow the Lord, I thought my surrender would be rewarded with a life of exciting adventure filled with the abounding joys of saving the world. Nothing could have been further from the truth.

Within months, I was depressed, discouraged and angry at God. I wanted to run away and quit. I believe the only reason I didn't was because of something I heard a professor of mine share.

He shared with our class the story about the Israelites and how they frequently murmured and complained; wanting to return to their bondage because they believed their oppression was greater than what they were experiencing. My professor shared that, in ministry, we too would be tempted to murmur, complain and desire to go back to where we once were. However, he reminded us that if we did we would be returning back to nothing more than bondage. Though I was miserable in my current circumstances, I really did not want to return to a place of captivity from which the Lord had drawn me out.

In time, I learned that before we can do great things for God, we must become bankrupt of ourselves so that we can become fully dependent on Him. In order for me to be able to endure the tests and challenges that would come my way in the future, I had to first go through some fiery trials where my faith could be refined. It was during those first years at the Mission that I was frequently reminded of the many lessons I had already learned and the ways in which God always remained faithful to provide.

One such memory marker was Christmas of 1980. Had this experience and others like it not taken place, I'm not sure I ever would have had the faith to step forward in managing a homeless shelter that I knew nothing about.

The parsonage my wife and I lived in was cold and drafty. It was also located in a rough, impoverished and crime ridden area of Kansas City where we knew no one. In all of our lives, I'm not sure we had ever felt so alone. We had little income, no food, and no presents under our artificial tree. My father was dying of cancer and Tami was nine months pregnant, expecting our first child.

Our circumstances were bleak, but a glimmer of excitement shone in our hearts as we anticipated Christmas Day. We had made plans with family and would be enjoying the day in Topeka celebrating the joy of Christ's birth. However, our plans quickly shifted when, on Christmas morning, I woke up with the stomach flu.

With every part of my being ravaged with pain, combined with the dark realities already in front of me, I quickly became even more depressed. Tami tried to cheer me up, but to no avail. In a prayer of bitterness I cried out to God, "So this is how You take care of people who have said they will serve You? You let them be broke, sick and unable to celebrate Christmas? You give them a father as a best friend, only to let him die of cancer? A wife who is pregnant with no food to eat and no money to buy it? And all this on Christmas? Really?" I fumed in my anguish and was sure He had turned a deaf ear.

We had $1.90 to our name. By this time Tami could hardly fit behind the wheel of our tiny car, but she squeezed herself in and drove down to the gas station. She came back with a small bottle of Pepto-Bismol and a bottle of 7-Up. For lunch that day we dined on 7-Up and crackers, while I drank the pink medicine.

Tami was so pregnant she could hardly move, but her attitude remained positive and was truly commendable. On the other hand I, all day long, chose to wallow in my self-pity while complaining to both her and God.

An unexpected knock on the door came around four o'clock, interrupting my saga of gloom. As we opened the door, we were greeted by a man and a woman standing there in the cold. We recognized them as neighbors from down the street. They knew we were going to the Bible School since we were staying in the old parsonage beside the church. They also had not seen us go anywhere or have anyone come by on this special day and wondered about us. "So," they said, "God placed it on our hearts to bring Christmas to you."

In their arms they held leftovers from their Christmas meal. The crackers we were saving for dinner were soon replaced with warm turkey, mashed potatoes, gravy, green beans, and pumpkin pie. They said they had experienced a really nice Christmas that morning and they wanted to share it with us.

They had taken the wrapping paper that had been on their presents and reused it to wrap presents for us. Inside several packages were food items and baby toys for our daughter who would be arriving shortly. All of the items were used, but in good condition. Even though there were no stores open, this couple had taken what they had available and given it to us.

They smiled as they told us they appreciated what we were doing with our lives and that they had felt God had shared His blessings with them so that they could share them with us. I was convicted, humbled and deeply grateful.

God clearly spoke to me that day and let me know that, even in the midst of my complaining and woe, He had not forgotten about me. "In spite of what you will go through," He said, "I will always meet you there." What started as the worst, turned out to be the best Christmas I'd ever had.

From that day forward my faith in God was strengthened and my trust in Him changed. It was obvious for where He was taking me that I needed to experience a number of lessons in faith. Prior to that event and others similar, I would have never had enough stamina to remain standing in the midst of the challenges I have since faced. How could I trust God to provide for others if I had never experienced great need and His provision for myself? I learned from His faithfulness and this couple's sacrifice that there would always be hope, as long as I was walking with Him.

One of my favorite promises in scripture is that God will work all things out according to the good for those who love Him and are called according to His purpose (Romans 8:28). I now believe, after meeting so many unique individuals, that each one of us are called with a God-given purpose in life. There is no one on this earth today that is purposeless in God. If we say yes to the Lord and begin walking with Him, this promise is one we can always be assured of.

I once lived in poverty and experienced great lack. I watched my family question as we wondered where our next meal would come from. I remember the anxiety I felt when the bills came and there was no money to pay them. I remember the sleepless nights wondering if I had missed God and questioning if things would ever change. However, I can look back now and know with all certainty that even through those trials, there was great purpose. Had I turned my back on the ministry and given up hope, I would have never experienced the richness of His miraculous provision, the best Christmas of my life, or the privilege of leading the Topeka Rescue Mission that stands as a testimony of God's goodness today.

There may be some unpleasant circumstances you are living in now. While they are rarely enjoyable as we go through them, we can find hope in His promise that each one will be turned around and used for the good. May your eyes shift from the despair of your current circumstance to the hope of tomorrow that lies just within your reach.

Dear Lord,

In all circumstances, help me to remain thankful. Thank You for the promise that You will turn all trials, as dark as they seem, around for Your good. Help me to focus on the good that will come versus the darkness I face. I trust You and thank You for a renewed sense of faith.

In Jesus' Name. Amen.

CHAPTER SIX

Cooking with Umbrellas

*"...Tribulation worketh patience;
and patience, experience; and
experience, hope."*
Romans 5:3-4

*Have you ever felt like there was no end to the trouble that
was coming your way; that the pressures of life only seemed to
mount and grow with each passing day? In the midst of our
greatest challenges comes some of our greatest opportunities to
grow and find the hope in life we so desire. It was through a
deteriorating kitchen that God showed me how...*

When I began working at the Topeka Rescue Mission,
divine intervention was needed daily in order for disaster
not to strike. As a result, I was learning more and more
about faith and true hope in God with each passing day.

I didn't realize how sparse our finances were until I
made my first trip to the kitchen. I watched as our volunteer
cooks stood for hours peeling potatoes with the back of
spoons; only because there was no extra money to purchase
a peeler. As I watched the creative carving take place, my
eyes drifted up to the ceiling above. I could see holes that
had been created as a result of the lack of proper ventilation.
Because there was no other source of heating in the area, the
oven was used by volunteers to warm the space.
Unfortunately, as the ovens became hot and the heat rose to

the ceiling, holes were formed that eventually developed fully through to the roof.

Things became increasingly interesting in the winter months when snow and ice would buildup on the roof. The continual heat from the oven would melt the contents, thus causing a steady stream of water to fall into the kitchen. Had the money been readily available, the holes may have gotten fixed. Instead, the same cooks who resourcefully used a spoon for the potatoes would bring umbrellas to work and hold them over the food to keep the next meal dry.

Though the food was protected from the melting snow that caused the falling rains inside, further damage was ensuing as a result. Because the streams were falling from the umbrellas to the floor, the floors would quickly become saturated with inches of water. Since the melting elements flowed so steadily, mops were not able to effectively keep up and absorb the amount of water that fell.

There were no drains in the floors so, to prevent excessive damage and potential collapse, the innovative cooks used hand drills to drill holes in the floor. Those same waters that poured from the roof through the ceiling, to the umbrella to the floor, were now streaming down into the basement. The basement would flood, but at least the food was kept safe and our workers were warm!

This was one of my first real tests in faith and I shook my head in disbelief at the realities of our situation. I could have easily chosen right then to walk away because the road seemed too impossible. However, I chose to persevere and continue trusting the Lord with one day at a time.

I used to ask the Lord why He seemingly allowed so many tribulations to come my way. Every day carried with it a new trial, a new test or a new crisis of some sort. Regardless of what I tried, the war wouldn't cease. Finally one day, He took me to Romans 5:3-4 and the challenges in my life began making more sense: *Suffering produces perseverance; perseverance, character; and character, hope.* I realized the Lord was trying to develop hope in my life, but I couldn't get there without persevering in Him first.

Everything we go through in life can be used as a process. If we focus on the suffering, we will move backwards and remain stuck in the place where we are. If we choose instead to move beyond the obstacles that stand in our way and persevere, then we can further develop into the men and women that He desires for us to become.

Now, when I am faced with obstacles, challenges and seemingly undeserved attacks in my life, I try to first look inwardly and ponder if there is another area of my character that the Lord wants to mold. If I will submit rather than complain about my circumstances, the Lord will be able to further shape me in areas I may have otherwise not seen.

What attacks seem to be coming at you in this season of your life? Before you try running away from them or praying for them to cease, let the Lord examine your heart and mind. Is there an area of your life He is trying to purify and develop? What the enemy plans for evil, God can turn for good. All we have to do is submit to the process and remain pliable in His hands.

Lord,

I submit to You and to the process before me. Rather than focusing on my circumstances, help me to focus on the change that You are desiring to do within me as I persevere. Thank You for the hope that awaits me in the end.

In Jesus' Name. Amen.

CHAPTER SEVEN

The 600-Year- Old Man

*"And let us not be weary in well
doing: for in due season we shall reap
a harvest if we faint not."*
Galatians 6:9

*Have you ever dealt with a challenge in life for so long that
you began doubting your situation could ever change? For years I
watched as a man, who struggled with homelessness for decades,
remained stuck and unable to move forward in life. Regardless of
the impossibilities, in time his circumstances were altered and both
his life and my own were forever changed...*

It wasn't long into my arrival at the Mission when I
first met Norm. He was a gentle older man who had lived in
the shelter for as long as anybody could remember. I later
found out that the Mission had been his home for well over
twenty years.

Prior to his coming, Norm served in World War II
and was an extremely intelligent equipment designer. He
was an airplane mechanic and also designed new and
innovative technology that was eventually used in military
flight machines. Norm used his skills not only in his military
experience, but also to bless the Mission.

Through his intellect and expertise, Norm invented
what would one day become a large recycling operation for
the Mission. He had grown up on a farm and was familiar

with the old farming equipment. One day he found an old hay bailer and skillfully converted it into a machine that could be used at the Mission. It was placed in our warehouse for the processing of rags which, after baling and selling them, allowed us to bring in extra revenue.

As brilliant as Norm was, it didn't take me long to recognize he was suffering in the area of mental health. He would often talk to himself and usually secluded himself at a distance from others. When he was in a group, there was typically an air of uneasiness and paranoia about him.

I did some research and was able to find out a little more about Norm's past. He had lived a normal childhood on a farm in Northeast Kansas. He was a pleasant child who was friendly towards all he met. Shortly out of high school, he joined the service and became an airplane mechanic with the Air Force. He served in World War II and was stationed in Germany. Norm never had any problems, until he came back from the war.

Norm's brother served as a pilot during the war. One tragic day his plane was shot down. He parachuted to the ground and landed in a German village behind enemy lines. Upon sight, he was murdered by local farmers in a way too gruesome to share. Because Norm was an airplane mechanic, he blamed himself for the disaster. He began caving into himself, fully believing that if he would have taken better care of his brother's plane, he would still be alive. From that point on, Norm was never the same.

He came back from the war very troubled. Over time, the family became concerned about the behaviors he was exhibiting and had him committed to treatment within a psychiatric institution through the Veteran's Administration (V.A.). Against medical advice, he eventually left and turned to the streets. It was somewhere between 1954 and 1960 that he was found in a drainage culvert, where he had been living for some time. He was brought to the Mission and remained at the shelter from then on.

Norm was a kind and gentle man; just disturbed. I did my best to help him, but even in my best attempts, he always refused services. I spoke to him several times about his mental health and resources available through the V.A., but each time both the paranoia he possessed and the fears of being locked up prevented him from accepting any help.

Through the process of time we began to realize that Norm, who had been receiving no income other than a small weekly stipend for his assistance at the Mission, was eligible for social security benefits and a large back settlement from the government for his military service and disability. The dollar amount he was eligible to receive was enough to purchase his own home and live comfortably for the rest of his life. I was extremely excited at the possibility of Norm being able to start afresh.

The day came when I, Norm, the staff from the V.A. and a local social worker all sat down to go over the paperwork that would make it possible for him to obtain his benefits. After reviewing everything in detail and explaining what he was entitled to, Norm looked at the paperwork and said matter-of-factly, "I can't sign this."

After decades of homelessness, I was in shock that this man would not be interested in doing whatever it took to get his life back. I asked him, "Why not?" and he responded, "Because that's not me."

I pointed to the paperwork and again went through all of the information with him. He confirmed the details of his demographics until I got to his birthday. "That's the problem," he said. "It's the right day but the wrong year." With a copy of his birth certificate in hand, we knew the date was correct, but Norm was adamant. When we asked what year he thought he was born he gave us a date that would have made him 300 years older than he was. He believed what he shared; and, in turn, would not sign the papers because he thought it would be dishonest. I tried everything I could to convince Norm otherwise but, regardless of my best endeavors, Norm stood his ground. He was certain that signing the papers would be lying and he refused to do such a thing.

I sat back and realized that either Norm was looking for an excuse to stay at the Mission, or he truly believed the words he spoke. I knew without his signature there was nothing more we could do. His money would remain locked up in an account and he would never have access. I left the meeting feeling hopeless while the papers remained unsigned.

After some time had passed, I asked Norm if he would write me up a bit of his life's story so I could understand him better. He did so willingly and gave me a nearly thirty-page document that was hard to comprehend and difficult to follow. Through it, I picked up a glimpse of the personal encounters he believed he had shared with George Washington, Abraham Lincoln, and a number of other historical figures. Norm now believed he was nearly 600-years-old.

We continued to try and find ways to obtain Norm's assistance for him over the years, but none of our efforts worked.

After about ten years, Norm began developing some health issues and suffered a serious heart attack. We tried connecting him with his family on the farm, but he didn't believe they were really his relatives. The Mission was now the only family he trusted and knew.

Kay Ireland had been volunteering at the Mission and had just recently come on board as a staff member. She saw the needs and immediately jumped in to reach out to Norm.

She worked with the medical personnel concerning his surgery issues and was there for support during his recovery once he returned to the Mission. Norm really connected to Kay and I began seeing him open up to her in ways I had never seen him do with anyone else before.

Over a period of time, it became obvious that Norm was not able to receive all of the care he needed at a homeless shelter. He truly needed the aid that assisted living would provide, but without the funds to sustain it, there was no way he could afford such a place.

As I was talking to him one day, I asked about his stay in the hospital. He shared it was okay and was feeling much better. I asked him about the hospital personnel and how they had treated him. His face lit up as he talked of how nice they were and raved about how great everyone had been. I then asked Norm if he knew how much it had cost for his heart surgery. When I told him $50,000, he was astonished. I reminded him that since he had no money, the bill would never be paid. He was saddened by this and said that it just wasn't fair. I solemnly agreed and shook my head with him.

While he was still pondering, I said, "Norm, I have an idea." His eyes perked up. "You know those papers I've been trying to get you to sign for all of these years?" "Yes," he said. "Well, you know we're only off by a few years. If you would go ahead and sign that paperwork, those kind people in the hospital who took really good care of you would get their money." Norm looked down and said, "You know I can't do that." I told him that I understood and left the room.

Norm came into my office later that day and, reflecting back on the hospital personnel, said, "You know, they took awfully good care of me and I wouldn't be alive if it wasn't for them." He went on to share that even though he was really 600-years-old and the papers had the wrong birthday listed, he would go ahead and sign them so the hospital could receive their money.

Norm followed through and signed all of the paperwork. It wasn't long before the funds were received. The hospital got paid and, through his new health insurance, he had the opportunity to explore housing outside of the Mission.

Kay began working with Norm to find the right place for him to live. After nearly thirty years of living at the Mission, he moved into his new home at an assisted living facility. While he was there he did well for a few months before being admitted back to the hospital with medical complications. It was obvious as he neared discharge that more intensive residential support was needed. Unfortunately, because of the cost of living in the formal facility, Norm had no finances left for such an arrangement. However, through Kay's diligent prayers, dedication and faithfulness to care for Norm, he was released from the hospital into an affluent hospice community where he received all of the care he needed... free of charge.

Norm eventually slipped into a coma before breathing his last breaths. Kay was able to get in contact with his brother and it was he who held his hand as Norm passed from this world into the next.

I had the honor of conducting Norm's funeral service and was able to share about one of the most unique lives I had ever encountered. I told of a very gentle man who served his country and came back terribly wounded; and of a government system that was designed to help him but was not able. I shared how the compassion of a community that created a place for someone like Norm to live, and a very kindhearted woman who was willing to take a forgotten man under her wing and sacrificially love, was able to provide this man a new life.

There were many times over those ten years of working with Norm that I was perplexed and my thought processes confused. I wondered how, with all of the challenges in place, we would ever help this man receive the support he needed. The struggle was so great that it truly seemed like there was no hope he would ever move on from the Mission.

We did have options. We could have set a deadline and kicked Norm out. We could have drawn up a plan and demanded he follow it in order to keep his bed. Instead, we chose to meet him where he was at and treat him with love to the best of our abilities.

We are told in Galatians 6:9, "Let us not be weary in well doing, for in due season, we shall reap if we faint not." Day after day, we reached out to Norm. We gave him a bed, meals, a place where he could work and a sense of dignity in his life. The struggles he experienced made it difficult on us all. But rather than giving up, we pressed forward in the Lord's strength.

What struggles are you faced with today? Is there an area of your life that has been in turmoil for so long that you've lost sight of the ability to believe anything will ever change?

For twelve years, a woman in the Bible suffered from an issue of blood. For over a decade she had spent all of her money on doctors, never to find a cure but only to grow worse. She had tried everything that she knew to do, but nothing ever worked. The struggle continued. The issue remained.

One day, she managed her way into the crowd. She saw Jesus and had heard of how He had touched and restored many. She pressed forward with anticipation and thought, "If only I could touch His clothes, then I would be well." She mustered the strength and reached out her hand. As soon as the hem from His garment touched the tip of her finger, she felt her body shift and knew the condition she had struggled through for so long was finally over (Mark 5:25-29, Luke 8:43-44).

Norm struggled in his life, and we struggled with him. Year after year, we wondered if his situation would ever change. We tried everything we knew, but nothing ever worked. We kept moving forward and kept our focus on Jesus.

One day, after years of striving and trying to make it happen, the struggle ceased. Norm did what he needed to do and his three decade stint of homelessness was complete.

Had Norm not spent all of those years at the Mission, we would have missed out on a lot. Our lives were changed by his integrity, gentleness and compassion. The Lord strengthened our resolve to persevere and showed us how in the end our efforts were not in vain. In addition, Norm was instrumental in developing a recycling operation that stands to this day and generates thousands of dollars in revenue for the Mission every year.

I never would have dreamed on the day I first met him, the impact Norm would have on my life and the ministry of the Topeka Rescue Mission. As we reached out to him, God used him in many ways to reach back and bless us.

There are experiences and seasons in life that are challenging and unpleasant. After we try everything we know to bring resolve, the situation only seems to get worse. We grow hopeless and weary, wondering when it will ever end.

Had the woman with the issue of blood given up completely, she would have never been able to touch the garment of Jesus and receive the fullness she obtained. Had we given up on Norm and failed to continue to embrace him in our home, he may have died on the streets with his inventions never birthed. If you were to give up hope in the challenge you face, you may miss out on the beauty of life and the blessings God has in store. May you never give into weariness, but instead continue pressing through until the day arrives when you can touch the hem of His garment and be restored once again.

Dear Lord,

There are times when I feel like I've tried everything and have nowhere else to turn. I'm tired and weary and need to feel Your touch. Come and breathe life into me and the challenges I face. Draw up a new sense of perseverance and drive within me and allow me to receive Your life and restoration afresh.

In Jesus' Name. Amen.

CHAPTER EIGHT

Learning to Love Those Who Are Different

*"There is neither Jew nor Greek, there
is neither bond nor free, there is
neither male nor female: for ye are all
one in Christ Jesus."*
Galatians 3:28

*Have you ever become so comfortable and acclimated in
your own culture that you realized you were not able to relate to
people who were seemingly different from you? Or so passionate
about the people group you work with that your eyes were
unknowingly blinded to others outside of that group? It was early
in my ministry at the Mission that God showed me the importance
of embracing all people, regardless of their backgrounds or
socioeconomic status in life...*

I came into the Topeka Rescue Mission knowing very
little about homelessness and I wasn't quite sure what I was
going to do. My heart's desire was to experience God at
work in the world today so, without understanding the
purpose, I followed His lead to serve among those who were
homeless and poor.

When I began, there were between fifteen and thirty
guests who stayed at the Mission on any given night. The
people who lived there and those coming in from off the
streets would cook the meals, do the laundry, answer
phones and provide security. There was no other paid staff
at the time and it was obvious that there were a lot of

changes which needed to be made. In order for that to occur, I knew I needed to learn a whole lot more about the Mission and the people occupying its walls. I also knew this was not something that could occur solely between the hours of nine and five.

I cannot express enough gratitude for the ways in which my family supported me during those early days. For many years they put up with a work schedule of mine that consisted of eighteen-plus hour days, seven days a week. For a wife with two small children, this was no small task. It seemed like the only time I was home was to spend the night and get ready for the next day.

Even though the population was small, the needs were great. It wasn't just the responsibility of keeping the Mission running and food on the table. The complexities of the lives I was beginning to learn of were not only overwhelming to those who lived them, but also to me.

When I served as a therapist in the mental health field or as minister in the church, I had help. I could walk away at the end of the day or pull in another to assist. Now, everything was different. Often the only one I could turn to was God.

Out of necessity, my education concerning the complexities and the challenges of what homeless individuals face was growing at warped speed. But what was also growing was a dangerous assimilation as I began to identify with the people who were before me. Without realizing it, I was beginning to develop an unhealthy identification with the people who were so troubled and in need.

Within a few months, I began to notice there was something wrong with me. I would go to church on Sunday mornings and feel like I didn't belong. I felt as though those around me couldn't really understand who I was or what I did. As this continued, I realized I was beginning to understand a small piece of how the people I worked with felt every day. Many had a hard time fitting into society and often believed they weren't understood or just didn't belong. It began to occur to me that this is why we often don't see people from the streets occupying our churches or other places of gathering. It's not because of rejection from good-hearted and loving members of the body of Christ. Many just didn't know how to reach out; and I was entering into a place where I didn't know how to do so either.

As I analyzed what was going on in my life, some realities hit me. I had not grown up in poverty. Apart from a short time after a tornado destroyed my home, I had never been homeless. I was never in jail, never addicted to drugs or alcohol, and I had never really suffered from any serious discrimination in my life. In spite of all of this, I was beginning to feel the way that people who had experienced all of these traumas felt. In a very rapid manner I began to understand why people who have been rejected and who have grown up in poverty react the way they do towards people who had never walked in similar shoes. There is a lack of understanding and ability to reach out, causing each one to remain in their shells of existence within the familiar places they know.

I realize now that I had to go through this inward struggle. Through it, I was able to obtain the balance needed to be effective in helping the homeless and poor of our community. It also helped me to better reach out and educate those who don't fit into the same category. God has allowed me to be a bridge, a voice, eyes and ears, to be able to express the needs of the poor to a community of compassionate people who desire to help. I've also been honored to serve in the same manner to those who are poor and homeless by letting them know there are people who love them and earnestly want to extend their hands.

I used to think my only purpose was to help those who were homeless and poor. What I realize now is that by getting caught up in my presumed call, I was inadvertently becoming prejudice towards those who could help me succeed in my endeavors to help. The Lord opened my eyes to see that I could have purpose and compassion for the poor while still loving those who were not. As He did, I was able to see the beauty of the unique relationships that God had created in our community between those who are hurting and in need with those who are affluent and caring.

There was a day when Jesus stopped for a rest at a well in Samaria. As He sat, a woman from Samaria came to the well to draw water for herself. Jesus turned to her and asked for a drink. The woman was shocked. "How is it that you, a Jew, would ask for a drink from me?" she asked; for she knew that Jews did not associate with Samaritans. Jesus spoke to her in love and through this encounter, a number of people came to know Him and the Gospel was spread (John 4:6-42).

We live in a society where different labels are assigned to our lives every day. We may be rich, poor, Christian or not, black, white, homeless or housed... and the list goes on and on. While it can be easy to become solely identified with the titles we've been branded, the Lord wants us to understand that in Him, there are no such boundaries. His love for the Samaritan is the same as the Jews; His love for those without homes is the same as for those who have.

While God may awaken our hearts to reach out more diligently to a particular people group in life, we must be careful that our love and thoughts towards those outside of that group remain pure.

I started off in my role at the Mission feeling uncomfortable around people who were different from who I perceived myself to be. There was nothing wrong with them, they just didn't fit into my supposed category and I no longer knew how to relate. What God showed me was that, regardless of our professions or stature in life, He has created us all to live together, work together and treat one another with love. Had I not been open to receive this lesson, I would have lost the beauty that God wanted to show me through so many people who care.

There are subtle ways through which hidden prejudices can sneak into our lives. Let's ask the Lord to examine our hearts and reveal any bias that may have taken residence in our hearts. May we embrace the Samaritans that come across our paths, and always treat one another in love.

Lord,

May I never become so consumed with my perceived purpose and plans that I fail to see the value in each person that crosses my path. I lay down my pride and humbly ask You to show me how to love each and every one, regardless of their status in life. May I see with new eyes as I reach out in love.

In Jesus' Name. Amen.

CHAPTER NINE

The Beauty and the Beast

*"...I have loved thee with an
everlasting love..."*
Jeremiah 31:3

Sometimes the ugliness of our faults seem so overwhelming that it is hard to comprehend anyone could ever love us or embrace us for who we really are. Regardless of how dark your life has been, there is a true love that awaits which is more glorious than any tale ever told...

I first met Bobby and Sue on Thanksgiving Day - my first at the Mission. I had no idea what this day was supposed to look like, but I did know we had no money for any extras. A turkey to feed the thirty-some guests we were anticipating had been donated and I asked the guys in the kitchen to do what they could with whatever else we had on hand to make the dinner special.

As I walked into the dining room that day, I immediately saw a young woman who had a healthy toddler bouncing happily on her lap. She couldn't have been much more than twenty and she wore a bright smile. Her child cooed and giggled and you could tell from their countenances that they were joyful and content. Across from them with his back facing me was a young man. From the way he was sitting I could only see his thick black flowing hair. He too seemed to be conversing delightfully and enjoying the day.

Surely they weren't guests of the Mission, I thought. I went up to the front desk to find out for sure. "Yes," I was informed, "they checked in late last night." I couldn't believe it. What would such a young vibrant family be doing in a homeless shelter? I hadn't worked with many homeless families before, but the ones I had encountered always seemed rugged and worn. This family appeared anything but that. The child was jubilant and healthy, and the parents were obviously in love with each other and their young son.

I went back into the dining hall and began approaching the family. I watched as the mother handed off the boy to his dad and the young child leapt eagerly into his father's arms. As soon as he did, his bright eyes looked into his face and he started to laugh. My heart was warmed and I was eager to meet the lovely trio who had captured my gaze.

I made my way through the small crowd to where they sat. The mother saw me coming and greeted me with a warm smile. When I turned to face them all for the first time my heart skipped a beat. I tried not to appear shocked but inside I was completely startled. The young father was missing half of his face. One eye was missing and only remnants of a nose, chin and mouth remained. His skin was concave and scarred like nothing I'd ever seen before.

The couple greeted me affectionately as their child continued to bounce and coo. I watched their interactions with both me and one another as we continued to converse. It stunned me the way they acted as though nothing was different between us. He spoke with a soft wispy voice but, aside from that, if you could not see the deformity of his face you would think this family was perfectly normal.

As we talked, I learned their story and the tragic reality of why they were now guests of the Mission.

Bobby entered the U.S. Army and began working as a vehicle technician just two years out of high school. He worked on all types of military vehicles and did exceptionally well in his trade. He married young and experienced a very stormy relationship with his first wife.

One afternoon, he came home and was enraged to find his wife in the arms of another man. Overwhelmed with hurt, anger and fury, Bobby ran into the bedroom and came out with a double barrel twelve-gauge shotgun. He was determined to take their lives. As he pointed the gun to the couple, he abruptly changed his mind and decided instead to turn it on himself. He put the shotgun under his chin and pulled the trigger. A shot fired and darkness filled his world.

Bobby woke up in the hospital where he began to undergo a series of surgeries. Though they tried their best, there was no surgery or pill that could fully repair the physical and psychological damage that had been done.

Bobby was discharged from the army, turned into an outcast in society, and wanted nothing more than to end his life. He continued with various suicide attempts but each one was unsuccessful, only landing him back in the hospital where he sank deeper in his pain. He believed his life was hopeless and ruined... until he met Sue.

Even upon first glance, Sue was able to see past Bobby's beastly appearance and fall in love with his heart. As their time together increased, her love for him grew and before long they were husband and wife. In time they gave birth to the handsome little boy that now bounced cheerfully in their laps. Sue's family was outraged that she would throw away her life on such a man and abruptly cut all communication ties. They saw only with their naked eyes, while she looked through the eyes of her heart.

Because of his condition, Bobby could not land a job. As a result, the family moved from state to state in attempt to find work. They found their refuge through homeless shelters in each city they went. I was amazed, regardless of the hardships and rejection they faced, at the joy and positivity that shone from their lives.

I became filled with an immense love and compassion for this young family and for the next six months I did everything I could to help Bobby find work. Sadly, our resources were scarce and nothing panned out. Though his resume was impressive, after each face-to-face interview that occurred, he was politely turned down. I understood the reasons why but I was frustrated within.

Eventually, through continued rejection and pain, Bobby once again began sinking deep into the depths of depression. Feelings of worthlessness consumed him as the inability to provide for his family pierced his heart. Sue began working part-time jobs in efforts to help, but in time Bobby was no longer able to care for their son on the days she was gone. She terminated each job and returned full-time to the Mission to care for her family.

I was outside as the family walked down the street one day. As they came nearer the familiar jokes from others nearby filled my ears, "Oh look, here comes the beauty and the beast." I watched as he put his head down and she did her best to ignore. What hope is left for this family, I wondered. Can anything good ever come of their lives?

As I watched Sue's optimism and her consistent love and affection, I continued to remain amazed. Regardless of how dark their lives were becoming or how awful her husband would act, her love remained genuine and pure.

"How do you do this?" I asked Sue one day. She smiled and said she really didn't know, apart from her relationship with God. She said He had placed such a love in her heart for Bobby that she was continually able to see through his actions and deep into his heart.

I thought of the Father's unconditional love for us. In spite of our ugliness, He sees past to our hearts. While our behaviors become uncomely and repulsive at times, He never walks away. He remains close to our sides lavishing us with a love that is so undeserved.

Bobby's depression continued to increase and, as the suicidal thoughts became more prominent, mental health services were able to intervene. Though he connected with professional counseling and support, nothing seemed to work. His heart remained heavy and his outlook was dark.

Just when I thought this story was going to have a tragic ending, God's glory broke through. After listening to the penetrating words of a minister who shared the Good News, Bobby finally understood the mystery of God's love. He handed his life over to the Lord and asked Jesus to come into his heart. From that moment on, transformation began. He walked out of the Mission's small chapel with a peace in his heart and a revelation of redemption he never thought possible. The guilt of his past was completely vanished and his fears washed away.

I watched over the next two months as an extremely hopeless situation transformed into a newness of life and opportunity like this precious family had never known. Bobby began applying for jobs again and rediscovered his worth. He had a new spring in his step and confidence in his walk.

I received a call from an employer who had interviewed Bobby previously. Apparently, Bobby had reapplied and requested a second interview. The employer was calling to ask me what I had done. He shared it wasn't his physical appearance that had caused them to not offer him the job previously; it was their lack of confidence in his ability to perform the job. "Now," he said, "we know he can." I testified of the hand of God in Bobby's life and let the employer know it was to Him that all glory was due.

Bobby accepted the job the employer had to offer and he and his family were then able to quickly obtain housing. They stayed in Topeka for about a year before another miracle occurred. God had softened the hearts of Sue's family and they invited them to come home. They moved back to the town they had originally lived and God continued to open up doors. Bobby found an even better job as they picked up the pieces and moved forward in life.

Unconditional love can be described as affection without limitations. When we love unconditionally, we love a person regardless of who he or she is or what they become. While we read about it in storybooks and fairytales, it is a kind of love that is rarely seen. As Sue embraced Bobby, regardless of his imperfections and faults, I witnessed the true definition of love stemming forth. Irrespective of what he had done, how he looked or how he behaved, her love never wavered. She continued to stay close, hold him in her arms, and believe in the man she always knew he was.

Does your heart long for that same kind of love? God's desire is for you to receive. Regardless of what you've done or how you've lived, He is still walking by your side ready to embrace you and reveal that there is hope for a brighter tomorrow.

Sue didn't know what the future would hold, but she had confidence in her husband and the God she served. God took her display of unconditional love and saved a man's life. Had she not opened herself up to see through to his heart, it is likely that Bobby would not be alive today.

In the original fairytale classic of "Beauty and the Beast" we know it was only by finding true love, despite his ugliness, that the curse over the Beast's life could be broken.

Just like Bobby and the Beast, we too need to taste of true love to be freed from the darkness that invades this current life. We can try other means to satisfy our hearts and give meaning to our lives, but it won't be until we receive the love which brings healing that our lives can fully be restored.

God has a deep measure of that love to give to you today. Regardless of what your life has looked like up to this point, what you have done or who you have become... God's heart is still beating for you and longing for you to receive His embrace. It's one that will bring transformation and life. Don't let another day go by without receiving of His greatest gift.

Dear Lord,

There are days when my life looks hideous in my sight. It's hard at times to believe that anyone would want to love me and give me their heart. Yet, I know that You see through my faults and into my depths. Help me to receive Your forgiveness and peace. I accept Your love and the life You have to give through Your Son, Jesus Christ. May I embrace and receive the transformation You have to bring.

In Jesus' Name. Amen.

CHAPTER TEN

Learning to Skate

*"But we have this treasure in earthen
vessels, that the excellency of the
power may be of God, and not of us."*
2 Corinthians 4:7

*There is treasure to be found in every person around us.
Sometimes the gold is buried by the stains of abuse, addiction or
mental illness; but even then the value and significance of a
person's life is never diminished. I had a friend who taught me
much about life through the embrace of his suffering. This story is
about the treasures found in my friend Joe who taught me to skate,
in more ways than one...*

I found myself in an awkward situation one evening
around 1976. I was supervising a skating party for
adolescents at one of our local skating rinks. The awkward
part was that I didn't skate. I think I would rather skydive
than attempt to roll around on eight tiny little wheels over
hard concrete. The kids were having a blast though and I
was amazed how skilled they were at rolling, spinning, and
turning around the rink. I had put on a pair of skates to look
the part, but had no intention of ever moving from off my
bench.

As I sat there, a cute little boy came up to me and
said, "Sir, my name is Joe and I don't know how to skate.
Would you please show me how?" I remember those sad

little eyes looking up at me and wondered how I could possibly say no to this child who was probably the only other person in the entire place who could not skate. I felt sorry for him and realized how lonely he must have felt. I paused for a moment and then by sheer guts and blind faith I said, "Joe, I'll hold your hand if you hold mine and we'll try to get around this rink just one time." The delight on this little guy's face was worth the impending pain and embarrassment I was about to face.

Here I was, twenty-years-old, holding the hand of a twelve-year-old little guy; both of us awkwardly shuffling ourselves on to what might as well been the surface of the moon. As we held hands and hugged the wall, we somehow managed to make an entire lap around the rink that night. What seemed like an eternity melted into a victory hug from little Joe when we made it back to the safety of the carpet and a sturdy bench to sit on. To my dismay, it wasn't over. He pleaded with me to go around one more time; then again... and again. For the rest of the night we held hands, hugged the wall, and had the time of our lives.

A few things occurred to me that night. I knew I would never put on a pair of skates again for as long as I lived (I have since kept that promise). It also felt really good to get out of my comfort zone and take a risk to help someone in need. Lastly, I knew I would probably never see little Joe again... how wrong I would be.

During the summer of 1980, my wife, Tami, was expecting our first child and we were in the process of moving to Kansas City to attend Bible School. Our good friends, Bill and Matie, arrived one hot and muggy morning to help us with the move and brought an extra helper with them. When Bill's younger brother stepped around the corner of the truck he looked at me as if he knew me. His eyes sparkled as the memory returned. "You taught me how to skate!" he exclaimed. I was shocked. This little kid, now older and much bigger, was my little friend from that night at the skating rink. I wondered at the end of our day if I would ever see him again.

Ten years after that night at the rink, Joe came back into my life. It was now his turn to show me what it really meant to skate around the turbulent rink of this world we call life.

I got a call one evening from my friend, Bill, who asked if I remembered his little brother. Joe was going through a really tough time and needed a place to stay. His brother wondered if there was anything that I could do to help.

I met up with Joe that evening down at the old Mission building. He had changed a lot. The young boy I had met years earlier was now a man greatly challenged with the anguish of mental and physical disability. Tormenting thoughts and emotions ran through his mind that stumped even the best in the medical community. Once again, Joe was asking for me to take his hand and help him make it around the rink. And once again, I was uncertain as to whether or not either one of us would be able to make it around even once.

The next few years were a real eye opener for me. Late nights at the emergency room and attempts to pry open a system that just did not seem to be there for Joe brought him and I together like brothers. As I continued to take Joe's hand, it was not long before he began to take mine. It was then he was able to show me the way of suffering that many experience in this life, but also the gold that could shine forth even in the midst of turmoil. With the support of Joe's family, friends, and his growing love for Jesus, he began to turn his sorrows into a fervent desire to use his infirmities to help others.

The meager facilities and minuscule programming available through the old Mission didn't bother Joe. He was grateful for his home and friends at the Mission. As we sought God's direction together on how to improve the Mission's services and environment, Joe was always there. Whether it was working the night desk, driving the van out to pick up a stranded homeless individual, or driving someone to the emergency room, Joe was always the first to be ready, eager and willing to serve.

Joe became an encourager to many lost souls and I often marveled at how men and women twice his age would seek him out for comfort and advice. His challenges were not hidden, but neither were his expressions of compassion and love for those who suffered. Joe became my right-hand man in those early days, helping to build a foundation for what eventually became the Topeka Rescue Mission we know today.

Over the years, Joe and I grew older and didn't get to see each other as much as we would have liked. Although I know it bothered him, he never complained. Even though his suffering would ebb and flow and take him to new and deeper pain, my friend always had a word of encouragement, wisdom, and love for me and everyone around him, especially those who were suffering or in need.

Joe died not long before the publication of this book and the pain of his suffering has finally ended. While I miss him, I can't help but envision him skating around the rink of heaven with a giddy smile on his face continuing to spread joy.

I learned a lot from my friend Joe. He taught me how to find the treasures within myself and others. He taught me how to be more understanding, more patient, more compassionate, and more loving. Joe helped me to become a better man... and taught me how to skate.

Today I still ask God why He allows the suffering we see in this world. But when I do, He often reminds me of Joe. Joe had many struggles throughout his life, but he never gave up and he never lost sight of the value in others regardless of what they were going through. While his personal pains and sufferings were immense, Joe continued to embrace life and do what he could to help others. While strangers may not have seen the gold within him at first glance, everyone who took the time to know him couldn't help but see him shine.

There is a treasure buried in each person who walks this earth. Some have already discovered their worth and their splendor shines bright. Others don't realize the value that lies deep within them. They look in the mirror and see only dirt. But what lies deep inside is a beauty and a treasure like nothing we've yet to behold.

Gold mining requires effort, patience and time. Rarely is gold found just lying in plain view. You have to look for it. You have to search within hard crevices and dig under layers of soil. While the labors take time, the value of the treasure, once it is found, cannot be compared.

Arise! Shine! Your light has come! (Isaiah 60:1, NKJV).

The treasures within us are not just for us, they are to be displayed so others are drawn to the Light of Jesus Christ (Matthew 5:16). How can we shed forth His light if we're not aware of what lies within us?

Your life is a treasure and a gift. God sees your beauty shining bright even when you do not. It may be buried beneath layers of darkness, soil and weight but it is there. Let the Lord reach down into the depths of your earth and draw out the treasure He's designed. As He does, may you make the effort to dig within the depths of others and find the gold that is buried deep within them as well.

Dear Lord,

When I look at my life, help me to move beyond the soil and stains to see the treasures that are buried deep within. May I see the gold not only in myself, but also in others I meet. Use my life to display the worth of Your splendor that You desire to shine forth.

In Jesus' Name. Amen.

CHAPTER ELEVEN

When I'm Tempted to Run

*"When my soul fainted within me I
remembered the Lord..."*
Jonah 2:7

*Have you ever experienced a trauma in life so great that all
you could think of was running away? While the temptation can
be great, the outcome that follows is rarely the best. What began as
one of my most traumatic days at the Mission ended in a victory
far greater than what would have been accomplished had I chosen
to walk away from it all...*

The month of February in 1987 was part of a cold, wet
and snowy winter in Topeka, KS. It was one of the winters
when you step outside and your breath is nearly taken away
because of the frigid stillness in the air; a time when your
body shakes to the core after spending just a few minutes
outside in the freezing air. It was during this time that
growing numbers of homeless individuals were finding their
way to the old drafty Rescue Mission building in hopes of
finding refuge from the cold.

One thing I had become aware was that when people
came to us they didn't just have homelessness as a problem.
Many also came struggling with addiction, mental illness
and a myriad of physical afflictions. There were no direct
connections with medical services at the time. As a result,
our only solutions were prayer and costly ambulance rides
to the emergency room when needs arose.

During that long arctic winter, a man and his wife were spending their days on an open boxcar as they traveled across the country. They were homeless with no form of heat other than the clothes on their backs and the plastic bags that they wore to keep dry in the snow. They were tired and desperate as they rode on the cold jarring train to a destination of which they were unaware.

When the husband began having difficulty breathing, they got off of the rails. They landed in Topeka and eventually made their way to us. His breathing was so labored and difficult that within 24-hours of their arrival we sent him to the emergency room for immediate intervention. It turned out he had active tuberculosis and had to be quarantined in the hospital for an extended period of time.

A few days later his wife came to my office. She timidly shared that her feet were hurting very badly. Since she had nowhere else to turn, she asked if I could take a look.

It was extra cold in the building that particular morning. Our heat didn't work well and a steady draft came in from all of the thin, aged windows. In an attempt to keep warm, the woman had on a very old fluffy coat that was covered with dirt and torn in many places. On her aching feet she wore heavy plastic boots with fake fur around the top that extended just over her calf.

I had already learned in working with individuals who were homeless that it was normal to encounter strange, sometimes repulsive smells as a result of many different reasons that extend far beyond the lack of proper hygiene. As the woman began to pull off her damp plastic boot that allowed for no ventilation inside, the pungent smell was beyond the norm. The odor that began to fill the room was almost more than I could bear. As horrific as the stench was, what happened next was even worse. As she finished pulling off her boot, my eyes widened in horror as two of her blackened frostbitten toes fell right off into the wet musty boot she held below.

I froze and everything seemed to go dark. It took all of the strength in me to keep from falling off my chair. My eyes were locked and my breath abated while I continued to watch. Before I could stop her, she pulled off her other boot magnifying the foul smell and uncovering another foot that appeared nearly as bad as the first.

I immediately called for help. Within minutes she was taken by ambulance to the hospital where a series of surgeries took place to spare what was left of her feet and help save her life.

As I prayed and pondered the tragic events that had unfolded since the couple's arrival, a sense of hopelessness ensued. There were obviously so many in need of medical care and our ability to provide anything onsite was nonexistent and far from possible in my eyes. I wanted to run the other direction and wallow in my grief as the drama of the morning continued to replay in my mind.

I was still trying to overcome the shock of what I had seen when a woman from the community arrived at the front desk and asked for me. I pulled myself together and was introduced for the first time to Rita Tracy, a professor at the Washburn University School of Nursing Department.

Rita entered my office and asked if the Mission ever had a need for medical aid. With the details of the morning so graphic in my mind, I knew this was a direct answer to prayer. Her ambition was astounding and, through her and many others in the field, a relationship was birthed between services that still exist today. A day that had begun with tragedy ended as one filled with breakthrough and hope.

Over time, a medical clinic was formed onsite at the Mission that continues to be a source of great support and blessing to the guests who come through our doors. Many others have followed in Rita's steps to make this possible, including Sharon Meissner who has faithfully served as the volunteer coordinator of the clinic for over twenty years. There guests not only have their medical needs assessed and treated, they also receive the love of Jesus and the goodness of His heart as they realize they are significant and valued enough to be cared for in every area of their lives. Whether they receive a bandage for a cut, pain reliever for a headache, or the referral and treatment for a more severe disease, each person is welcomed and lovingly cared for.

There may be seasons in our lives when we, like the couple who were riding the rails, travel through life unsure of the place we are going or where we will land. It is only when we put our trust in Jesus and give our lives to Him that we can find our direction. Even more so, we can look forward in anticipation and assurance that our eternal destination to come will be free from suffering, absent of tears, and glorious beyond our realm of comprehension.

Jonah was a runner. He had been given direction by God but, when it didn't line up with what he desired, he tried to go the other way. While God could have taken his life, he was miraculously spared and given another chance to live and obey. After he declared to the Ninevites the words of warning he had been given, Jonah sat back and awaited their destruction. The Ninevites situation seemed hopeless and bleak but, through their repentance and God's loving forgiveness, their lives were restored. The events didn't unfold as Jonah had expected, but God had a better plan (Jonah 1:1-4:11).

When the husband with the difficulty breathing came to the Mission it was my first experience with a guest who had active tuberculosis. I knew how quickly the contagious infection could spread and how, without immediate intervention, the Mission and all of the people inside were in trouble. Just as we seemed to get that situation under control, his wife came to me with her frostbitten feet. Could the circumstances get any worse? I too wanted to run and hide, but God had a better plan.

As disasters were mounting, God was intervening and what began as a tragedy unfolded into triumph. God took a situation that was beyond my comprehension and turned it into a gift that has since brought life and restoration to thousands. Had I walked away because of what I had seen or the outcomes I didn't understand, lives could have been lost and so much of His goodness would have been missed.

Regardless of what you have experienced or are currently encountering in life, don't give in to the temptation to ever run away. While the other direction might seem easier, that isn't always the case. Jonah learned that lesson the hard way when he ended up being cast into the sea (Jonah 1:15). Don't make the same mistake. Keep moving forward and know that God sees the bigger picture and always has a greater plan.

Lord,

When my eyes are filled with tears and I cannot seem to see any glimmer of hope around me, help me to turn my eyes to You and find peace and rest. I give my tragedies and pain to You; and I give You my heart to heal and make new once again. Thank You for taking every crisis and using it to bring peace and blessing, even in the coldest of nights.

In Jesus' Name. Amen.

CHAPTER TWELVE

Ground Beef

"...Ask and it shall be given you;
seek, and you shall find; knock, and it
shall be opened unto you. For
everyone that asketh receiveth and he
that seeketh findeth; and to him that
knocketh it shall be opened."
Luke 11:9-10

I used to doubt that God wanted to intervene in every area
of my life. It took a donation of ground beef to show me how very
wrong I was...

Cecil Dain was a humble man who hungered for God, had a tremendous servant's heart, and was willing to do whatever was asked of him. He was also the first paid cook at the Mission after I arrived.

Shortly after he began, Cecil came to me with a grave concern. He explained to me that he had bread and potato chips, but there was nothing to put in between the bread for sandwiches and no money to purchase food for dinner that night. We had approximately fifty hungry people to feed and no meat in our kitchen to serve.

Cecil looked at me with desperation in his eyes and asked what I was going to do. Still a novice in both running a homeless shelter and walking by faith, I was dumbfounded and didn't know how to respond. After a few seconds of silence, Cecil's eyebrows raised and he leaned closer towards me. "Well," he said, "aren't we supposed to pray?"

It was already three-thirty in the afternoon and dinner was scheduled to begin at six. With no money and no meat, there was no way we could come up with a solution before then. I was embarrassed by my lack of faith but reluctantly agreed to pray. I sighed before I began; believing deep down that no prayer of mine was going to do any good. We needed a miracle in less than three hours and, to me, that just seemed impossible.

My simple prayer began. "God, we need meat and we need it really quick for dinner tonight..." I tried to continue but was taken aback when Cecil interrupted my words. "You need to be more specific," he said. Both irritated and shocked because no one had ever interrupted my praying before, I candidly asked him what he was talking about. He told me that as a cook, he could do more in the kitchen with ground hamburger meat than he could with pot roast. With the ground meat he could make tacos, sloppy Joes or chili, but with pot roast his options were slim. I stared at Cecil in unbelief before rolling my eyes and continuing my prayer. "Lord, Cecil says we need hamburger and we need it quick..." I wondered sarcastically if that had been specific enough.

Cecil and I prayed for the next thirty minutes and then I went to a scheduled meeting. I returned to my office just before five.

When I sat down at my desk, the phone rang almost immediately. On the other end of the receiver was a grocery store calling from Carbondale, Kansas. The caller asked if there was any chance the Mission could use 900 pounds of ground beef right away. My forehead crinkled in question as I asked what was wrong with the meat. They told me there was nothing wrong and that it was in fact high quality. They just had made a mistake in their ordering and had no place to store the extra. If we weren't able to take it they'd be throwing it away. The meat was all prepackaged neatly in two-pound bundles and it was ready for us to pick up if we were interested and able.

My jaw dropped as I realized what had just occurred. Though dinner was a little bit late that night, God had come through and miraculously provided abundantly for our need at hand. All we had to do was ask.

Jesus and His disciples were walking along one day when Bartimeus, a blind beggar, heard they were near and began crying out. Those close by rebuked him but, the harder they tried to bring silence to his pleas, the louder he cried. Jesus called the man near. "What is it you want me to do for you?" he asked. The man looked up with his pupils of white and humbly replied, "Rabbi, I want to see." Immediately Jesus responded and his vision was restored (Mark 10:46-52).

My faith was hardly as strong as that of Bartimeus, but I believe Cecil's was. He knew that if we were standing in need, we should go to Jesus with our request. When we looked up at Him and shared what we desired, He brought forth a near-immediate response and our needs were supplied.

Though I doubted as we prayed, God still heard our cries. It wasn't because of my righteousness or faith, but because of His mercy and love.

What do you stand in need of today? Sometimes we are afraid to go to the Lord with our requests. We might believe our needs or desires are insignificant in light of the other seemingly more prevalent needs around us. The fact of the matter is that, regardless of the other tragedies that might be going on in the world, the Lord is still asking the question, "What do *you* want Me to do?"

Don't worry about anything: instead, pray about everything. Tell God what you need, and thank Him for all He has done (Philippians 4:6, NLT).

When we find ourselves lying on the ground blinded by worry and sorrow, we might not see Him but Jesus passes by. He looks down, leans towards us and asks with compassion and love, "What is it that you want Me to do for you?"

Bartimeus responded and his prayer was fulfilled. May you experience the same as you cry out to Him.

Lord,

I confess my needs and cry out to You, humbly asking that You would intervene in a way that only You can. I believe in Your Word that says if I ask I will receive; if I seek, I will find. I long for You and thank you for revealing Yourself in an ever greater way to me in the days ahead.

In Jesus' Name. Amen.

CHAPTER THIRTEEN

Eggs, Milk and Butter

"For My thoughts are not your thoughts, neither are your ways My ways, saith the Lord."
Isaiah 55:8

Have you ever expected God to move in such a way, only to be disappointed when the answers did not come as you had hoped? After experiencing His miraculous hand of provision concerning ground beef, I thought I had God all figured out. When He didn't move in the way I thought He should in the next challenge I faced, my faith began to falter and doubts began to crowd my mind. While it wasn't what I expected, I later realized that God still had the situation under control all along...

Two weeks after the miraculous provision of ground beef, I thought I had the strategy for prayer pretty well figured out: we have a need, we present it to the Lord, and immediately He responds. When Cecil came to me and shared that we had no food for breakfast the next morning and still no money to purchase it, I was confident in what I thought I knew and was ready to see my new formula put to the test.

What we needed was eggs, milk and butter. With the victory of the meat delivery still fresh on our minds, we eagerly prayed and asked the Lord for another timely miracle.

Like clockwork, I went to my scheduled four o'clock meeting and then directly returned to my office. I sat down at my desk awaiting the phone call I truly believed would come from someone offering us food. As I sat in my office waiting for the call, I watched the minutes shift to hours as no calls came. Finally, at seven o'clock the phone rang. I eagerly answered with a smile, ready for another swift answer from God. After I said, "Hello," I was surprised by the voice which responded on the other line. It was my wife wondering when I'd be home.

I got off of the phone with Tami and continued to wait. Over the next thirty minutes my faith began to falter and my intellect had me fully convinced that the event with the ground beef, which had occurred just two weeks before, was nothing more than sheer coincidence. I rationalized that if it truly had been God answering prayer, then surely He would have done it again tonight in the same way I expected.

My mind was dark and my outlook grey. I felt abandoned, alone and as if the weight of the world was resting on my shoulders. I had no faith, no answers and absolutely no idea what to do. I left the Mission that night feeling totally defeated and depressed.

While I wanted to stay in bed and not face the day, I forced myself up and drove into the Mission the next morning. As I walked in, I immediately noticed the dozens of guests who were eating the breakfast that just hours prior I thought for sure we weren't able to serve.

Cecil spotted me and ran up to me with childlike glee. "It came!" he exclaimed, practically jumping up and down with excitement in the process. I smiled but was confused and unsure so asked him to explain.

He had come in that morning still not sure of what he was going to do about breakfast. As he looked through the bare shelves and refrigerator, he received a call from the front desk. A family was there to see him and asked if he could come outside right away. He met them at their large utility vehicle and when they opened the back he was amazed. Inside was a plethora of milk and eggs, all fresh and stacked neatly in cases. They shared that they had been blessed with abundance and had felt just that morning the Lord was leading them to share. Cecil reeled with delight as they carried the food to the kitchen and he cooked up the feast for that morning.

I was excited about the timely provision but wondered about the rest. "Where's the butter?" I asked. Cecil shrugged his shoulders and said it had not yet arrived. Instead he was able to make do without.

The next day a woman walked into the Mission with a 50-pound slab of butter and all of our prayers for provision were both answered and complete. While I stood amazed yet again at the way God provided, I was a little taken back by the way it hadn't looked like I expected.

In 1 Kings 17:8-16, we read of a widowed mother who was overwhelmed with depression and hopelessness. Nearly everything she possessed was now gone. She knew tonight's meal would be the last for her and her son as she collected the sticks for a fire.

Elijah approached her and asked for a drink, then a meal. Sighing, she admitted her struggle and apologized she couldn't oblige. "Don't worry about a thing," Elijah replied. "Go make me a little cake with what you have and use the leftovers for you and your son... as surely as the Lord lives, your cup will not run dry." The mother must have been confused as she prepared the small cakes. But just as the prophet had spoken, her jars didn't run dry.

I have often wondered why God met the need for milk and eggs but waited two days before delivering the butter. I still don't know the answer, but I have come to learn that He knows what we stand in need of and, when the timing is right, He will supply.

The widowed mother thought for sure she and her son were soon to die. God knew they were in need and could have performed a myriad of miracles to sustain them and provide. Instead, He chose to multiply the little they had to meet the needs that were before them.

I believe God did the same thing with our breakfast. We needed eggs, milk and butter. While I expected Him to respond in the manner and timeframe that I anticipated, He chose a different route and instead provided according to His plan and not mine.

God's ways are beyond what we know. Just when we think we have Him all figured out, He allows something to occur that leaves us scratching our heads. While it might not always look like we thought or come when we expect, God always provides. May your eyes be open to see the many ways He already has provided and the way He will continue as you go forward in this life.

Dear Lord,

Your timing is perfect and I trust You to provide. While I often think I know what I need and when, I know that You know my true needs. Thank You for the assurance I can have in knowing that while my ways are not always Your ways, You love me and will always provide for my every need.

In Jesus' Name. Amen.

CHAPTER FOURTEEN

Shredded Lettuce

*"But God hath chosen the
foolish things of the world to
confound the wise..."*
1 Corinthians 1:27

*Before working at the Topeka Rescue Mission, I would have
never thought God could use a bag of shredded lettuce to save
someone's life. It was through this encounter I realized that God's
love is so immense that He will use whatever means necessary to
shed forth His light...*

Before his downward spiral began, Don had a
successful career as a professional chef and enjoyed a stable
family life. The turmoil began with a depression that led to
alcoholism. It was not long after that he was fired from his
job and his wife and children walked away. Homelessness
soon followed, which eventually brought him to our doors.

Whether homeless or not, Don still knew how to cook.
He saw the needs the Mission had and agreed to help out,
but only under one condition... that I agreed not to talk to
him about God. His heart had hardened over the years and
he had no trace of belief left. I agreed to his request but
warned him that, at times, God chooses to speak for Himself.

One morning, I was in the dining area having coffee
with some colleagues and friends when Don approached
me. He was in need of some money to purchase shredded
lettuce for the sanchos he was preparing for dinner. Because

of the tight finances at the time, there was still no extra money for food. I apologized and reminded him that we could only use what was donated. He had forgotten but respected the position we were in.

Before Don walked away to go back into the kitchen, a woman timidly walked into the dining room and looked around. In her hands she held a huge Ziploc bag filled with shredded lettuce.

I walked up to the woman and asked how I could help her. She seemed embarrassed and nervous as she spoke. Her church had hosted a dinner the night before and a large amount of lettuce was leftover. They were going to throw it away, but she felt the strong conviction that the Lord wanted her to take it to the Mission instead. Now that she was here, she thought it to be silly and apologized for bothering us and wasting our time on something so insignificant and small.

I smiled as I called over to Don. Once he approached I turned to the woman and said, "Ma'am, your gift is *very* significant. You heard from God." The sweet woman began to cry as she then realized she really had heard His voice. Tears then began running from my eyes. I looked over and saw the eyes of the men sitting at the table doing the same. Don just stood there puzzled. I turned to him and asked, "Didn't you just ask for shredded lettuce? God loves you and is showing you by answering your need."

The woman reached out her hands and handed the lettuce to Don. He mechanically told her, "Thanks," and then turned and walked away. I was discouraged by Don's listless response to this obvious encounter from God. I shook my head in despair realizing just how hardened his heart must have been.

Two days after the lettuce arrived, Don approached me and asked if we could talk. He told me he couldn't get the situation with the lettuce off of his mind. We talked for some time and as we did the Lord touched his heart. Before our visit came to an end, Don accepted Jesus Christ into his heart and began a new walk with the Lord.

When we are tempted to give up on ourselves or one another, God has a way of shining forth His truth and light in a way we never imagined. I saw the hardness of Don's heart and wondered if there was a way for it to ever change. Never would I have guessed that God would use a bag of lettuce to soften his heart and change his life.

Balaam was heading in a direction God didn't want him to go. He sent an angel to deter him but Balaam's eyes were not opened to see. When his donkey saw the figure, he veered off the trail. Three times, Balaam got angry and struck him because he didn't understand. When Balaam continued to try and go forward in the way he thought was right, God opened up the donkey's mouth and intelligible words came forth. It wasn't until then that Balaam finally saw and understood (Numbers 22:21-35).

God had to use something that seemed foolish to get these two men to finally see. If the donkey had chosen to continue on the path, the angel said that he surely would have killed Balaam (Numbers 22:33). If the woman would not have obeyed the nudge from the Lord she felt was silly, Don may have never come to Christ. It was a donkey that saved Balaam's life and a bag of lettuce that saved Don's. Two seemingly foolish means that brought life to two men who were traveling the wrong way.

God speaks to us every day. While it might not be through a loud audible voice, there are promptings He lays on our hearts all of time. Don't underestimate the nudging you may one day hear. Like the woman who sensed God's leading to bring the shredded lettuce, it might very well be God's way of choosing the foolish to confound and save the life of the wise. As you follow and obey, may you experience the blessing of knowing that the Creator of the universe has chosen *you* to take part in His eternal plan.

Dear Lord,

May I become even more sensitive to what it is Your Spirit is speaking to me. May I never be ashamed to follow what I believe You are guiding me to do, even if it makes me look foolish in the eyes of man. Reveal what it is You are asking of me and help me to clearly hear Your voice.

In Jesus' Name. Amen.

CHAPTER FIFTEEN

Homeless in Chicago

*"... though He was rich, yet for your
sakes He became poor, that ye through
His poverty might be rich."*
2 Corinthians 8:9

*Spending three days homeless on the streets of Chicago
helped me to better identify with the struggles that many people
endure every day. There were times when I was scared and fearful
for my life. However, I found comfort in knowing that, regardless
of where I was or what I encountered, I was never alone...*

I was still working for the Topeka State Hospital
when I received my first phone call from our local
newspaper, the Topeka Capital-Journal. Stan Freidman, a
Christian reporter with a passion for his work, was on the
other line. Having never been interviewed before, I was
perplexed at his request to conduct one and asked him the
obvious question, "Why?" I was about to become the new
Executive Director of the Mission and that, he said, was
something people would want to hear about.

I was extremely nervous as we talked and stumbled
over my words quite a bit. I wasn't sure what it meant to be
the director of a rescue mission so I certainly didn't have
much to say to a reporter. Stan picked up on my
inexperience and helped me through the call. He quickly
became a close friend and personal media coach.

Stan had a special interest in the Topeka Rescue Mission and homelessness. Just a year prior he had gone undercover as a homeless man and stayed in the Mission for a few days. Afterwards, he did a feature story on his experiences and developed an even greater interest in homelessness within our country.

After I had been serving at the Mission for just over a year, Stan came into my office one day and challenged me. "In order for you to really know how to help the homeless," he said, "you need to experience homelessness yourself." I felt like I had come as close as I wanted to in 1983 when a tornado took our home and we had to live with friends for a couple of weeks before relocating. Stan shook his head and assured me that wasn't good enough. I needed to go to the streets and live there.

I was intrigued by the idea and agreed with one condition. I would become homeless for a few days, if he did so with me. He agreed. My wheels starting turning and I suggested some local places in Topeka where I thought we could sleep. "Oh no," he said with a smile. "That isn't good enough... we're going to Chicago." In order for me to experience what it was really like, Stan explained that I needed to go to an unfamiliar place where I had no family, friends, or knowledge of resources.

A few days later we hopped onto a plane, landed at O'Hare airport and hit the streets. I was excited about our adventure. I walked the streets of downtown Chicago that September afternoon with a smile on my face and exhilaration in my heart.

I recognized very quickly that people in Chicago don't make eye contact with you. As a matter of fact, many looked as if something was wrong with me when I smiled and said hello. It didn't take long for me to realize, we weren't in Kansas anymore.

Our adventure was planned to last three days. My smile started to fade when I witnessed an elderly man on the corner. The intersection was busy and on it stood four limousines, each carrying wealthy executives to jobs in the fast-paced city life. The man, obviously homeless and hungry, was searching through the open trash receptacles, taking out and eating whatever remnants of food had been left behind by the rushed passersby. The contrast between rich and poor America that filled my eyes was glaring and heart wrenching.

I learned as the days progressed that life on the streets could be dangerous and risky. My first experience of such occurred when I innocently sat down on a public bus stop bench. Within seconds, a big and burly man with flowing white hair and a dirty beard came running my way. He belligerently approached me screaming over and over, "You're on my bench! You're on my bench!" I looked at him in shock... and got up from his bench.

Over the course of the next three days, I was threatened, taunted, and chased out of alleyways and doorways by many. There were two times when I thought I would not only be assaulted, but quite possibly lose my life. It was mean and rough, but I was hungry for the realities that so many face and wanted to experience as much as I could.

We decided to make shelter arrangements rather than sleep on the streets and stayed on the floor of a communal living area through the ministry "Jesus People USA." They lived in a way that they believed mirrored the New Testament church by living together and sharing everything they had (Acts 2:44-45). It was there that nearly 800 people lived in an impoverished communal high-rise, and it was there that we ate and slept.

Back home, the Mission had been serving around fifty people at dinner and there were nights when even that seemed overwhelming. Here, over 1,600 people came through the dining hall for food. I will never forget seeing the large line that stretched down the street and around the block. In addition to the hundreds that lived at the complex, another 800 who were homeless or in need lined the street and tables for a free meal.

When not in the commune, we would stay out on the streets until late. Within blocks there was a large rubble area where a high-rise once stood. Out in the middle of the large field of debris sat a solitary desk and a chair. I was curious of its purpose and walked by the field several times. During our first night as it was getting dark, I watched as a man sat down and a line quickly began to form. People seemed to come from every direction as they then took their place and waited for their turn to approach the desk. I stood back in the darkness by myself as I timidly watched, wondering what was taking place. By the time two o'clock in the morning arrived and I went inside, over 200 people had filled the field.

The next morning I returned early to the same grounds. As the sun began to rise, my eyes fixated on between thirty and forty people who now lied in the rubble. Within minutes, a police car and ambulance drove up as if almost on cue. Officers got out and began walking around with their nightsticks, poking those who slept to arise. The ones who got up slowly stumbled away; the others were loaded into the ambulance on stretchers. It appeared that some may have not survived through the night. What I had witnessed the night prior was a drug dealer's enterprise. The field had been turned into a horrid business where hundreds came nightly to buy and use drugs. The identical scene unfolded all three nights I was there.

On Sunday we decided to attend a chapel service that was taking place in the basement of the large high-rise commune. I raised my eyebrows as the preacher came out. I was reminded of the Beach Boys when I surveyed the man with long, gray hair, big bushy beard, Bermuda shorts, half-unbuttoned Hawaiian shirt, sneakers without laces, and Bible in hand. He preached from the Word of God and, although I had never seen a preacher quite like him before, I was inspired.

The basement was filled with a combination of people who were either homeless, members of the Jesus People Movement, or men dressed in three-piece suits. Who caught my attention most though was a young woman, probably in her twenties, who sat immobile in a wheelchair. She was quadriplegic and appeared to be suffering from cerebral palsy. I was intrigued by the band she wore around her forehead and the long stick attached. I watched as she used this to communicate with others by moving her forehead and typing out words on the old typewriter that rested in her lap.

As this woman sat and listened to the message being shared, she wore an incredible smile on her face. Each time the Name of Jesus was mentioned, bursts of glee filled her countenance as she did what she could to raise her hand slightly in the air and lean her head back with a laugh of pleasure, excitement, worship and joy. As I watched her antics of praise, I smiled… and wept.

After the service I went up to one of the staff and asked of the young lady's story. I found out that she too was an employee and that everybody who came to reside at the commune received some type of job. Hers was typing letters. Though she was restrained by a body filled with pain and suffering, she had a brilliant mind, loved Jesus and did what she could to offer service for Him.

My heart was in awe as I approached the woman who had inspired me so. I told her she had ministered immensely to me that day and that I could see the love of God in her face. A smile welled up on her face as she threw her head back with a gesture of joy and delight. Though I could not speak her language, her language spoke profoundly to me; reminding me once again that God could work in and through anyone.

That afternoon, I freshened up and headed back to the airport. While I waited in line to board the plane, something strange was happening to me. I didn't feel like I belonged. There were normal people standing in line waiting with their suitcases in hand and families at their side, but for some strange reason I just felt peculiar. I couldn't put my finger on it, but I knew I was not the same. It wasn't until later that I read of research that had been on the psychological impact of homelessness. It was found that being homeless for only 72-hours or less could be so problematic that the devastation from the experience could negatively impact some for years. Though I wasn't actually homeless, I had caught a glimpse of the effects and what millions endure every day.

I can't say that I know now in its entirety what it's like to be homeless. Only those who experience it can truly attest to the realities it contains. As I became likened to those whom I serve, however, I received a deeper understanding of the struggles that are bore and how to better reach those who are suffering and in need.

There are times when we feel all alone and as if no one understands the struggles we face or sometimes live with every day. We can try to isolate and hide but there is One who has an understanding we can never escape. Jesus chose to come into this earth to live with us and become like us so that we could be reminded that there will always be at least one who understands our sorrows and pain.

My three days of homelessness could hardly compare to the 33-year lifestyle of Christ, but through my experience I gained a deeper appreciation and revelation of the life He once lived. He gave up His comforts and home to be like us. There were nights where He had no home in which to lay His head (Luke 9:58). He was ridiculed, misunderstood, mocked and abandoned. He chose to be like us so that He could acquaint more personally to our needs. He didn't have to choose that walk, but He did... all out of love for you.

If you've felt all alone, like no one understands or cares, be reminded today that you don't walk by yourself. Standing next to you in this life is a King so great that became a servant so meek, just to come closer to you. He has been where you walk and can relate to your pain. All He requires is that we open our hearts to receive the love He so freely gives. As we invite Him to make His home in our hearts, we can rest in the assurance of knowing that, though lonely at times, we are never alone.

Dear Lord,

You sacrificed so much for me. In my life may I walk with a willingness in my heart to do the same for others. Make Your home in my heart. Take up residence within me that I may never walk alone again.

In Jesus' Name. Amen.

CHAPTER SIXTEEN

The Worst Disease

*"... for He hath said, I will never
leave thee, nor forsake thee."*
Hebrews 13:5

*Isolation and loneliness can cause us to hide away and
surrender to the devastation of our hurts and suffering. Rather
than receiving the help we had to give, Cheri repetitively pushed us
away and continued in her downward spiral of despair. As we
persisted in love, a light which would free her from darkness finally
came forth...*

On a day not significantly different than the others, I
received an unexpected call from a woman who lived in
Central Topeka. She shared that there was a young homeless
woman living in a garage in the alleyway down from her
home. She had witnessed the woman going into the garage
and staying through the night. In addition to her presumed
homelessness, she was also concerned that something was
physically wrong with the woman. Throughout the night
strange sounds could be heard coming from the garage, as if
the woman was in agony.

I received the address from the caller and then
contacted a local mental health caseworker to see if she
could meet me at the location. We picked the time and
arrived separately at the detached garage which could be

entered only from the alley. The day was hot and sticky, and the leaky garage was musty and smelled of mold. We walked in through the open door and saw a table, lopsided chair that was missing one of its legs, a blanket, half-eaten apple and left-over bite of hamburger that was covered in dirt and appeared to have been retrieved from a dumpster. From the setup and contents, it was obvious that someone was staying inside.

The caseworker and I stood in the garage for about thirty minutes while I relayed the details of the call I had received and we waited for the woman to arrive. As we stepped out of the garage and were getting ready to leave, we spotted an attractive young woman walking down the alley towards us. From a distance she looked well-kept and alert so we assumed she was just a neighbor and proceeded to leave. The nearer she came, the more obvious the woman's tattered clothes and soiled face became. We could also then see that the pile of clothes she held in her arms was concealing a stomach which was obviously in the latter days of pregnancy. We then realized that the dreadful moans that the neighbors had heard through the night were actually labor pains from a young mother who was about ready to give birth.

The woman arrived at the place where we stood and immediately became very angry, demanding with a stressed out look on her face, "What are you doing in my house?!" When I carefully asked her if she lived in the garage, she proceeded to say, "Yes," and again asked us what we were doing in her home. I apologized and shared of my call received from a neighbor who was concerned. I introduced both myself and the caseworker and told her that we were there to see how we could help. The woman became even more agitated and enraged, immediately demanding that we get off of "her" property at once.

We left at that moment but returned several times throughout the day to attempt to reach out and see if we could assist. Each time we were greeted with defiance and hostility as she adamantly proclaimed that she was not homeless and did not need mental health services, though the obvious needs were evident to us both. Regardless of the factual knowledge we had which said otherwise, this woman was convinced that the garage belonged to her and that we were intruding in her home.

As much as we tried, she was not able to receive mental health services or shelter because of her lack of belief that she was actually in need. However, because of her pregnant state and the child in her womb that was to soon be delivered, we were able to solicit support from both child and adult protective services who kept an eye on her during those last weeks of pregnancy.

Through the effective collaborations and assistance from neighbors, we were able to be at the garage at just the right time to get the young mother to the hospital where she successfully delivered her first child. Two days after the birth, she abruptly left the hospital and abandoned her son leaving no indication of where she could be found. After months of searching, we finally caught up with her again while she was living on the streets. She remembered me from the past and finally agreed to accept shelter at the Mission.

The woman's name was Cheri. I eventually got to know her more and came across records from her past. In doing so, I was able to contact her parents who were living in Emporia, KS; the town I later found out she was from. They gasped in relief when they answered my call and shared they had been looking for their daughter for quite a long time.

Cheri had been an exceptionally bright student all of her life. She graduated from Emporia State University with a positive outlook for her future and a degree in business. However, about a year before we had met, she had begun to develop what her parents described as bizarre behavior. While family and friends attempted to reach out to her, she always refused. It was not until months later that she was officially labeled with the severe diagnosis of schizophrenia. There was no known family history of such a disease and not a trace of symptoms that had been displayed earlier in her life. It was not until the age of twenty-four that her behaviors began to shift and the family began their saga of great anguish regarding how to effectively help their child.

Prior to her arrival at the Mission, Cheri's physical beauty had gotten her invited into the homes of various men. While there, she would be used to fulfill their unwholesome desires but, when they were done, they would kick her out of their homes. On the streets she would remain until finding the temporary solace from another man. As a result of this pattern, Cheri became pregnant by three different men; each child lost in a system of foster care and adoption after her repetitive abandonment during postpartum hospital stays.

Cheri's ability to navigate through life while struggling with the innumerable traumas of both visual and auditory hallucinations made her life hellacious. I witnessed this one day as she stood on the back stairwell of the outdoor fire escape of the old building. She had left with the intention of going down the stairs but as she got halfway, the voices in her mind cautioned her to stay right where she was. As she listened and became preoccupied with the instructions she heard, she became stuck and could do nothing to finish the seven-foot walk down the remaining stairs.

As soon as I became aware of the situation, I went out to assist. When I did, I found Cheri in a completely catatonic state of being. She was deafened to my words and could do nothing but stare straight ahead as she held tight to the banister with all of her strength. Several of the other guests at the Mission tried with me to usher her down but, regardless of our best attempts, she remained frozen with no resolve of movement in any direction.

While I attempted to find help through both law enforcement and mental health services I was left with no answers. Law enforcement said the only way they could physically remove her was if I would press charges for trespassing. Mental health services said there was nothing they could do because she was not, at this point, a danger to herself or others. As day progressed into evening, and evening into night, Cheri stood locked in place and there was nothing I could do but pray.

For over 24-hours Cheri remained in that place. It was near evening the next day when we finally realized that because of her location on the stairs she was technically blocking a fire escape. Law enforcement was then able to come and forcibly remove her. Cheri was committed into the hospital and for the first time received treatment for a mental illness that had spiraled well beyond her control.

After becoming stabilized on medications, Cheri returned to the Mission. While she remained on her medications, she would thrive and do well. But sadly, as many suffering from mental disease often do, when she began feeling better she would quit taking her medications and fall back into the grips of hallucinations, trauma and despair.

Cheri floated in and out of the Mission for a number of years. Due to her illness, she would often view those of us who were trying hard to help her as the enemy. She would become paranoid and angry and again flee into the streets of darkness and the beds of strangers.

After seven years of abuse, rape, beatings, as well as living on the streets, in homeless shelters and abandoned homes, Cheri became tired and began expressing the desire to unite with her family once again. In spite of the previous resistance and life of darkness she had lived, they welcomed her back into their lives. The last news I received was that Cheri had returned to her hometown and was living in a group home close to her family, doing well.

I have heard the stereotype often voiced that all individuals experiencing homelessness are "lazy" and should simply "go get a job." While this solution is a viable option for some, there are others who are struggling in their minds or bodies to such a degree that they cannot tend to the daily function of buttoning their shirt, let alone the responsibilities tied to obtaining or maintaining a job.

At first glance from afar, Cheri appeared to have it all together as she walked through the alleyway towards the place where I stood. Had I not taken the opportunity to see her up close, I would have never seen the struggles she was facing or the battles that were raging within her mind. Cheri, like many others in her situation, stood before me alone and in need but was only able to respond through a reaction of bitterness and opposition.

Mother Teresa, who spent her life caring for the most crippled and needy of persons, once said that of all the diseases she had encountered, loneliness was the worst. The symptoms are not only isolation and despair, but often suspicion and mistrust towards anyone that would try to come in and break down the walls that have been built. While the challenges can be difficult, it is only when someone comes along and is willing to consistently step into another's darkness, that this devastating infirmity can possibly be healed.

When Jesus walked this earth, He knew rejection and despair (Isaiah 53:3-4). When He was approached by His captors in the Garden of Gethsemane, He experienced what it was like to feel abandoned and alone (Matthew 26:56). Rather than retorting with disdain or anger towards those who had left Him, He moved forward and entrusted His future into the hands of the Father. When we are struggling, He encourages us to do the same.

So do not fear, for I am with you; do not be dismayed, for I am your God. I will strengthen you and help you; I will uphold you with My righteous right hand (Isaiah 41:10, NIV).

In many ways, Cheri was alone and distraught. While she was rejected by many, she was never rejected by God. Regardless of the poor decisions she made or the negative attitude and actions she portrayed, His love for her remained great. While we too could have turned our backs when she tried pushing us away, we instead chose to love with the same kind of love that our Father so freely gives.

There are thousands like Cheri who are struggling in similar situations all over our world today. In order for them to receive the healing and freedom they need, we must be willing to love as Christ loved and reach out our hands. It is through our persistent pursuit that God will be able to shed forth His light to bring change. We may have no medicine to cure them or service to offer, but we can always continue to offer ourselves through the strength that God daily gives us. Rather than rejecting and walking away, He asks us to stop for the one before us and simply love.

As we receive His peace and deliverance from loneliness and despair in our own lives, may we go forth and give the same gift to those around us. Receive of His light so that you can shine forth upon others who need to find their way through the darkness in which they live.

Dear Lord,

It is only Your light that can penetrate through my darkness and bring comfort in my places of despair. Where there is loneliness, bring the assurance of Your presence and love. Where there is darkness, bring light. May I take all that You bestow upon me and unreservedly give to others in need.

In Jesus' Name. Amen.

CHAPTER SEVENTEEN

The Intruder

> *"For we wrestle not against flesh and*
> *blood, but against principalities,*
> *against powers, against the rulers of*
> *the darkness of this world, against*
> *spiritual wickedness in high places."*
> Ephesians 6:12

An intruder came into the Mission late at night breathing murderous threats. While I still don't fully understand the outcome, I am reminded that in all circumstances we can still turn to God...

In my early years of service at the Mission, it was not uncommon to get calls at home during all hours of the day and night. Because there was no additional paid staff, we relied heavily on the support of the guests to keep the ministry running. As a result, it was not infrequent for me to have to stop what I was doing and drive to the Mission.

It was two o'clock in the morning on one such occasion when I was jolted awake by the ringing phone. On the other end was a frantic guest, Joe, who was watching a devastating scene unfold. A gun was being held to the head of a young guest who was also serving overnight as the front deskman. Joe was the only one awake and, after ducking into my office undetected by the assailant, he was desperately calling me to find out what he should do.

After ensuring the police were contacted, I stayed on the line and tried my best at keeping Joe calm. As he peeked through my office window, which sat directly behind the front desk, Joe described the man who had the barrel up against the young man's temple. In fits of rage the infuriated man was shouting repetitively, "I'm going to blow your brains out!" The young man sat still, locked in a state of shock and disbelief. Joe continued to watch in a quiet hysteria as the drama continued to unfold.

My thoughts kept wandering to the man who had been innocently serving at the front desk when the attacker appeared. He was probably not quite twenty-years-old and had a childlike and innocent look about him. His blond hair and pristine features gave him more of the look of a model than a homeless man. My heart broke for him.

As Joe and I continued on the phone, I began to hear in the background the all too often problematic sound of a train passing through. Because the Mission was boxed in by the railroad tracks and the river, there was no other way for emergency personnel to get to the building. It would easily be between fifteen and twenty minutes before the train would be gone and the police could come through. My heart raced knowing the sirens were forced to remain still and as a result many inside the shelter were in even greater danger of devastation and possible death.

A sound I had never heard before at the Mission began coming through the phone. The wings of a flying helicopter buzzed overhead and I began to breathe a brief sigh of relief. Unfortunately, as Joe spoke on the other line to the 9-1-1 emergency personnel, he was told there was not enough clearance for the copter to land and that all of the other vehicles were stuck behind the train. Joe, doing his best to muffle his voice and hide in the office, continued to frightfully ask me, "What are we going to do!?" I felt responsible but had no solutions.

The entire time we were on the phone I was assessing our options and praying for an answer. When none came I realized the only option we had was to pray and ask the Lord to intervene. Joe and I began praying deeply and intensely over the phone. We prayed for what seemed like hours as we waited anxiously for the train to pass.

Though praying for God's hand to bring peace, I was still prepared to hear the sounds of gunshots at any moment. Instead, I was amazed to hear Joe whisper excitedly that the train had passed and he could hear the police nearing the building. As soon as those words left Joe's mouth, he watched as the once belligerent man placed his gun on the desk and stood calmly as he waited for the police to come in and arrest him. Truly God had done a miraculous work.

I got off of the phone with Joe and immediately rushed down to the Mission. We were all obviously shaken but more than that, we were all grateful. As I spoke with Joe and the young man, who just moments before had a gun held to his head, we all knew we had to stop and pray. We thanked God for the way He had intervened and for the lives that were spared. The more we prayed, the more our hearts turned towards the man who so disconcertingly had come in and brought fear. None of us knew who he was but we each began to develop a genuine compassion and concern for him. We asked the Lord to come in and touch him and to radically transform his life. We never saw him again after the police took him away that night.

I don't fully understand the reasons why lives were spared that night, but others since then have been lost to a multitude of tragedies. While it's common in such situations to question God, I recognize that the evil which occurs in this world is not caused by Him. God didn't make the irate man come into the Mission in the middle of the night and pull out a gun. We live in a fallen world. While God and His

Presence are very real, His oppressor, the devil, is very real as well. While Christ is ultimately victorious over him, people in this world are still given the free will to choose who they will follow.

Sadly, there are still many in this world who choose to follow the ways of darkness, bringing harm to innocent and undeserving people as they do. It is not because of God that these tragedies occur; it is because of evils of this world that have been inspired by satan since the fall of man (Genesis 3).

Paul was a disciple of Christ and missionary who faced much oppression in his day. He was tortured and watched as friends and fellow believers were murdered and experiencing the same. Despite the gruesome horrors that he witnessed and personally experienced, he asked the question. "Who shall separate us from the love of Christ? Shall trouble or hardship or persecution or famine or nakedness or danger or sword?" (Romans 8:35, NIV). Rather than giving up on God or backing out of his service to Him, Paul continued to trust God regardless of the persecution and evil that came his way. He recognized that in spite of, he was still more than a conqueror because of the victory promised in the end through Jesus Christ (Romans 8:37).

We can praise God because lives were not lost when the intruder entered in through the Mission's doors late at night. But would we have still been able to praise Him if the circumstances would have been different? While it would have been devastatingly tragic, there still would have been nowhere else for us to turn in our sorrow. It is only He who is able to turn our mourning into dancing and our sorrow into joy (Psalm 30:11).

God wants us to turn to Him in triumph and tragedy, in gladness and despair. There is still hope for our lives even when things don't turn out like we planned or the most devastating of tragedies occur. Rejoice with Him in the good, but know that you are free to weep to Him in your times of despair as well. Not one tear has escaped His sight and He cares about every concern that pierces your heart.

Even when life is not good, God is. And regardless of what tragedies you have encountered, He has not left you or forsaken you. I pray that you will be able to release any bitterness that you may feel towards God for the circumstances you have experienced. He is the One who is able to bring healing and peace. The fullness of that won't be found through any other means.

If you have experienced loss and question God for the reasons why it occurred, I encourage you to surrender your understanding and place your trust in Him. He loves you and longs for you to find your true victory through Christ.

No matter what you have faced, the darkness will not last forever. Eventually the sun will rise and the dawn will break. Until then, do not give up on life and don't give up on God. Whether you sense Him or not, His presence is with you and even in the most tragic of circumstances, you are never alone.

Dear Lord,

When I feel consumed by darkness, please shine forth Your light. Help me to praise and trust in You through good times and bad. Thank You that You are for me, not against me and that ultimate victory will come through Jesus Christ. Help me to take every crisis I face and use it as a catalyst that draws me even closer and nearer to You.

In Jesus' Name. Amen.

CHAPTER EIGHTEEN

One Vet's Story

*"When my father and my mother
forsake me, then the Lord
will take me up."*
Psalm 27:10

When going through difficult times, we often hear the familiar words – "there's always hope." When we look at the lives of those suffering around us, do we believe it? Is there really hope in the situations that seem impossible? In the lives that seem so lost? For me, it was a man named Johnny who helped me to realize that, even in the most devastating of circumstances, there is always hope and our Father's love is always near...

Johnny came to the Topeka Rescue Mission in 1987. Just like many of the others who walk through our doors he was desperate, tired, and felt utterly hopeless.

Johnny was one of our more difficult guests. He was continually breaking the rules and not following through with the assignments that were given to help him. Through all of his apparent rebellion and faults, there was something extremely likeable about Johnny. Once you got to know him, you could tell that this 56-year-old man just wanted to be loved. As he began sharing with me about where his homelessness, alcoholism, drug-addiction and multiple broken relationships had begun, I came to see Johnny from a completely different perspective.

In 1950, when Johnny was just nineteen years of age, he was drafted out of his rural community in Northeast Kansas and sent into a very serious and difficult situation in Korea. The effects of what he experienced during that time forever changed his life. Johnny saw more death and suffering than can be put into words. While in combat, he was captured by the enemy and spent a year of his life in the darkness and anguish of a North Korean Prisoner of War camp. While imprisoned, he saw fellow soldiers and friends tortured and put to death. While he too suffered extreme physical and emotional abuse, he managed to survive.

When Johnny was finally rescued and recovered from his injuries, he was sent back home. With great excitement and anticipation he stepped up onto the front porch of his family's home. Before he made it to the door, the screen door was opened and Johnny's intoxicated father walked out. Without any emotion or greeting, his father coldly shared that his older brother had been killed in action in Korea. He heartlessly declared that while his brother was a hero, Johnny was nothing but a traitor. Johnny stood on the porch, shocked and bewildered, as his father yelled at him and angrily called him a coward. He told him the only reason he was alive was because he must have told the enemy what they wanted to know. Silent and stunned, Johnny could feel the life draining out of his body as his father continued. "I had two sons... one who died a hero, the other a traitor." "Johnny," he cruelly spoke, "you are dead to me. I never want to see you again." The door was slammed in Johnny's face and he never saw his father again.

Numb and crushed beyond words, Johnny walked off the porch and soon made his way into the local tavern. There began his thirty-five year journey of addiction and abuse; one that led to a $350 a day heroin addiction that could only be supported through theft; one that caused him to spend countless nights sleeping in dumpsters and abandoned buildings. This was the journey that brought him to the Topeka Rescue Mission.

Over the course of several months, Johnny and I became quite close as he shared with me more of the traumas of his past. Once I received a deeper understanding of why Johnny acted in some of the ways he did, I also received a deeper compassion and knowledge which encouraged me to further explore how we could help him.

I'll never forget the day Johnny came to me, twenty-five years my senior, asking me for a favor. Humbly and earnestly Johnny looked at me hopefully and slowly asked, "Would you mind if I called you... *Dad*?" Johnny was old enough to be my father, but I saw the sincerity in his eyes and I now knew his story. I looked at him with compassion, gently smiled, and nodded my head. From that day on in our relationship, I was no longer Barry... I had become Dad.

A fatherly love for him grew and as the days continued to pass, I saw a gradual change beginning to come forth. His heart was softening and the thick walls he had built for so long were beginning to fall. One night while allowing himself to be open to the possibility of a new life, Johnny sat in a chapel service and handed his life over to the Lord. He found another new Father that night and his life was never the same.

Even though Johnny remained rough around the edges and a bit more ornery than most people appreciated, Johnny quickly became a new man with a transformed life. I watched as Johnny the alcoholic, Johnny the drug-addict, and Johnny the thief became one of the most loving, giving and compassionate men I have ever known.

As he moved forward in recovery, he discovered numerous gifts that had been buried deep within. He found skills in the area of food service and loved sharing his abilities at the kitchen in the Mission. His new life caused him to also give of his time and talents in his church where he began working with young people through Sunday School and summer youth camp programs. His service was so commendable and far-reaching that, together with a former guest of the Mission who later became his wife, Johnny was recognized throughout the community of Topeka for his devotion in helping others who suffer to find comfort and purpose.

One Saturday morning, while Johnny was volunteering at the Mission serving breakfast, his heart stopped beating. This man, who had given his heart to Christ and his life for others, was now ready to fully embrace the true rewards of his service.

Johnny had been forsaken in life. His family turned their backs and cruelly pushed him aside. For decades the pain associated with that rejection plagued him and nearly cost him his life. However, when his life was at its worst, the Lord reached down into his circumstances and gave him a new life. Though his beginnings were very difficult and sad, his end was filled with life, joy and fulfillment.

Many of us have suffered rejection from people we respected and once loved the most. The wounds can be so deep that they cause us to put up walls all around, never letting anyone close again.

Johnny was a good wall-builder. He clung to the negative words his biological father had spoken and began believing they were true. Rather than risking the pain of rejection and abandonment again, he shut down, looked for unhealthy ways to soothe his pain, and rejected everyone around him. He wasn't able to receive healing from his wounds until he allowed his walls to be lowered enough for someone else to come in. Once the love of God began penetrating his heart he was then able to realize that, regardless of how his earthly father treated him, he now had a heavenly Father who approved of him, loved him and forgave him for all of his past mistakes.

Rejection is devastating. It causes your heart to hurt in places you didn't even know existed. It causes your mind to think thoughts that you would have never dared believe before. But it's not the final word for your life.

Regardless of the wounds from past betrayal, rejection and hurt, you are not alone and you do have a compassionate Father of whom you can turn. While His love can be hard to comprehend, especially if you have suffered at the hands of your earthly father, know that it's real and it's available to you. Don't spend another day believing the negative words or lies that have been spoken over your life, regardless of whose mouth they came from.

The Lord calls you His child. He is a father to the fatherless... He places the lonely in families, sets the prisoners free and gives them joy (Psalm 68:5-6). Don't ever believe that you're worthless or that you've been permanently rejected ever again. You have been adopted, you have been accepted and you are tremendously loved.

Lord,

Thank You that I can call You Dad. Thank You that during the times when I just need to be loved, Your arms are there holding me close. Help me feel the warmth of Your embrace and the security of Your love. Heal me from past wounds as I step away and choose to no longer believe the lies. Thank You for adopting me and allowing me to be Your child.

In Jesus' Name. Amen.

CHAPTER NINETEEN

Desperation

"Thou wilt shew me the path of life..."
Psalm 16:11

The decisions I had to make concerning Matt were some of the most difficult I had ever encountered. My back was up against the wall and I didn't know what else to do. Yet, even in the most extreme of conditions, I witnessed the Lord's hand at work...

It was the coldest winter that Topeka had experienced in years. Temperatures had dipped down into the negative twenties and were accompanied by an even more extreme wind chill factor. The snow was piled high and continued to fall. Standing outside for even short periods of time was unbearable at best.

The insulation of the old Mission building was horrible and the windows were brittle and thin. As the winds whistled and blew, the thin glass rattled and fought to keep the gusts outdoors. Drafts filled the building and made the temperatures even harder to bear. Even with the furnace on high, it was necessary to layer with coats, hats and gloves in an attempt to keep warm.

During this season, the Mission served as a lifesaver in more ways than one for the sixty-some individuals who sought refuge inside. It would have been impossible for anyone to survive a few hours, let alone an entire night outside in the cold. Fortunately, most of the guests staying with us were grateful and compliant with the structure in place. It was Matt, however, who became the exception.

The longer Matt stayed with us, the more my mind flashed back to a few months prior when the demands of my role at the Mission had become seemingly too much to bear. I confessed one night to Ron, a Board member and friend, I didn't think I could go on. I was distraught about the difficult decisions which I repeatedly had to make concerning people's lives; many of which were often matters of life and death. I was over-burdened and worn, uncertain of how I could possibly continue to face the challenges before me.

Ron gave a lot of meaningful counsel to me that night but what I remember most was a question he had asked. He affirmed that the position I was in was a challenging one, but reminded me someone had to fill it. "Was I that 'someone' or not?" he asked. If I wasn't and this wasn't my assignment after all, he encouraged me to quit and get out of the way so the right person could step up. "But if this is what you're supposed to be doing," he said, "then accept it and do it."

I went home that night and emptied myself out once again before God, asking Him to make the answer perfectly clear. As I prayed, the confirmations quickly came and I realized that this was where He had placed me. As much as I still to this day dislike making the hard decisions that affect other people's lives, I know it remains a part of my assignment as long as the Lord has me positioned at the Mission.

Matt came to Kansas from California after running away from legal concerns and becoming estranged from his family due to his hostile behaviors. When he first arrived in

Topeka, he was homeless and lived on the streets; but as the frigid temperatures began, he found haven with us.

Matt was an intimidating man who was nearly six-and-a-half feet tall with a strong, muscular build. Severe alcoholism and anger ravished his life and his intolerance of the Mission's rules was a continual challenge. Whenever any type of income was received, Matt would use it to feed his addiction and then come back to the Mission drunk. There was a zero-tolerance policy regarding alcohol consumption in place but because of the severe weather, we were continually faced with the same intense dilemma. Everyone knew that Matt had nowhere else to go.

I appealed to Matt on numerous occasions in attempts to help with his addiction. Each time he adamantly refused. Instead, the same cycle would continue and he would return to us more intoxicated than the night before. With his already combative nature intensified by the effects of alcohol, Matt was beginning to become disruptive to the entire ministry. In addition to the rules that were consistently broken, many were feeling threatened in their safety and challenged in their own sobriety. It was becoming apparent that as long as I continued to let him in our doors, Matt was going to keep drinking to his death. I knew in spite of the hazardous weather outside, the time had come for me to make one of the hardest decisions of my life.

Matt walked through our doors late on one especially bitter-cold afternoon. He was drunk as usual, but coherent enough to understand. I pulled him aside and told him bravely that we could no longer go on with the same patterns. If he was going to continue to refuse help and disrupt the peace of the Mission, he could no longer stay with us. I let him know he could spend the night but warned him if he walked through the doors the next day after his usual binge, he would not be allowed to come in.   Matt shrugged his shoulder in apparent disinterest and walked away.

Hopeful but unsure of whether or not Matt had taken my threat seriously, I anxiously came in early the next morning to follow-up with him. I took another staff member with me to remind him of the stance which was effective that day. Anger began to fill his face. "You know I can't quit drinking!" he exclaimed. I calmly reminded him that he very well could if he would receive the help we had been offering all along. With confidence he looked at me and returned the threat. "I *will* be coming back here tonight, and it *will* be after I drink." Minutes of sparring back and forth ensued. I told him that I would be testing him for alcohol consumption when he came back and that, if there was any detected, he would be spending the night outdoors where it was predicted to hit minus twenty-six degrees.

I was desperate to help the defensive man who stood before me, but didn't know what else to do. I knew without some type of motivation, however harsh it seemed, he was simply not going to quit drinking on his own. With all my heart I hoped and prayed that he would make the right decision and I would not have to put him out, as I feared the result would be tragic.

Matt got up from his chair and slammed it hard into the table. He forcefully put on the hat and gloves we had given him and strutted towards the door. Before he walked out, he turned around, glared fiercely, and yelled with all boldness and sincerity, "I'm going to write a note and put it on my body. When they find out what you did to me, you're going to jail!" He stormed out and slammed the door behind. I felt sick.

It was nine in the morning when Matt left the Mission. Throughout that day I prayed as hard as I have ever prayed that he would experience a wake-up call and do what was necessary. As it got closer to the dinner hour when Matt usually arrived, the dread and trepidation within me grew. It seemed like the longest day of my life as I wondered and worried about what I might see come through the door.

Five o'clock came, and then six. The sky outside was dark, the snow was blowing and the temperatures were steadily dropping both outside and in. My mind whirled as I wondered what happened to Matt. *Did I send him to his death?* I pleaded earnestly with the Lord. I left the shelter of the Mission and went outside in the blizzard conditions to search for him. My attempts were fruitless and he was nowhere to be seen. As the night grew darker and the hour later I wondered, "What have I possibly done?!?" My conscious and emotions were in complete turmoil.

Finally, at around eight o'clock at night, Matt walked through the door. I was relieved, but at the same time nervous and anxious not knowing how I would respond. *Could I really send him back into the cold if he had been drinking?* I thought if I did he would quite possibly die but, at the same time, felt confident I had no other choice but to stand my ground. My insides shook with apprehension as I walked up to Matt. I felt like I was dangling off of a cliff while hanging onto nothing more than a small thread that was ready to break.

With his head down, Matt softly said, "I haven't been drinking and I know I need help." I was stunned and couldn't believe my ears. The breathalyzer test confirmed what he spoke was true. There was no measureable trace of alcohol in his system.

Matt told me he could not remember having a sober day for the past three years. He admitted he didn't know if I was serious about putting him out in the cold or not, but that he didn't want to find out. He apologized for the trouble he had caused and humbly asked, "Will you please help me to quit drinking?"

I eagerly placed a call to the detoxification unit to request a bed for Matt. Unfortunately, they wouldn't accept him because in order to be admitted, he had to be intoxicated. Though he had spent the past three years of his life in a constant state of drunkenness, his current sobriety disqualified him from receiving their help.

Hopelessness for the man standing before me began taking over but was quickly interrupted by a group of men staying at the Mission who came forward. Each one had been where Matt once stood and had been able to overcome the wicked snares of addiction. Unreservedly, they offered to help him make it through the same journey. Broken and ready, Matt's new road to recovery immediately began.

Severe withdrawal consumed Matt's being for the next two weeks inside our cold, frigid walls. Through it all, the faithful men never left his side. We filled him with lots of apricot juice, honey and nutritious food; but mostly we held his hand, covered him with prayer, and showered him with genuine love. It was remarkable to see how the men, filled with their own issues and challenges in life, served in the same capacity, if not greater, than any trained clinicians I had ever encountered in the field. At the end of fourteen days, Matt was successfully detoxed and beginning to feel human again for the first time in years.

It was soon afterwards that Matt was befriended by then Board member, George Spotts, who also volunteered his time by completing donation pick-ups for the Mission. George took him under his wing, loved him unconditionally, discipled him and helped hold him accountable. The two quickly became good friends. It was through George's advocacy and high esteem for him that Matt eventually became hired as the Mission's full-time truck driver where he served faithfully for numerous months.

The true definition of compassion is not just hoping someone doesn't suffer; it's about laying down your life in the midst of their suffering. That is exactly what George did and continued to do for many years even after Matt left the Mission.

Through the friendship and support received by George, the guests who helped him to detox, and many others at the Mission, Matt's receptiveness to addressing other issues in his life began to excel. In time he welcomed Jesus into his heart as his personal Lord and Savior and his new life fully began.

After some time had passed, Matt asked if I would have really put him out in the cold that one fateful night. I told him that I'd rather not answer. He smiled and responded that he'd rather not know. He went on to say if I had put him out, he knew now it would have been because I loved him. He shared it was because of the love I and the others had shown, that he was able to realize for the first time, regardless of his failures, God loved him too.

Through his growth and rehabilitation Matt eventually realized it was time to face his history head-on. He reconnected with his family and made strides towards addressing the legal concerns he had run from in the past. He knew it was time to return home and when he did so, he went as a different person.

The day Matt left the Mission was bittersweet. While our beginnings had been difficult, Matt had become a new man over time and it was now difficult to see him go. We smiled as we reminisced on how far he had come since the cold winter night and both thanked God for the many ways in which his life had been spared.

If any man be in Christ, he is a new creature: old things are passed away; behold, all things are become new (2 Corinthians 5:17).

When Matt first came to the Mission, he was angry, violent and addicted. He was headed for destruction in more ways than one. I tried to love and accept him where he was, but it came to a point where I knew more was needed. His eyes had been blinded to the reality that his actions were producing. Though it hurt my heart to handle the situation the way that I did, it was the only way I knew of that would help him to see.

There are times in life when we, like Matt, begin traveling down the wrong path. While the Lord and others may be able to see the pending destruction we will face if we continue, our vision is not always as clear. Sometimes it takes a startling response from our Father to open our eyes and help us navigate the right direction.

For Matt, the door to the Mission had to be closed. Leaving it open would have not only potentially destroyed him, but also others who would become witness to his ways. At first, Matt became angry and bitter. He thought I should have just accepted who he thought he was... a hopeless alcoholic with no future or plan. But I was blessed to see beyond his hard exterior and knew there was potential for change. I couldn't force him to accept what I saw; it was a choice he had to make on his own. Rather than remaining hostile towards me and risking death in the storm, he accepted what I had spoken and made the decision to move forward in life.

God allows doors in our lives to close as well. We may be going through life thinking everything is just fine, when suddenly we become faced with a crossroad we didn't even know existed. God uses these times to guide us and help us reach the fullness of who He has created us to be. All of us run the risk of becoming stagnant in our lives, accepting our shortcomings and assuming our circumstances can never change. That's never true though. Even the darkest of circumstances are not too dark for God (Psalm 139:12). Everyone and every circumstance is capable of change. Sometimes it takes the Lord closing a door before we are willing to consider. When those doors close, we face the same decisions as Matt. Do we become remorseful and bitter towards God or do we humbly accept that His ways are higher than ours? Do we give up and choose to die in the storm or do we move forward in the new path that He has formed?

I hoped and prayed that Matt would make the right decision but I couldn't force him to do so. It was a decision that he had to make. God is the same way with us. He'll never force His own way, but He will always allow us to make the choice for ourselves. One path will bring life, the other destruction.

If you have made the wrong choices in your past, it's never too late to turn around and start afresh. God isn't mad at you. Instead, He loves you and will always give another chance to do what's right.

If there's a door that's been closed, don't be angry with God. Trust that He loves you and always has your best interest at heart. He never closes doors to bring harm, but only to help us choose the new path that will bring life and fruitfulness to our days. How we will respond is up to us. We can become bitter and fight to stay on the same road, or we can trust in the Lord's goodness and accept the new plan that awaits. I pray you choose the latter. In doing so, I'm confident that your future will be greater than your past.

Lord,

Help me to accept the doors that You have closed and humbly embrace Your purposes behind each one. Help me not to fight back with resentment or anger. Instead, open my eyes to see as You see and trust that my life can move in the direction You know is best. May I rely on Your strength in the process I pray.

In Jesus' Name. Amen.

CHAPTER TWENTY

The Freezer

*"Finally, my brethren, be strong in
the Lord, and in the power
of His might."*
Ephesians 6:10

The fears of the unknown can often grip us to such a degree that we become afraid of moving forward in life. It was through a donation of food and the purchase of a freezer that God was able to teach me a valuable lesson in moving beyond fear to faith...

During my first couple of years at the Mission, the Memorial Hospital in Topeka was preparing to close. In doing so, they placed a call to us to see if we would be interested in receiving a large donation consisting of all their leftover food and kitchen items including paper products, utensils, dishes and more. Though the need at the Mission for these items was great, I knew after viewing everything that we didn't have enough storage space in our current freezers to hold all of the food.

I spoke with the representative from the hospital and told him we would like the donations but that we couldn't receive everything due to space. Because of their need to disburse the items quickly, the man let me know that if we were not able to receive everything, they would have to give it to another organization. He would wait for me to call back.

I went before the Mission team and we estimated that we could purchase a freezer large enough to store all of the food for approximately $3000. While we had almost exactly that amount in our bank account, those finances were allotted to all of the bills due later that month. If the finances were spent on the freezer, there would be no money left over to pay the bills.

When one of the long-term Board members, Dean Hurst, heard about the situation he told me assuredly I could not expect to receive God's blessings unless I positioned myself to receive them. In other words, I could not expect to receive this blessing of food if I wasn't first willing to take a step of faith and purchase the freezer needed in order to store the food.

By faith, the approval to utilize the money for the purchase of the freezer was made and the donation in its fullness was received from the hospital. While this was a tremendous blessing which would be used to feed everyone coming to the Mission for at least two months, the crisis of having zero dollars to pay bills was glaring.

The bills were due and all of our money was gone. As I sat in my office the day after we purchased the freezer contemplating the pending doom that would come upon the ministry if the bills were not paid on time, my thoughts were interrupted by a woman who knocked on my door. She shared that she had some money to donate and wanted it to specifically be used towards the purchase of food. Before accepting the gift, I explained the current dilemma and asked if the donation could be applied towards the current needs resulting from the purchase of the freezer instead. She agreed and handed me an envelope that had been sealed before her arrival. As I opened it, I found a check made out for $3,000 - the exact amount that had been needed to purchase the freezer and pay the bills.

Because of God's provision and our willingness to put action to our faith, the freezer was purchased, the food was delivered, the shelves of the Mission were busting at the seams and all of our bills were paid. For months, the donated food was utilized to feed everyone and once again I learned a valuable lesson in faith. "Don't expect to receive a blessing from God if you're not prepared to receive the blessing."

David was a shepherd boy. He spent many days alone as he tended to his sheep. He may have been content, but he also may have been a little restless wondering when life was going to get a little bit more exciting. One day when no one else was around, some action occurred. A lion came from seemingly out of nowhere and tried to attack David's flock. Though he was just a boy, the protector within him rose up. He faced his fears knowing the danger he faced and fought the beast. Victory was won and his strength was heightened. When a bear later approached, this time with a bit more confidence, David pressed forward beyond fear and did what was necessary.

As time progressed, David heard people murmuring in fear of a giant who was tormenting the land. He remembered the victories the Lord had previously given and knew if he once again walked forward in faith a victory would be wrought. The people were amazed when the enemy fell to the ground, but David just smiled. He knew it was God who had delivered the victories into his hands. The battles he had won in the wilderness had prepared him to continue moving forward when danger and uncertainty appeared in the future (1 Samuel 17:34-58).

Sometimes a situation occurs that looks like a crisis to us when, in reality, it is actually a method God is using to strengthen us and prepare us for the victory He knows lies ahead. We go through seasons when we wonder if there is really a purpose for what we are doing in life. What we don't always see is the opportunity that lies just before us if we will continue to face our challenges head-on instead of turning and running the other way.

There was an enemy called fear who stood in front of me when the blessing of provision was just within reach. He tried to paralyze me as I looked at the uncertainties of finance that stood in my way. I could turn around and just remain in the place we had been, or I could tackle the enemy of fear and move forward in confidence knowing in the end God would supply the victory.

Sometimes we get afraid to move forward, even with good things in life, because we're not sure of what will happen in other areas if we accept the blessing that is before us. We can recognize the gift is coming from the Lord and trust Him to not lead us astray, or we can decide to stay where we are and miss out on the victory and blessing God has prepared.

God is not going to take you down the wrong path. He won't lead you in a direction that brings destruction. He loves you. He sees the strength He's placed in you and the victory that waits in the end. He wants to use your current circumstances to prepare you for the day when you will receive your blessings in full. Don't be afraid to receive His goodness. It's a gift He has prepared that waits solely for you.

Lord,

May my confidence be in You and not in the uncertainties I often see. Where there is fear, replace it with faith. Where there is idleness, replace it with action. Help me to move forward in all that You have for me to do.

In Jesus' Name. Amen.

CHAPTER TWENTY-ONE

The Lure of Compromise

*"There is a way which seemeth right
unto a man, but the end thereof
are the ways of death."*
Proverbs 14:12

While it can be reassuring to turn to friends for comfort and advice in our times of need, I have learned we must make sure that the first counsel we seek is from God Himself. Practical solutions and intellectual advisement may sound great, but if they are not lining up with what He is speaking, the only result that will ultimately come is destruction and harm...

Before the old Mission building began falling down, I was receiving counsel and support from a group of former colleagues and friends whom I had worked with in the mental health field years prior. As they observed and heard of the many challenges the Mission was facing, they began using their logic and intellect to offer solutions.

The most rational answer to our issues at hand was, in their minds, for the Mission to begin accepting government funding. Doing so would bring in a surplus of additional finance which would allow for the necessary repairs to be made and programs to be built.

Another solution that they believed to be sound was for the Mission to begin toning down the visible Christianity our ministry displayed. According to them, the community would embrace us more if the constant foundation of

Christianity was more hidden or relinquished and, as a result, public support would be increased. As I looked at their faces, each one seemed sure and confident in their counsel. These were men and women whom I trusted but my spirit was vexed. I knew I would have to seek the Lord in order to know what to do. The war within me raged on.

I was at home one morning washing dishes. With each dish I cleaned, my mind seemed to wander and my spirit struggle even more. I was deeply troubled. I didn't want to walk in pride and refuse to accept government funding without any real reason. However, I also knew the main crux of the ministry was based on the foundation of Jesus Christ. I struggled immensely with the possible ramifications of taking our focus off of the Lord and no longer having the ability to freely minister the Gospel within the confines of the Mission.

As I wrestled, my prayer turned into travail and the tears began to fall. In desperation, I pleaded with God for a sign. Almost immediately I felt the soft touch of a finger on my cheek. It was as if it was gently turning my head to the left. As it did, my eyes landed on a small plaque hanging on the wall next to the stove. I read the inscription: *In all of thy ways acknowledge Him, and He shall direct thy paths. Proverbs 3:6.*

It was the first time I had ever seen the plaque hanging in our home. I quickly called out to my wife and asked where she had gotten it. She told me that she had picked it up at a yard sale. When I asked how recently it had been hung, she told me it had been there for nearly a year. Somehow my eyes had been blinded from seeing the clear message God had been speaking all along.

Job suffered great tragedy in his life. Through it all, he asked the Lord many questions to try and discern what he had done to land in the ashes where he laid. In the midst of his uncertainty, three friends came to visit him; each one boasting of why they believed he was in the predicament he was. Their knowledge was great and their answers made sense, but in the end they were rebuked by God (Job 42:7). It was not the counsel of man Job had needed; it was a word from the Lord.

The counsel given by former colleagues to tone down our Christian witness and accept government funding made practical sense. We needed finances in numerous areas and following their suggestions seemed like it would work. However, what made sense to them and what had been spoken by God were completely different. God understood our dilemma but He didn't want us to put our confidence in government structure, He wanted us to put our trust in Him.

As the gentle touch from God I was not expecting came forth, my once veiled vision became clear... In *everything* we do, we are to acknowledge Him. I knew from that moment on the Mission could never compromise. My eyes were opened, my spirit was settled and the decision was made. Our foundation has been and our future will remain to put God first and never try to hide the fact that the Topeka Rescue Mission belongs to God. Since we have continued to move forward maintaining our focus on God, He has been faithful to cover us, protect us and ensure that every need remains met.

The lure of compromise is a subtle foe that comes in almost undetectable ways in our lives. A path may seem right and make sense, friends may even say that it's correct, but if it doesn't line up with the counsel of God, the end of that path is destruction.

Don't underestimate your ability to hear clearly from God. He is able to get our attention in the subtlest of ways; but if we are caught up in the whirlwind of what everyone else around us says, we may miss His voice.

If there are decisions you are faced with or answers you seek, draw near to the Lord. He has a way of making Himself known in even the gentlest of whispers. May your ears be open to hear all that He has to say.

Lord,

Forgive me for the times when I have sought the counsel and approval of man before You. Help me to trust in Your direction even when it does not make sense to me or those around me. I seek You for guidance and direction and I thank You for Your voice that still speaks. May my ears be open afresh each day to hear all that You have to say.

In Jesus' Name. Amen.

CHAPTER TWENTY-TWO

The Man with the Gun

"And be ye kind to one another,
tenderhearted, forgiving one another,
even as God for Christ's sake
has forgiven you."
Ephesians 4:32

My life was threatened and the safety of the Mission's guests compromised. Even through the trauma of this event, God opened my eyes in a new way to the awareness of His peace and the power of forgiveness...

It was a quiet afternoon as I sat in my office, which was then located behind the front desk in the old Mission building. The weather was sunny and comfortable and many guests stood outside enjoying the day. Suddenly, I was jolted and alarmed by the words of our front deskman as I heard him shout, "There's a man outside with a gun!"

I rushed out the door and there just south of the railroad tracks, about forty feet from the Mission, was a middle aged man theatrically moving about with a gun held tight in his hand. As he moved, he mimicked the actions of one who was in a gunfight back in the old western films. He would stand for a moment, twirl around while aiming his gun with both hands and then crouch down on one knee as he squinted and honed in on someone close by. He would then dramatically pretend to shoot and continue his dance.

The dozens of men, women and children lining the sidewalk and street frightfully held on to each other as they feared for their lives. The police had been contacted and I began doing what I could to keep the guests safe. Slowly, I began ushering people into the building one by one, all the while keeping a close eye on our visitor so as to not draw attention. Joe Masqua, our volunteer chaplain at the time, was right by my side doing his best to remain calm and assist. As we continued to sneak people inside, the man's eyes fixed on ours. He began walking towards us as his arms flailed and words I could not comprehend came roaring from his mouth.

We got all of the guests safely inside and our plan was to follow in suit. We were going to barricade the doors and remain locked inside until the police could arrive and remedy the scene. As Joe walked through the door the man continued closer and was now just twenty feet away. I stepped up on the curb to go in through the door when I heard the cold command, "Freeze... don't move." My back was now turned to the man, but I could hear his steps quickly approaching and knew he was near. He demanded I put my hands up and turn slowly around.

I did what he said and heard the faint sound of sirens approaching in the distance. As he pointed the gun right at my chest I wondered if they would get there in time. I looked into his red swollen eyes. He glared while he spoke, "If you know Jesus you will not be afraid."

I was confused and taken aback by his words. *Was this all just a test to see how I would respond?*

My thoughts raced as I realized there was a very real possibility the trigger would be pulled at any moment. As I stood there, I became aware of God's presence. Despite the likely chance of being killed any second, this man's wicked intent was being superseded by the undeniable peace of God.

We stood there for what seemed like hours as my gaze shifted back and forth from his eyes to his pistol. I realized then, more than ever before, how important it was to always be right with God and ready for eternity. Truly, none of us knows when our time will come.

Finally, the screaming sirens came nearer and I saw flashing lights coming our way. Like a scene out of a movie, five police cars raced across the railroad tracks; each one literally flying through the air as they hit the first edge of the track. They each came down with a thud as they scattered through the street barely coming to a stop before officers began pouring out with their guns drawn. As they directed the man to drop his weapon, I knew either he'd listen or he would shoot me instead. I waited.

Gradually, he lowered his gun down to his waist and away from my chest. I quickly stepped away as the brave policemen approached, but the gunman fiercely fought back. It took all five of them to apprehend the man and confiscate the pistol from his hand. After a long battle, they were able to place cuffs onto his wrists and force him into the back of a police car.

As I watched them whisk the offender away, the moments were surreal. Gratitude for God's protection welled up in my heart. I was thankful I would have the opportunity that night to go home and embrace my family. I was even more grateful for the confidence I held that, had the trigger been pulled, I had a Savior who was waiting to greet me into my new eternal home.

Where would you spend eternity if the trigger had been pulled on you?

I found out later that the man who was so disturbed suffered from a severe form of mental illness. While in jail he received treatment and was released in a very short period of time. With nowhere to go, he returned back to the Mission. This time there was no gun in his hand. Instead, he offered repetitive and humble words of apology for the actions he displayed and the trauma he had caused. He was now homeless, in need, and asking for help.

There were many in my life who were legitimately dismayed that the man would even consider asking the Mission for assistance after all he had done. We barely escaped without any casualties the first time he was near, why would we willingly invite him through our doors now? While the concerns were all valid, I was reminded of my Savior, Jesus Christ, and the reality of the faithful God who graciously gives each of us chances over and over again when we fall. As He so freely offers forgiveness and welcomes us back, should not we as His servants do the same?

We prayed and assessed all of the safety concerns. After doing so we knew the Lord was urging us to give this troubled man a second chance and a place to stay.

He entered the doors of the Mission as a guest and was polite and apologetic the entire time he stayed. Sadly, he could not even recall most of the details from the former encounter that had taken place. He disappeared one day without a word and never returned again.

I think back to one of the questions that ran through my mind as his gun was once pointed to my chest. *Was this a test and if so, had I passed?*

When Jesus hung on the cross, He had been beaten and scorned. Those who once followed Him had spread lies, betrayal and mockery. If anyone would have been justified in not offering his offenders a second chance, it would have been Him. By our standards, He had every right to be offended and held the power to bring judgment upon each one.

As He hung and breathed His last breath, it wasn't a curse that He spoke or disdain that He felt. Instead, He turned to His Father and asked for their forgiveness, for He recognized they had not known what they'd done (Luke 23:34).

The man that once held a gun to my chest and threatened to take my life had not known what he had done. He wasn't aware of the pain he had caused or the traumatic effects his actions had upon so many. Was it my job to scorn him and make sure he paid for what he had done? Or had God through Christ asked me to love and forgive him just as He had forgiven and died for me?

Maybe you've never had a gun held to your chest or been threatened with your life. But have you ever been hurt, abused, or betrayed so deeply that you were sure you could never forgive?

When we hold on to unforgiveness it's like a fierce disease that takes hold of our insides. The longer it grows, the more damage it brings; not to the offender, but to us. Forgiveness is the only remedy that will bring healing to the pain. It may seem unwarranted and our bitterness justified but, the more we hold on to the remorse, the more diseased we will become.

Jesus Christ came, endured shame and humiliation, abuse and agony, and died for you. When people came against Him, He didn't retaliate; He forgave. He forgave them and He forgives you, regardless of what you may have done. What He asks in return is that we give others that same gift. It's the only way that our hearts will become healed and we will be able to experience true freedom in this life.

Who is it in your life that God is placing on your heart right now and asking you to forgive? Release the past to Him. Release the hurt and pain that it caused. Allow God to reach in to the depths of your being and help you to truly forgive the ones who have hurt you so deeply. As you do, may you begin to experience a new sense of peace and freedom from the One who truly forgave the most. Choose to walk in His freedom today.

Lord,

Show me those who are in need of forgiveness from me. Bring me to the place where I can forgive not just with my mouth, but with a deep sincerity and depth from my heart. I choose to let go of the pain they have caused and the bitterness I have clenched. I forgive them and welcome Your peace as You free me from every past hurt.

In Jesus' Name. Amen.

CHAPTER TWENTY-THREE

From Awkward to Amazing

*"... He hath no form nor comeliness;
and when we shall see Him,
there is no beauty that we
should desire Him."*
Isaiah 53:2

Often we allow the external shells of people we encounter to prevent us from seeing the beauty that truly lies within them. Through an awkward man named Tim, God allowed me to see His Spirit at work in a way that I would have otherwise never dreamt possible...

Life's hardships, rejection, alcohol, and the traumas of active duty during war had taken much of Tim's life. When he arrived at the Mission, it appeared by looking at him that he had always been the odd man out. His appearance was unkempt and his mannerisms awkward. Sores from eczema covered his face and body. Atop his scarred and peeling face sat greasy hair that was always scattered and uncombed. The old dirty glasses he wore were held together with duct tape and were so crooked that it was amazing they still stayed on his face. His posture was hunched and he walked with a limp. When he spoke, the highest and squeakiest voice I ever heard came forth.

Around the time Tim first came to us, I was frequently invited to give formal presentations at churches who were interested in learning more about the Mission. In addition to a musician and myself, a tight-knit group of nine guests who were staying in the long-term program of the Mission regularly accompanied me to the churches to share their testimonies.

A presentation at a local church was scheduled for one summer evening and the agenda was set. As I began loading the van with our equipment, the team from the Mission approached me and said they wanted Tim to come along. He had recently become a part of the long-term program and, while I had not yet received the opportunity to get to know him, the rest of the group had welcomed and quickly grafted him into their family.

I had seen him around and, based on his appearance, I didn't think he was quite ready to come and share his testimony. I politely turned down their request and returned to loading the van. Unfortunately, they didn't give up that easily and continued to make a strong appeal on behalf of their newest friend.

I was irritated. The evening was planned, a great presentation was ready, and I truly believed bringing along someone like Tim who I didn't know would just mess everything up. I again turned the group down. They were visibly frustrated at my stance and resentfully walked away.

The group returned just as it was time for the van to pull away to go to the church. Instead of piling in, they all stood in front of me with their arms crossed and their heads held high. "If Tim doesn't go, we don't go," one of the guests declared. The rest of the team nodded their heads in agreement. I couldn't believe it. I felt like I was being held hostage by my own allies.

I took a deep breath, realizing now I had a huge problem. There was a two-hour presentation scheduled and if this group didn't go, it would be up to me and the vocalist to fill the entire space; not something I felt confident we could do. I said a quick inner prayer and then reluctantly agreed to let Tim come, but only to observe. They shook their heads letting me know they weren't satisfied with my conditions. They wanted Tim to share his testimony right alongside of the rest of them.

I had never heard Tim's testimony and could only imagine what the presentation would be like. In compromise, I told them the agenda was already set but if by chance there was extra time at the end, Tim could share. Though I had no intention of allowing enough time at the end for him to really speak, the joy within the team at the possibility was great and they all climbed happily with Tim into the van.

The program was going wonderful. The music was great, my message was clear, and the testimonies were phenomenal. As the last guest began finishing what he had to share, I was both astonished and horrified to look at my watch and realize we still had ten minutes to spare. Thinking no one else in the group would notice, I tried ignoring the clock but to no avail. Nine pairs of penetrating eyes stared intently at me as they cleared their throats and motioned towards Tim. I looked at him in dismay. He was sitting hunched over in the pew with his dirty plaid shirt and oversized pants. His broken glasses were falling off of his face and his oily disheveled hair was going in forty-five different directions. I feared the worst and thought for sure his high squeaky voice would ruin the night.

Hesitantly, I returned to the stage and with microphone in hand gave a little disclaimer. "I don't know this guy… but he really wanted to come tonight and share his testimony." I introduced him by name and handed the microphone into his rough, crusted hand. As I walked down to my seat I bowed my head in prayer and asked the Lord to please help us through what was sure to be a disaster.

As Tim began to speak, what I had feared became a reality. His pitchy voice over the microphone sounded irritating, his words were hard to hear, his speech was filled with stops and stuttering, and I was certain no one would get anything out of this grand finale.

Bravely, Tim began to do his best to share about what his life had been during his near fifty years of rejection. He talked about the challenges of abuse, poverty, homelessness, hunger, alcoholism and failure he had faced. Then he went on to share about the new family he had found at the Topeka Rescue Mission. He called each member out by name and talked of the love and embrace he received from each one. I was surprised and ashamed when he even included me. He shared how he had only heard about Jesus Christ in his past but now, because of the love he had received, he fully knew Him as his personal Lord and Savior.

My head was still bowed when my ears tuned in beyond Tim's voice to the sounds of quiet rustling in the crowd behind me. While the auditorium was silent and still, the sound of purses and bags being opened caught my attention. When my curiosity could take it no more, I turned around slowly and looked. Men and woman across the packed sanctuary were pulling tissues and handkerchiefs out of their pockets and handbags to wipe the now steady flowing tears from their eyes. Hundreds cried profusely as they continued to listen to the most powerful testimony of the night. While the content was not much different from what the others had shared, I realized that God's Holy Spirit was using Tim to touch hearts in a way I would have never dreamt possible.

Tim had been broken by the misfortunes which had characterized his entire life. Developing a sense of worthlessness from childhood on, he lost pride in himself and the ability to maintain his appearance. It wasn't his fault he had sores on his face or a voice some found irritating. It was a piece of his external shell that covered the true beauty which resonated from within.

When I first met him, I admit I couldn't immediately see past it. I was concerned about what others would think if I allowed him to present and didn't want his awkwardness to mess up what I had planned. Thankfully, the Lord had a better idea. Rather than using the carefully articulated speech I gave, the perfectly melodic songs that were sung, or the rest of the perfect program I had planned, the Holy Spirit chose to breathe upon a person who I hadn't even believed belonged. In doing so, He showed me that in order to walk humbly before Him, there is no room for judgment because of the way a person looks, how they talk, or what they have done in their past. Instead, we are to look inwardly as God does.

When the Jews anticipated their coming Messiah, they envisioned the external royalty and splendor found in their current and historic kings. Many had a hard time accepting Jesus for who He was because He didn't fit into the description of what they thought. He was born in a stable, not in a palace. He grew up in poverty, not in wealth. He lived His life as a servant, not a master. Yet, God chose His meek and humble life to save ours.

God can use any one, at any time, for any reason... even when it doesn't make sense to us.

It's not the clothes we wear, the beauty of our faces, or the eloquent words we prepare that leave the most lasting impressions in this world. It's Jesus Christ in us. Only when we humbly lay our ordinary lives down at His feet will we begin to see the Lord's extraordinary goodness pouring forth.

Tim wasn't striving to be someone extraordinary when he stood up on the pulpit that night. He simply came as he was and shared. Through his humility, God moved and hundreds of lives were touched.

Don't be afraid to be different or ordinary. Don't be afraid to be you. Doing so will bring forth more amazing results than any striving could ever produce.

You are beautiful. You are blessed. And if you humbly lay your life down, God will extraordinarily use you.

Dear Lord,

I lay down my life and all of my imperfections. I let go of striving and perfectionism and instead ask that You would simply use me just as I am. Help me to recognize the beauty that You've placed within me and everyone who crosses my path.

In Jesus' Name. Amen.

CHAPTER TWENTY-FOUR

The Kiss

*"A new commandment I give unto
you, That ye love one another as I
have loved you, that ye also
love one another."*
John 13:34

*Sometimes out of frustration, anger or a lack of alternatives
we make decisions in life that may negatively impact others. While
I knew no other solution and was trying to bring protection and
not harm, I once turned away a man in fury. It wasn't until
decades later that the Lord was able to teach me a lesson through
one of the most unique relationships I may have ever had...*

Charles was a tall and muscular man who came to the
Mission numerous times while battling with mental illness
and alcoholism. He was in denial about both and refused all
of our help. While we did our best to accommodate him, his
behaviors became such that we could no longer tolerate the
risks being posed upon our other guests. He would stalk
women on the streets and harass those staying with us. No
female could walk by without an inappropriate comment
being made. While his assaults were all verbal and no one
ever got hurt, his near seven-foot frame was intimidating
and most of the people who saw him became sorely afraid.

After numerous interventions between mental health
services and law enforcement failed, we finally had to ask
Charles to leave. It was clear his behaviors were becoming
much too hazardous and he was refusing any help.

Charles left the Mission amicably but afterwards he still always seemed to be around. We tried banning him from the property but he would instead hang out on the public sidewalk that lined our buildings. He would peer in through the windows and continue to make inappropriate comments to those passing by. I was concerned about the guests in our care and becoming increasingly frustrated with his lack of desire to change and unwillingness to go away.

One day when another detailed report of Charles' inapt behavior came to me, I had reached my tolerance limit and could take it no more. I grabbed my colleague, Cecil, and we went outside to try and reason with him once and for all.

As soon as I saw him, it was clear Charles had been drinking again. He denied it and so I furiously reached into his pocket and grabbed the bottle he had tried unsuccessfully to conceal. Jolting him into a level of sobriety and shock, I smashed the bottle on the ground.

He looked at me with big widened eyes as I told him with seriousness and anger he was coming with me. I pointed towards the Kansas Avenue Bridge and told him we were taking a walk. In silence, Charles, Cecil and I made the solemn trek to the bridge. When we stepped onto it the months of frustration I had bottled up inside came gushing out. I looked at Charles and then pointed south. "Go," I told him, "and don't ever come back." He stood stunned and the expression in his eyes told me he could not believe his ears. I motioned again for him to go. In a dazed state, he slowly turned around and walked across the bridge.

While I had wished there was another way I could have handled the situation, I knew I had an obligation to protect the others under my care and I saw no other alternative. For months I had been exploring multiple venues and solutions, but each one proved unsuccessful. I felt very alone and it seemed as though no one else was interested in helping. I wasn't proud of my actions but was honestly relieved they had worked. From that day forward, Charles was nowhere to be seen. It wasn't until several months later I saw sight of him again.

I was on my way to a meeting and walking out of a store in downtown Topeka when I looked and spotted Charles' large figure walking towards me on the sidewalk. I held my breath, not sure of what the encounter would entail. Charles pleasantly greeted me with the familiar aura of intoxication. After I told him hello, he asked if I would give him a dollar so he could get a cab to go to the detoxification unit and get help. I knew he was lying and that, as in most similar cases when people are asking for money, it was not wise to give him the cash. I have actually always made it a practice to never give money to people on the streets who ask. If they are hungry or in need of shelter, I will do my best to make them aware of services nearby but I never open my wallet to give, mainly because I cannot be certain that the money I give won't just be used to further indulge a bad habit. I knew if I gave Charles a dollar, it would likely go towards another drink and that was not something I wanted to support.

I stood on the sidewalk and was stuck. I was in a hurry to get to my meeting and had no services left to offer. Going against my better judgment and the personal rule I had always followed, I very reluctantly pulled out my billfold. When I opened it, I realized the only cash I had was a five dollar bill. I bit my tongue, clinched my teeth, reached in and pulled it out.

When I handed Charles the bill, immediately his face lit up with a glee and excitement I would only expect to see from a young child. He held up the bill and looked at it with wonder and delight. Dancing up and down he began boisterously exclaiming, "Five dollars! Five dollars!" He reached out and threw his arms around me, picked my six-foot-four frame from off of the ground and then gave me a huge sloppy kiss on my cheek. He started shaking me up and down and wouldn't let go as he yelled loud enough for the whole downtown to hear, "I love you! I love you!" Shock and mortification filled every inch of my being.

After what seemed like an eternity, I finally freed myself from Charles' grip and brushed myself off. I took a step back and, as loud as I could, told Charles to go get his cab so he could get the help he needed at detox. He thanked me and I dashed rapidly around the corner to my truck.

Relieved and believing the embarrassing encounter was over, I got in my truck and began driving down the street. I hadn't gotten but a few feet before I heard shouting coming from behind. The humiliation continued as I looked in my rearview mirror and saw Charles. He was running down the street, blowing kisses my way, and screaming over and over again, "Barry, I love you!" I was not sure my face would ever return to its normal color again.

It wasn't until over twenty years later that I ever saw Charles again. I walked past the front desk of the Mission one day and there he stood. He was much older and more serene at the time, but once again asking for shelter and aid.

As our eyes locked, he smiled and said, "Hey, I know you... you gave me money." I braced myself for another extreme embrace but instead he went on to tell me about his life. He said he had spent many years in California but, when it didn't work out, he decided to come back to Topeka.

Though he was still suffering tremendously in his mental health, Charles' aggression had ceased and he was ready for help. For the first time in over two decades, we were able to effectively introduce him to services, the unfailing love of God, and the compassion of people.

Charles became involved in a local church and turned into a different man than the one we formerly knew. His former belligerence turned into submission, and his harassment towards people turned into support. He frequently shared of his gratitude for the Mission and the Topeka community.

Charles did well while he stayed with us and then one day without warning, he disappeared into the streets. Though I trust our paths will cross once again, I have not seen him since.

When I think back to my experiences with Charles, I still have to shake my head and laugh. While he had challenged me more than any other who had come through our doors to that point, he taught me some things I will never forget.

While his behaviors were far from holy, a portion of his life represented to me the life of Jesus Christ. Not because of his actions or conduct, but because of his response to the actions that were brought against him.

I had threatened Charles, reprimanded him, and rejected him. While I did my best to accept him and tried all I knew to work with him at first, over time I became irritated with him and embarrassed to be near him. In spite of my negative actions, Charles always greeted me in love and never held my unseemly actions against me.

How many times have I done the same in my relationship with Jesus? I can think back shamefully on the times that I have become angry with Him, tried to walk away from Him, or been embarrassed by His presence in my life. Yet He has always welcomed me back.

The Gospels tell us of the pain Jesus endured. His best friends deserted and betrayed him. They were embarrassed by Him and ashamed to be associated with Him. He was lied about and unfairly judged. In all of these situations He chose to forgive and, rather than choosing revenge, He chose to love.

There are relationships in our lives we have with people who are difficult to love. Maybe they've used us. Maybe they've betrayed us, stolen from us, rejected or scorned us. In all of those situations, we are still called to love.

Love one another as I have loved you (John 13:34).

Forgive one another even as God for Christ's sake hath forgiven you (Ephesians 4:32).

We all have a choice. We can choose to love and forgive, or to avoid and ignore.

Regardless of what we choose, what we've done or where we've been, Christ still stands waiting for us with open arms. It doesn't matter how rough we've been, how many times we've rejected Him, tried to ignore or avoid Him; our Lord is still there. If you've found yourself living at a distance, may your lives reconnect and your eyes lock with His once again.

Dear Lord,

I am so sorry for the times I have treated You poorly, been embarrassed by You, and tried to hide from Your presence. May I never be ashamed to acknowledge and call You my Savior and Lord. Deepen my awareness of how I treat others and may I be reminded in each encounter that as I treat them, so I treat You. Help me at all times to choose to love and forgive the way You have loved and forgiven me.

In Jesus' Name. Amen.

CHAPTER TWENTY-FIVE

Laying Down Their Lives

"Greater love hath no man than this,
that a man lay down his life
for his friends."
John 15:13

Many times I have read the scripture about laying our lives down for the sake of our friends. It wasn't until I met Rod and Judy Say that I really realized the entirety of what that scripture entailed...

When I first met them, Rod and Judy were just average citizens who were working hard and doing their best at raising their two young boys. They later became two of the most remarkable people I have ever met in my life.

Once carefree and innocent, their oldest son, Brad, grew up and began suffering from the torment of a seizure disorder which prevented him from being able to function normally in life. In time, he eventually experienced circumstances that caused him and his parents to turn to the Mission for help. Rather than becoming hopeless or walking away, his parents made it their personal mission to reach out and do whatever it took to meet him right where he was at. In doing so, they were able to find their true purpose in life.

Brad was only twenty years of age when he came to us. His disorder was severe and the challenges he endured as a result were great. In spite of his challenges, Brad pressed forward and entered into the Mission's long-term program. There he found camaraderie from his peers and continued nurturing from his parents.

My hands were filled with many other responsibilities at the time. Rather than sit idly by, Brad's parents saw the needs for mentorship within their son's new group of friends and unofficially became the new leaders. Quickly they began hosting Bible studies, creating outings for the group, inviting them into their home, and keeping in contact nearly every day. They took each and every member under their wings and showered them with acceptance and unconditional love.

The team that Rod and Judy led consisted of a unique blend of individuals who ranged in age from their early twenties to mid-sixties. In addition to their son, the new family consisted of Joe, Steve, John, Ronald, Tim, Peggy, Sue, Kitty and Paul. Each one had their own set of distinctive circumstances that brought them to the Mission but each one became intricately knit together through the bonds of their friendship and love.

Joe was a challenged man who had been receiving mental health services for the majority of his life.

Steve had been a financial administrator of a large corporation. He became homeless for the first time after being released from jail for the embezzlement of funds.

John was a Korean War veteran who had turned to the comforts of drugs and alcohol to mask the many emotional torments of his past.

Ronald was trying to find an escape from life after having eleven children and choosing to walk away from the responsibility of each one.

Tim was just awkward and slow.

Peggy was one who had never received love or a chance at life because of her uncomely appearance.

Sue had spent most of her life in and out of state hospitals. She came to the Mission after being discovered in a field while suffering from a severe mental breakdown.

Kitty was weathered and worn after years of prostitution and drug abuse.

Paul had been a professional social worker with the Veteran's Administration. After damaging his back and experiencing immense pain, he turned to alcohol in attempts to manage his suffering and eventually became homeless as a result.

All of these individuals, as different and challenged as they were, received the consistent love and embrace that Rod and Judy had to give. It was a love so nurturing that it brought permanent change into each one of their lives.

While it was their son that had first drawn them to the Mission and the team, even after Brad left they continued their unfailing walk of sacrificial love with each individual. The members learned how to depend on themselves and one another as they grew in life but their faithful coaches, Rod and Judy, were always there cheering them on.

As I watched how the couple persevered with each team member I was consistently reminded of the words spoken to us from our Savior, "Love each other as I have loved you. Greater love has no one than this: to lay down one's life for one's friends" (John 15:12-13, NIV). Never before had I seen people so perfectly illustrate what it was Jesus was saying in this scripture. I watched as Rod and Judy allowed their lives to be put aside for the sake of their new family and the friends they had made. They centered their lives around sharing love with each individual on the team and there was not one celebration or tragedy in which they were not present.

For over twenty-five years, this couple has attended every graduation, wedding and funeral. They have made visits during every hospital stay and even visited the jail, mental health facility, and emergency room when the walk for some became rough. Though many tears have been shed and most of the team members have since died, including their son, Rod and Judy have never given up hope. They took the words of Christ seriously and truly, without reservation, laid down their lives. The fruit has been lives saved and forever transformed because they were willing to give of themselves and offer their love.

I think we sometimes believe we have to do something extraordinary to receive God's approval or really gain his love. Jesus told us that He calls us friends when we do one simple thing... love (John 15:13-14). It doesn't get any simpler than that, but it also doesn't get more challenging.

Jesus embraced many who were challenged during His life on this earth. There were times when the pompous Scribes and Pharisees looked at Jesus with disdain. "Why is He eating with *them*?" they asked the disciples in disgust one day as Jesus dined with some sinners. Jesus answered the question for them by saying, "They that are whole have no need of the physician, but they that are sick" (Mark 2:15-17). He didn't come to love just those who were blameless and righteous, but those who were struggling and lost. And He commanded us to do the same.

As I have loved you, so lay down your life and love (John 15:12-13, paraphrased).

I believe Rod and Judy not only understood, but truly lived out what Jesus asked. It wasn't without hardships at times, but each day they awoke they recognized their purpose in life – to lay down their lives and love the ones God had placed in their paths.

Many of us struggle with purpose when the core purpose for all of our lives is the same. *Lay down our lives and love.* The question is, are we bold enough to embrace it and are we willing to walk it out?

Who has been placed before you? May you find the boldness to lay down your life, walk out His instructions, and love the ones He has placed in your path.

Lord,

Help me to follow Your direction and follow Your words. Thank You, Jesus, for laying down Your life for me that I may lay down my life for others. May I fearlessly, sacrificially and boldly do just that.

In Your Name. Amen.

CHAPTER TWENTY-SIX

Standing in the Midst of Falling

*"For He shall give His angels charge
over thee, to keep thee in
all thy ways."*
Psalm 91:11

I didn't realize it at the time, but in hindsight I was able to see there was no logical reason why our old building didn't fall down before construction of our new facility was complete. Through the discovery of what actually kept the collapsing wall standing tall, I was able to once again see the ways in which God strengthens and protects us, even when we are not aware...

I can still vividly recall the details of the call I received in March of 1989. A staff member was frantically calling to let me know a huge limestone rock had just fallen through the drop ceiling of the shelter. The large rock had crashed down directly on top of a chair a guest was sitting in just seconds before. Because of the size of the rock and the weight of the impact, all that remained of the chair was a shattered pile of rubble. If the guest hadn't moved, he would have been crushed and either severely injured or killed.

When the city inspectors came out to examine, they confirmed the building had begun shifting and that the collapsing section needed to be evacuated. Permission was given for the approximately seventy men who were staying on the top floor to relocate downstairs into the dining area as a sleeping alternative.

For two days, time was spent hauling our belongings to the first floor. When two of the men reached the bottom of the staircase with the last load, the entire north side ceiling of the second floor *immediately* caved in. The building was deteriorating greatly and because of the poor financial status of the Mission, there was nothing anyone could do to fix it.

When the top floor began to collapse, I have to admit my first instinct was not faith but fear. However, God was faithful to help me through. It was during that time I received a phone call from a dear friend and intercessor, Mickie. Not knowing what was going on with the building or the struggle I was having in my faith, she matter-of-factly relayed to me the message she had received from the Lord. I wasn't to worry about anything because there were three very large angels holding up the north wall of the building and it would not collapse.

My analytical mind was amused. I had never given much thought to angels working in that way before and thought the notion of having three assigned to the collapsing building was a little bit absurd. However, as the days progressed I found a lot of great comfort in the possibility that the brittle two-and-a-half story wall would never fall.

Two and a half years passed. A new shelter was developed, we transitioned all of our services into the new building and the old wall never fell. As part of the excavating endeavors, demolition expert George Champney and his crew were tearing down the old structure. After they had taken it down to the supporting floor joists, George called me over. He showed me what should have been the major support system for the large structure and pointed out how the floor beams had been corroded by floods, age and termites. He told me he had torn down a lot of buildings in his day and experience told him our old building wall should have collapsed a long time ago. My eyes widened when he then pointed to the support that was holding the entire north side of the building up... old, rotten wood measuring no more than a quarter-inch thick. George looked at me and said he considered this a miracle. He smiled and nudged me as he went on to add, "Kinda makes you think there's a God, doesn't it?"

I smiled and shook my head in disbelief as I recalled the phone call from Mickie. While I had first mused at the words she shared, I was now able to thank God once again for His faithfulness in the midst of my unbelief.

Outside of God and His sovereign protection, there is no reason why the man who sat in the chair just before the huge limestone fell got up and moved. He did not know what was about to occur. Had he waited even thirty more seconds, he would have been crushed.

When we spent two days hauling belongings down into the first floor, there was no indication the ceiling would soon fall. Yet, the entire north ceiling collapsed the second the two men were safely down the basement stairs.

For more than two years, the Mission's old wall structure was held up by nothing but decaying, unsteady wood. Regardless of the impossibility, the frame never fell.

While each one of these instances could be brushed aside as coincidence, I am confident each one was evidence of God's steady hand at work.

Many times I have been guilty of looking at situations on the surface and thinking all hope is lost. I have looked at my own weakness and failed to recognize His intervention and strength. While it's difficult for my analytical mind to sometimes comprehend, I recognize these are areas where I just need to let go and trust God. He is working behind the scenes in ways we can never fully imagine.

The deteriorating floor joists that held up the walls of a two-and-a-half story building were decayed, withered and weak. On their own, there is no possible way rotten wood could have supported the weight of the heavy wall attached to a large building filled with people. Yet, as impossible as it was, God used the feeble and deteriorating joists to support an entire structure which in essence saved lives.

There may be days when you feel like those brittle and worn wooden beams. They once stood strong and firm, but the wear they endured through floods, attacks, and time left them dilapidated and weak. You might feel in your weakness the weight of a two-and-a-half story building is resting on your shoulders. The walls may be caving in and there may be nothing you can do to stop it. It is in those times God tells you to imitate those feeble joists and just *stand* (Ephesians 6:13). His angels will bear you up (Psalm 91:11) and He will be your strength (2 Corinthians 12:10).

Regardless of how heavy the load may become, don't allow yourself to collapse and give in. The Lord wants to be your strength and He has assigned His angels to help you in ways you do not know. Though your body may be weary and your emotions weak, you don't stand alone and you will make it through.

Dear Lord,

Thank You that You are my strength when I am weak. Though the walls seem to be collapsing around me and I sometimes wonder if I can stand, thank You that You don't ask me to stand alone. Thank You for Your angels that guard me and Your strength that sustains me. Help me to be aware of Your presence in all I go through.

In Jesus' Name. Amen.

CHAPTER TWENTY-SEVEN

Acquiring the Impossible

*"… The things which are impossible
with men are possible with God."*
Luke 18:27

*The idea of building a new shelter was far from possible in
the natural. Numerous times I was told that "it can't be done" and
throughout the years of development, my faith continued to falter.
However, as I did my best to stand firm on what I believed we were
supposed to do, I witnessed God turn the impossible into the
possible time and time again…*

In was 1989 and the old building was falling down,
but the needs for shelter and food remained before us. Our
options were to go out of business and quit, or to trust God
and build something new. As the Board of Directors and I
prayed, we knew the Lord did not want us to give up.
Though the obstacles were huge, we began moving forward
in Him.

The plans were drawn up and the blueprint for the
new shelter was $1.5 million. Our annual budget was less
than $200,000 each year. *How could we possibly dream of a
million dollar expansion, let alone the cost to sustain it?*

As we put our fears aside, our prayers shifted from
"What?" to "Where?" We continued to pray for direction
and a strong consensus among us came. Across the street

from the then current building stood five dilapidated buildings. It was there where we believed God was showing us the next Mission building would stand.

By faith, we slowly walked forward and drew up the plans for the new building. We had not yet gone public with the direction we felt we had been given, when the City of Topeka announced they were going to be condemning all five of the buildings we had hoped to purchase and tear down. Timidly, I made my first call to the City to share of our desire to purchase the grounds. I was told the Mission could bid on the properties but that we would *never* receive them because of a $50,000 lien attached and the numerous other legal entanglements which would prevent anyone from ever purchasing them.

While others around me appeared to be standing firm, my faith was faltering and I was beginning to doubt if we had really heard from God. Every day I would take the floor plans for the new building and drive around the city. In doing so, I would ask the Lord where it was that He wanted us to build. I contacted property owners and explored several options but none of them ever came together. By the end of each day I would drive back to the Mission exhausted, discouraged and frustrated.

After completing the rounds throughout the city one day, I returned to the Mission. Again, I had taken hours out of my day to drive around and try to figure out where we were supposed to build. As I stepped out of my car, I felt like the Lord asked me a question. "Why are you wasting all of this time? I told you where it was going to be built." This time I listened. Regardless of how impossible it seemed, I knew the shelter would either be built there or not at all. From that day on I pressed forward and stood upon what I believed the Lord had shown and asked us to do.

In time, we found out that costs were estimated at $20,000 to purchase the properties but the City would then be spending an additional $70,000 to demolish them. Knowing the odds were still against us based on my previous call, I took a chance and placed another. I spoke to the planning department and asked if they would be willing to entertain a trade in which we would tear down the buildings for free in exchange for the property deeds, essentially saving the City $50,000. As the Lord would have it, the City agreed and after a short period of time, the properties became ours.

Once the announcement became public that we were preparing to build, God continued to come forth in extraordinary ways and every ounce of provision needed was supplied. One such way was through a stranger who walked into my office unannounced.

The man looked ordinary, wearing jeans, a white T-shirt and tennis shoes. Upon my first impression, I assumed this man was one of the guests staying at the Mission. Rather than introducing himself, he quickly began asking questions about the building and the construction details that were in place. He first inquired of what the outside of the building would be made of. When I responded by telling him it would be made of metal, he retorted by telling me that was a bad idea and suggested we use concrete instead. I held my breath while he proceeded to ask me what the inside of the building would consist of. As I confidently told him we were planning on sheet rock, again he replied that the idea was bad and it too needed to be made of concrete block. I could sense the irritation within me beginning to rise so, in an attempt to end the conversation, I politely told the man that, bad idea or not, the Mission could simply not afford the purchase of the concrete block he was suggesting. He looked at me nonchalantly and answered calmly, "Yes, you can."

Before I could offer any further rebuttal, he went on to introduce himself as Jim Browning of Capitol Concrete. I was stunned. He said that it was because of all the Lord had done for him in his life that he was going to donate all of the gray concrete block which was needed.

After the building was built, Jim came to me once again. He wondered what I thought of the color of the unpainted concrete blocks he and his company had supplied. Being accustomed to the dreary paneling and bare rock that filled the old building, I shrugged my shoulders and responded that it looked okay to me. He shook his head, smiled and then suggested that everything be painted with the paint he was going to donate.

With each new phase of development, our seemingly "impossible" endeavor became more and more plausible. Throughout the course of two years, I witnessed countless interventions as God sovereignly orchestrated the development on the land which He had told us to build. When we began moving forward, we had no idea how it would all come to pass and the oppression was great along the way. However, as we put our trust in Him and stood on what we believed to be His voice, all of His plans continued to succeed and over time a new shelter was complete.

A rich young ruler came to Jesus and asked Him the key to eternal life. After reminding him of some commandments for living which the young man said he had followed, Jesus told him to sell all that he had and give it to the poor; then he would have treasure in heaven and be able to fully follow Christ. The rich man was sorrowful. He was attached to his possessions and did not want to give (Luke 18:18-23).

Jesus saw the sorrow of the young ruler's heart and told his disciples it would be easier for a camel to pass through the eye of a needle than for a rich man to enter into the Kingdom of God. Troubled, they asked the question, "Then who can be saved?" Jesus told them this truth, "The things that are impossible with men are possible with God" (Luke 18:24-27).

The ruler in the story must have felt hopeless and distraught. Scripture tells us he was sorrowful and actually walked away from Jesus (Matthew 19:22). To him, Jesus was just asking too much. There was no way he knew how to move forward in what was being asked. But, while it was impossible for him to do what Jesus required in his own strength, it wasn't too hard for God.

There may be times in our lives when we feel like God is asking too much. We give of ourselves until we feel there is nothing left to give and yet at the end of the day we sense God is still asking for more. As impossible as it may seem, there is always a way when we are trusting in Him.

When I stared at a building budget of over one millions dollars and then looked at the current circumstances we were in, I thought it was crazy. "You want me to do what, God?" was a frequent question in my heart. There was no way I could have made it happen on my own, but God through His provision and sovereignty brought forth all of the pieces needed to ensure His plans would succeed.

He touched the heart of a faithful business man and asked him to give. Rather than becoming sorrowful at the Lord's request and walking away, Jim followed His direction and gave to the poor. Many others were used and followed Jesus' command to give in the same way. As a result of the obedient hearts and refusal to walk away, a state-of-the-art shelter was built that has housed thousands of people who were homeless, poor and in need over the years.

Nothing is impossible with God. No direction He gives; no circumstance you find yourself in. God has a way of coming in and orchestrating our lives in ways we never would expect. All He asks of us is to not turn away but instead follow Him.

Lord,

Thank You for the many ways that You take the impossible and make it possible. May I see Your hand of provision and faithfulness come forth as I look past the obstacles and trust You for Your purposes to be established. I let go of worry and grab hold of faith.

In Jesus' Name. Amen.

CHAPTER TWENTY-EIGHT

The Praying Man

*"... The effectual fervent prayer of a
righteous man availeth much."*
James 5:16

*One of the most unique and serious-about-Jesus guys I
have ever met was Bob Steffes. He deeply loved the Lord but he
wasn't what you might call "warm and fuzzy" about it. He simply
told it like it was and believed God. "If this is what Jesus said we
should do, then this is what we'll do." Bob is the one God used to
help cast the true foundation of the importance of prayer in my life
and I can say beyond certainty that if it wasn't for him, the first
new Mission building would have never been built...*

We were about to embark upon our first building
campaign. The blueprints had been drawn and we needed to
raise over $1.5 million for the vision of a new facility to come
to pass. In the search for a campaign coordinator, I was
contacted by someone who referred me to a well-known
man of influence and prosperity from our community. He
was a successful business leader and had raised significant
amounts of money in the past. Since I had never attempted
to tackle such a feat, I was thrilled when I learned he was
interested in coordinating the endeavors for free.

I learned a little bit more about the reputable man and
found he was the owner of a business the Mission had a
conflict of interest with. With so many individuals coming

through our doors caught up in the battles of addiction, we had never linked arms with the manufacturers or distributors of alcohol. This man who was volunteering to do such a great deed for the Mission was the owner of just that. I was in a real quandary. I had many coming to me saying this man could easily and effectively get the funds raised, but at the same time I was troubled by the message it would possibly send. I prayed and searched earnestly for the heart of Christ on the matter. In doing so I saw the eyes of the ones who were battling addiction, as well as their families. I knew that, in spite of the compassion and generosity in this kind man, I would have to reject his offer.

Darkness surrounded me when I came out of prayer. I was certain the man would not understand and believed some in the community would scorn me after having rejected such an invaluable offer.

The man was contacted and, to my relief, responded with understanding and respect. The negative publicity I had anticipated from some in the community was nonexistent also. I felt at peace knowing God had answered my cries, but now faced the question of what to do next.

I began carefully observing the people around me, trying to discern who the Lord wanted to chair this huge campaign. I was intrigued by Bob Steffes. He was a mature Christian and sharp dresser who drove a yellow convertible clad with a personalized license plate that screamed, "JESUS." I didn't know him personally but assumed by his appearance he was not only a Christian but a man of great wealth. When I talked with those who knew him better, they all confirmed my suspicions and said, "That is the man you want chairing your campaign!" I felt optimistic as they gave me his phone number and I placed the first call.

Bob listened intently as I first shared my heart, but was also perplexed wondering why I would want him to chair the campaign. I told him truthfully that he came highly recommended. Many had spoken of their confidence in both his ability to organize such a task and his sincere love for God and people. Bob seemed surprised at the offer, but agreed to accept.

What I didn't share with him that day was that I had observed, and others confirmed, he was a great man of wealth. It wasn't until later I found that the prosperity others spoke of was his wealth in the spirit, not financial. I also hadn't realized he had never led a campaign like this before. Only then did his perplexity at my request make perfect sense. Once again I wondered if I had made a huge mistake.

Rather than telling him I had changed my mind and turn him away, I met with Bob and asked what he was going to do as the official chairman of this campaign. He looked at me with eyebrows raised and shrugged his shoulders as he calmly said, "I have no idea… other than pray."

Inside I was discouraged and thought, "Good grief!" I knew we needed prayer, but that as a sole objective seemed to fall short of what I had envisioned necessary to meet the needs before us. Though I was battling immensely, I knew I couldn't turn this man away.

The odds were against us regarding our great plans to build. We still had not acquired the property needed, due to legal entanglements, and officials were telling us we never would. We had moved forward by faith when we decided to start the campaign and now I had a man in charge who knew nothing about it, other than to pray. I felt hopeless and stuck with no choice left but to trust God.

Over time, as Bob prayed and the money began coming in, I realized God had orchestrated the leadership of our campaign in a very different way than what I anticipated. While I thought the predominant factor in establishing the right leader was wealth, God showed me the more powerful resource was prayer. Through the next two years of the campaign, we teetered through challenges and successes, but through each one Bob remained faithful to prayer and God supplied everything we needed.

One of the challenges we faced was the devastation experienced when we heard of the necessary halt in demolition, due to the danger found in underground fuel tanks. It was Bob who I contacted when the news first came. Together with Eugene Shoemaker, over sixty different prayer warriors were gathered and what became known as the Spiritual SWAT-Team was formed. What happened as a result of the combined prayers was nothing short of a miracle. (For more on this story, see chapter 29).

I was on the go excessively during the campaign and though my body should have grown weary, I could feel the power of God's strength carrying me. I knew the Lord was honoring the petitions of the praying man who had assigned himself as intercessor to my life. Bob remained faithful to that role as the years progressed and through each encounter, I saw his prayers answered.

The campaign was over and I was in my office preparing for the new building's dedication banquet taking place the next day. I had decided to put together a 45-minute film documentary but I couldn't get the project to come together. Hours of filming had taken place and I was now working with loaned equipment trying to splice all of the pictures together. Wires were going everywhere and I was frustrated and distraught. For the life of me I could not get the equipment to work. I had been trying for days and was about to give up.

Unaware of the situation, Bob stopped by my muddled office that afternoon and found me in the middle of my trial. I shared my frustrations. After listening quietly he reached into his jacket and said, "No problem." Bob pulled out a bottle of anointing oil, put some on his finger and then began dabbling it around, making the sign of the cross on the different pieces of equipment while praying in Jesus' Name that it would all come together. As soon as he walked out the door, I knew what to do. What had taken me days, now came together in minutes. The banquet went smoothly and the documentary was a success.

Years later, my wife and I were trying to sell our house. We had experienced great difficulty so decided to take it off the market. Bob knew what was going on and wanted to help. Every morning for two weeks as the sun began to rise, he came to our house and prayed. He would start on our front porch, get out his oil and proceed to pray as he walked around the house. I can still remember my girls waking up in the morning and looking out the window exclaiming over their shoulders, "The praying man is outside again!" At the end of two weeks a "For Sale by Owner" sign was placed in the yard. Before day's end, a man came and paid cash for the house. I stood in awe as I recognized once again the fruit of a faithful man's prayers.

Before I met Bob, I had spent time in prayer. I knew the importance of taking our challenges and triumphs to God and had seen the evidence of doing so. However, it wasn't until Bob came into my life that I recognized the true intimacy we could develop with Christ if we shared every area of our lives with Him.

Somehow I had disregarded the scripture that tells us to "pray without ceasing" (1 Thessalonians 5:17). In my mind the only way this was possible was to stow away in a monastery somewhere. Bob showed me another way. He taught me it was possible to know God so intimately through scripture that we could believe every word He spoke. When a challenge arose, Bob didn't fret; he took it to the Lord and acknowledged the promises already spoken.

I used to stand in awe of the way in which God honored Bob's prayers, but now I recognize that He was just honoring His word. Jesus said, "That's why I tell you to have faith that you have already received whatever you pray for, and it will be yours" (Mark 11:24, ESV). I never saw Bob falter in prayer or have his faith waver. He was intimate with God and knew Him deeply. He trusted in His goodness and stood on His Word. It wasn't that God loved Bob more than me; Bob just had a greater revelation of His heart than I.

I have come to recognize the deeper we delve into God's Word, the more we will begin to see and understand His true heart. That is when we draw deeper into fellowship and begin recognizing His hand in every decision we make.

Bob's passion for Christ and his commitment to prayer stirred my heart and challenged my walk. I pray it does the same for you. May you learn to pray without ceasing and see the abundant hand of His love manifest greatly in your life the nearer you draw to Him.

Dear Lord,

I long to dwell in Your presence and find myself praying without ceasing; fully acknowledging and communing with You throughout every day of my life. Show me how to dive into even deeper relationship with You. Give me a hunger for Your Word and a desire to know You more. As I do, thank You for revealing Yourself in even greater ways.

In Jesus' Name. Amen.

Underground Fuel Tanks

*"... all things are possible
to him that believeth."*
Mark 9:23

There are times in life when situations seem so difficult we believe a change can never occur. While we may have experienced victories in the past, our present hopelessness consumes us and prevents us from grabbing ahold of the ability to trust God with our impossibilities. I've been there more than once. What I witnessed through some underground fuel tanks served as another great reminder that, regardless of what may seem impossible to me, nothing is impossible with God...

The Lord had revealed the land where the new building was to stand and, as details began to unfold, we enthusiastically moved forward in our adventurous walk of faith. The City of Topeka had agreed to give us the deeds to the properties we desired as long as we fulfilled our commitment and demolished the five run-down buildings that stood on the land. Confident in the approvals promised, we went ahead and scheduled for an army of volunteers to arrive and begin tearing down the buildings on September 17, 1989.

As the months turned into weeks and the weeks into days, anxieties began to rise as we inched towards our big day. With only 48-hours to spare, the news of legal permissions was received and authorization to move forward with our demolition plans came through. A sigh of relief was had by us all.

As planned, a mass of volunteers arrived at the scheduled time and the project began. Though the labor was intense, spirits were high and the excavation was going well. For the first few days everything seemed to be perfect until I received a visit from Ben Schmidtlein, the owner of Schmidtlein Excavating, Inc. who was helping with the work. He put his head down as he walked into my office and grimly shared two underground storage tanks were found which were filled with contaminants. As a result, the excavation would need to be halted and the Kansas Department of Health and Environment and the Environmental Protection Agency contacted immediately.

The ground needed to be tested for contaminants and there was a possibility that the estimated cost to correct the problem would be a couple of million dollars. I knew this would not be an option. Our efforts ceased and from my bleak perspective there was no hope in sight. I had been assured by one of the environmental officials it would be impossible for contaminants to not be present due to the age of the tanks. After all of the time, work and efforts we had put into the project it truly seemed as though it had come to an end. Once again, a sinking feeling came upon me and I was tempted to completely lose faith.

Before fully giving up, I contacted our Spiritual SWAT Team for prayer and they in turn placed a similar call throughout the city (see Chapter 28). Within 24-hours of doing so, contact from the environmental agencies performing the tests was received. They informed us that based on everything that was evaluated, the contaminants should have leaked into the ground leading to damage and a costly resolution to the problem. However, to their astonishment, when they tested the land they found not one trace of contamination had leaked into the soil. As a result, they were able to safely remove the tanks with no excessive costs. With man, this would have been impossible, but with God, I was learning all things truly were possible!

Our situation with the new Mission building and the underground fuel tanks reminded me of a similar situation Moses and the Israelites experienced. They had been fleeing from the oppressive hand of Pharaoh when they came upon the Red Sea. Staring into the vast extremity of its waters, they thought they were doomed. Instead, God parted the sea and allowed them to safely pass through (Exodus 14:21-22).

When they reached dry land and saw their foes had been vanquished, surely they believed victory had been won. As they continued to walk, however, they ended up further into wilderness. One battle was over but another was before them. They were now thirsty and tired but there was no water to drink. For three days they wandered with no liquid to quench their thirst. They looked ahead and saw the waters of Marah. Elated, they rushed to the water only to spit out what they drank. The waters were bitter and could not be consumed (Exodus 15:23)

The situation was impossible. Contaminants filled the water and there was nothing they could do to change that. Rather than give up hope, Moses prayed. When he did, God intervened. He showed Moses a tree he was to throw into the water and when he did, the waters became clean. What looked like a hopeless situation was now another testimony to the Israeli people of God's great provision and love (Exodus 15:25).

I don't know what God did in the soil around the underground fuel tanks to remove the toxins and purify the ground. All I know is one day our project was stopped due to a hazardous concern and after much intercession and prayer, the contaminants were gone.

God had brought us through the challenge we faced with obtaining the approvals, He had conquered the needs for provision, and now He had cleansed our ground. The same faithfulness He had shown to Moses and the Israelites, He was now showing to me and everyone involved. Truly His provision is limitless and His love without bounds!

There is no barrier, challenge or difficulty we can face that is too hard for God. While the enemy pursues us and tries to capture our faith, God remains in control and knows just when and how to intervene. As we cry out to Him, He is faithful to respond. Sometimes in ways that make sense; other times in ways that do not.

Whatever you are faced with remember that the more challenging the situation, the greater the opportunity for God to work a miracle. Don't limit His ability to intervene and don't ever underestimate His great love for you.

Lord,

I trust You and I place my impossibilities into Your hands. Thank You for allowing hope to arise within me once again as I step away from fear and into the confidence that truly nothing is impossible for You. May I see Your hand of intervention in my life and be reminded once again of Your great provision and love.

In Jesus' Name. Amen.

CHAPTER THIRTY

Finding Rest - The Story of George

*"Come unto Me, all ye that labour
and are heavy laden, and I will
give you rest. Take My yoke upon you
and learn of Me; for I am meek and
lowly in heart and ye shall find
rest unto your souls.
For My yoke is easy,
and My burden is light."*
Matthew 11:28-30

Have you ever felt so worn, weak and depleted that you wondered how you would ever carry on? For most of my relationship with George, that was exactly how I felt. I tried my hardest to fix the complicated challenges he faced but to no avail. Finally, after many sleepless nights and stress-filled days, God intervened and my heavy burdens were turned to rest...

George was a short, stout and gentle man. He was in his fifties when he came to the Mission and had been homeless for most of his life. He had entered into our long-term program and was doing well until a few months into his program when he began to deteriorate. Suddenly a serious increase in confusion and delusions began controlling his behaviors. I became concerned and tried everything my past psychiatric training had taught me to do. Sadly, George was getting worse with each passing day.

After working in the field for over ten years, I knew my way around the social service delivery system fairly well. It was during this time, however, that mental health reform was beginning and many of the options I once knew were rapidly changing. In an attempt to move individuals out of hospitalized care settings and into the community, it was no longer as easy for people to receive help. With the new philosophies emerging, unless a person was able to clearly demonstrate their need for intensive support (which was evidenced only through a clear plan to bring harm to either themselves or others), they would not be qualified to receive involuntary hospitalized care. This was regardless of the other symptoms manifesting in their lives. While the concept of deinstitutionalizing individuals was a noble one, sadly there were consequences which would inadvertently bring harm to others in the process and leave individuals like George falling between the cracks.

For days I did my best to work with George and establish the psychological support that was needed. He was one of the kindest and gentlest men I knew and I could never envision him bringing harm upon others. However, with the behaviors I was witnessing, I was quickly beginning to fear the hurt he was at risk for causing to himself. I watched helplessly as George continued to move speedily in the direction of self-destruction but, with the new systems in place, I could not get him the adequate assistance I knew was so needed.

After several days of drama and increased intensity, George took a turn for the worst. Somehow I managed to convince him of his need and, with high hopes, drove him to the emergency room. While we were there he began to believe the sun was exploding and that it would soon burn up the earth. As a result of his fear, he completely disrobed and began frantically pacing the emergency room. Instead of seeing this as a sign of desperate need, I was taken aside and told that I needed to take control of George and we both needed to leave. Defeated, we drove back to the Mission.

For the next three days I don't think George or I got any sleep. I was beginning to feel a bit delusional myself and was increasingly frustrated with the system in front of me that seemed to be failing both George and the community.

George was now spending most of his days walking from the Mission through downtown which required him to repeatedly cross over bridges. Because I was aware of the gravity of the situation and the potential danger he was in, I knew of nothing else to do but to faithfully get into my car and follow him around. One day I was forced to pull over on the side of the Kansas Avenue Bridge and coax him down. He was on the ledge, ready to jump, and I had to use all of my mental and physical strength to pull him from the railing where he stood ready to take his life.

During these times, I couldn't help but think back to the days when I worked in the mental health field and the ways in which individuals like George would have been hospitalized and getting care well before the situation had progressed to this point. I was frustrated and hopeless. My prayers were continual for God to intervene. Finally by no small miracle, after many days of struggling, George agreed in the middle of the night to go get help.

At three o'clock in the morning me, George and my faithful friend Joe from the Mission, piled into the car to drive to the nearby state hospital. We began the short drive but as we were pulling up to the admissions building, George changed his mind. While sitting next to me in the front seat, he spontaneously grabbed the steering wheel and began turning us straight towards a large support pillar. I thought for sure a head-on collision was inevitable. As George panicked, Joe was able to fend him off from behind and I was able to gain control of the car. Fortunately, as the events occurred, there were some hospital staff waiting for us outside who witnessed the whole episode. This was what it finally took to get George a bed in the hospital.

As I walked back to the car after George was admitted, I felt like such a failure. Certainly there must have been something more I could have done to help this man before taking this long and nearly getting all three of us killed. I had been awake for the majority of three days and was tired, frustrated, angry, and depleted. As I slumped behind the wheel I sighed deeply and asked the Lord, "God, what am I doing wrong?" Out of nowhere an unexplainable peace came over me and these words were breathed into my heart, "You are doing the best that you can, that's all I ask. I will take care of the rest."

For nearly a quarter of a century I have drawn strength and life from the words I believe were spoken into my spirit by God Himself. I don't often know all of the answers but what I do know is that my calling, like many others, is to simply do the best I can and trust and know God will take care of the rest.

George finally got the help he needed through that hospitalization and was eventually discharged to a well-run group home. There he received appropriate care and was able to comfortably live the remainder of his days. Thankfully, after a lifelong battle, he never became homeless again. While my struggles to help him get what he needed were intense, I learned the battle was never solely mine.

Jesus tells us to come to Him when we are worn out and heavy laden and He will give us rest. He says that His yoke is easy and His burden is light. He offers the same to us and says as we learn of His ways, we will find rest for our souls (Matthew 11:28-30).

I've looked at that scripture at times and thought surely it is one that is easier said than done. So often we become burdened and feel like there is always more we should be doing on any given day. Those burdens of responsibility and guilt leave us feeling helpless and burnt-out until over time we are ready to give up.

How do we truly place our burdens into His hands? We must recognize that He is there with His hands open wide, ready to lift off our weights. He's not shaking His head in disappointment or shame in the areas we think we have failed. He's beckoning us to come and rest in His Presence so that we can receive of His strength to carry on.

One by one, examine the weights that are pulling you down and, through prayer, handover and allow Him to remove each one. We are all placed in difficult circumstances from time to time but God never intended for us to try and figure them out all alone.

Jesus came so we would no longer have to trudge through life feeling as though we are just barely getting by. As you invite Him in, He eagerly comes alongside and provides the strength and grace you can pull from on each given day. He is ushering you closer today and asking for the burdens you carry. May you unreservedly place them in His hands and receive rest for your soul.

Lord,

There are days when I feel I am in this world all alone and that the weight of all burdens rests solely on my shoulders. Thank You for Your desire and willingness to take the weight off and for allowing me to find my rest in You. Come into my life and be my strength for all of my days as I eagerly place my life and my burdens into Your hands.

In Jesus' Name. Amen.

CHAPTER THIRTY-ONE

Kitty – An Unlikely Messenger

*"...Of a truth I perceive
that God is no respecter of persons."*
Acts 10:34

Sometimes we use our pasts as an excuse for not moving forward in the future. While we might see only the stains and horrors of previous mistakes, God sees beyond to the newness of life promised through Jesus Christ. When Kitty came to the Mission, I was blinded by my knowledge of her past. Through a supernatural encounter from God, I was able to see the new creation she had become...

Kitty spent many years barely surviving on the streets of California and became caught up in the downward spiral of both drugs and prostitution. She moved back to Topeka hoping for a new start but when plans didn't work out as she hoped, she found herself homeless and in need.

By the time she arrived, her once agile body was ravished with stains of affliction and abuse. After years of destructive living her mind, body, and resources were fully expended. Her body was now covered with lesions and she suffered from many other physical ailments. There was very little hair left on her head and she looked more the age of seventy-five than her much younger fifty-something self.

Out of her need for shelter, Kitty came to the Mission; but in return she found forgiveness, hope and a new life in

Jesus Christ. She was welcomed into the long-term program and immediately found a new family. Eagerly, she embraced the unconditional love so many had to give.

Kitty was staying with us during the time we were first developing plans to build the new Mission building. While our plans were moving forward, I was perplexed on two fronts. How would we get all of the money needed to develop a new shelter and where would we build?

When we started off, it appeared that a total of $1.5 million would be needed to complete the project. The number was overwhelming to me and I had no idea how all of the funds would come forth. I had never tackled such a project before and doubted it could really be done. All I knew was that there was a need and if we did not want to close our doors, this new building was something we had to pursue. I had seen many universities and medical institutions construct buildings solely from the support of just a few major donors so I began petitioning God for the same. If just a handful of major donations were received to support the entire project, our campaign would be much easier and a tremendous amount of worry and stress would be alleviated.

In addition to the quandary of finance, there was also uncertainty as to where the building would be located. I believed the Lord had shown me where it was supposed to stand, but there was a tremendous amount of opposition with property issues and I was told numerous times that the site I envisioned would be impossible. I wondered why God would lead us to build if there was no place to construct the facility. Nothing seemed to be making sense.

My repetitive and sincere prayers concerning the challenges I faced were, "Lord, where are we to build?" and, "Once You show me that, can You just send three or four donors to fund the whole thing?" Though I felt unsure of myself, I was confident in the Lord and positive He would answer my prayer the way that I desired.

One morning, after our building began falling down, I was on the second floor in the portion that was still habitable. As I walked through the living room, the door to one of the family rooms opened wide. Kitty walked out. She had on her fuzzy bathrobe and what little hair she had left was rolled up in curlers.

She warmly said, "Good morning," and then shared that God had spoken to her the previous night. I had a hard time believing she had an actual encounter with God but I humored her and politely asked what He had said. Her room faced Kansas Avenue and she had a window that looked out upon the property I originally believed God had shown us to build. Kitty claimed that God told her I was going to build a new building across the street on the ground He had originally showed me. As a result, she told me I was to quit worrying about it.

While that may have been impactful for some, I really wasn't too affected. In fact, I pretty much brushed it off thinking she had probably just overheard the plans to build and the previous rejections received from the advisors. She was a sweet lady and I figured in return for all she had received from the Mission, she was probably just trying to give back by being an encouragement to me.

I thanked her for her words and turned to walk away. As I did, Kitty's memory was jolted and she told me God had told her to tell me something else. I turned around to face her once again. With deep sincerity in her eyes, Kitty told me that God shared with her it was not going to be three or four big donors who would fund the building endeavors, but it was instead going to be a lot of little gifts. Now I was stunned. I had not shared that prayer or desire with a single soul.

My mind went everywhere. First, I had somewhat of an inward sulk not wanting to have to endure the project with just little gifts. I really was hoping to get it over quickly through the help of just a few. Then I wondered how Kitty possibly knew about my prayer. If it was through God, why would He use a woman who had been caught up in addiction and prostitution to speak to me?

I was so startled I couldn't muster any response, other than to give Kitty an emotionless word of thanks. As I walked away, rather than excitement at hearing from God, I felt troubled. My analytical mind kept going back to wondering how she could have known the information she did. Surely there was an explanation.

I talked to the Lord about the bizarre conversation and pondered it over in my mind. Over time I dismissed it entirely. It was only over the next number of months I was able to see the true fruit from our living room encounter.

There was not one advisor who told us it would be possible to build on the land we had pursued. Each one said there would be no way and that we were attempting an impossible feat. However, through a lot of sorting out with local officials, property owners around the nation, and even a national senator, the acquisition of the land slowly began to become a reality. In time, with a final cost of just over $1.7 million, the new facility was built exactly where the Lord had revealed. And, just like Kitty had shared, it was not through the generosity of a few major donors. Once everything was tallied, we found that it was the combined giving of 6,700 unique donors who made the development of the new building possible.

As I have reflected back on this situation over the years I have come to realize two things. One is it was truly the wisdom of a loving God not to send three or four people who would fund the project in its entirety. Instead, He moved on the hearts of thousands to establish a necessary team of contributors who would help us to not only build, but to become invaluable partners in the day-to-day operations of the Mission. Where we had only a handful of supporters before, God gave us an immense group of citizens of compassion He knew would be needed in the days ahead.

The other has become an extraordinarily valuable lesson: God truly is no respecter of persons. Regardless of a person's background, challenges or physique, every person who lives on this earth is cherished and valuable to Him.

God chose to speak clearly to me through a former prostitute, drug addict and dealer who had humbly given her life, and all that was left of it, over to Him. While I wasn't expecting it, God used her pure and full surrender to teach me what could have never been taught through another.

A woman similar to Kitty came to Jesus and, as an act of worship, chose to break an expensive jar of oil at His feet. Out of her love and faith in Him, she offered the best of what she had. While others around Him scorned her, Jesus exalted her by forgiving her and saying wherever the Gospel is preached, her story would also be shared (Matthew 26:13). Her broken life which she unreservedly laid at His feet was a greater sacrifice than others could possibly give.

There is no sin from our past so great that it disqualifies us from being used of God. I know many individuals who have felt, even after giving their lives over to the Lord, they could never be used by Him because of guilt and stains of their past. The Bible tells us that once we confess our sins, He is faithful and just to forgive our sins and cleanse us from *all* unrighteousness (1 John 1:9). If our past has been cleansed, we can then embrace the righteousness through our new life in Christ.

God honors a life of humility and surrender. Regardless of what you have done or what type of lifestyle you have lived, once you humble yourself before Him and confess your faults, they are remembered no more. As far as the east is from the west, so far does God remove your transgressions from you (Psalm 103:12). That means that they're forgiven, vanquished, gone. Quit holding onto the belief that you have to live in shame for the rest of your life based on some poor decisions you may have made in your past. God forgives you, He loves you and He is still able to use you!

God used Kitty, an unlikely messenger in my eyes, to dramatically speak into my life. While I saw her past, God saw her purity in Christ and used her for His glory. Likewise, God used another woman with a tarnished past to show us what true worship and humility really is.

Whatever you've been through, now is the time to relinquish your past and walk forward in the purity that awaits. Because of Jesus, you are good enough. And as you surrender your life to Him, you too will be used for His glory.

Lord,

I lay down my past and ask that You would forgive me for the mistakes I have made. I set aside the guilt and shame that has tormented my mind and allow You to fill me with Your righteousness and peace. Thank You that, even though it's hard at times to comprehend, I can still be used by You.

In Jesus' Name. Amen.

CHAPTER THIRTY-TWO

Hope in the Storm

*"For Thou hast been a strength to the
poor, a strength to the needy in his
distress, a refuge from the storm, a
shadow from the heat..."*
Isaiah 25:4

*Even in the most severe of storms, there is always a place
where we can go to experience refuge and shelter. When Nancy
found that place, she experienced not only peace but also a new
home, new perspective, and new chance at life. The same awaits for
each one of us...*

Nancy came to Topeka with the promise of a good job
and a new life. Everything was going well until serious
health problems set in and her employment was terminated.
Six months later when she found herself unable to pay for
her utilities and rent, she received the devastating yet
expected news of eviction.

New to the community with no family or friends, she
knew of nowhere to go for refuge. It was a cold and wet
October evening when she packed all of her belongings into
her small car. A neighbor saw her hopeless state and told her
about the Mission. Nancy began her journey to the north
side of Topeka but in her distress had forgotten to ask for an
address, phone number or clear directions. As darkness
began to fall, she found herself driving through the streets of
downtown Topeka feeling hopelessness, fear, and despair.

As she inched through the streets, the condensation continued to build on the windshield of Nancy's tiny car. Her defroster was broken and without continually wiping a small circle to peer through, it was impossible to see where she was going through the dark and rain. As she drove, questions began to torment her mind. If she did find the Mission, what would it look like? Would they have room? Would they be friendly? Would she be safe? She cried in panic and fear as she continued her anxious search for the only hope of shelter from the wet and cold. She had never felt so lonely, frightened, forgotten and hopeless.

In a desperate plea, after hours of searching and tears streaming down her face, Nancy cried out, "God, do not forget me... please save me and show me this place called the Topeka Rescue Mission." Not knowing where she was in the darkness, rain and fog, she turned the corner and through the small circle of her foggy windshield Nancy saw the illuminated words "Jesus Saves" shining in the distance. The old neon cross that had been transported on the roof of a car by the former director of the Mission in 1959 still stood strong and bright twenty-eight years later, continuing to convey a bright message of hope.

Through the rain, fear and tears of desperation, Nancy now knew God had not forgotten her. Not only did she find the shelter she had been seeking underneath that cross, but she also found the eternal message that God loves her and Jesus saves.

The welcome Nancy received when she came into this unfamiliar chapter of her life set her at ease for the next several months. Nancy learned of God's love for her, His plan for her, and her purpose in life. Nancy resided at the Mission for a number of months until her health improved and a new opportunity for employment was found.

Two years after her initial trek through the cold, a large group of people had gathered to explore the possibility of building a new homeless shelter because the old building was crumbling. One of the attendees in the meeting that evening asked what would be done with the old neon cross after the original building was torn down. I paused, not sure of how my audience would respond to the message of the Cross, nor the idea of keeping something old and putting it on a new building. During my brief silence, a woman sitting in the back stood up and asked if she could share.

Nancy came forward and shared what that cross meant to her. By the time she was done, there wasn't a dry eye in the room. I then asked the question to the crowd, "What do you think we should do with that old cross?" A resounding and unanimous declaration to keep it, refurbish it and do whatever it took to make sure that old cross stood tall atop the new building swept through the room.

Decades later, the old cross continues to light up every night as a beacon of hope to show people where they can find refuge and to communicate the message of God's unfailing love through His gift of Jesus Christ who still saves today. That cross led a broken, hopeless and scared stranger named Nancy to shelter, safety and refuge. Thousands have followed in her footsteps since.

There are many times in our lives when the storms seem to continually rage. We, like Nancy, find ourselves fearful and afraid of how we will ever escape. Just as the light of the old neon cross still shines bright atop the Mission, so does Christ's love.

A dear friend of mine recently shared of a vision the Lord had shown her when going through a difficult time. As she talked to God about the turmoils of life beating against her, He showed her a picture of a fierce storm. The clouds were dark, the rains intense, and the thunder and lightning were bold. Winds were howling, hail was plummeting and there appeared to be no refuge or way to escape. As she watched the intensity of the storm continuing to rage, God began to elevate her eyesight to see what was occurring just above the dark clouds. The more she ascended the less threatening the storms became and there above the clouds was the sun shining bright, as if unaware of the storms raging just below. She knew as she watched it would only be a matter of time before the clouds would begin to dissipate and move out, revealing once again the warmth of the sun that had never stopped shining.

She thought of her life, the situations that seemed dark and the circumstances that appeared hopeless. While she was focusing on the damaging winds and threatening rains, the light of the Son was still shining bright above; the clouds of life had just blocked her view from being able to see Him. While it was true the intensity of the storms were great, God assured her that, just as no storm on this earth will ever last forever, neither will any storm in our lives.

We may experience seasons where the days seem dark and cold but in time as we continue looking up, we will begin to see the clouds part and once again feel the warmth of the Son shining through.

Nancy was experiencing a severe storm in her life as she drove through the streets in the darkness and rain. Hopelessness consumed her until she cried out to God. As she did, He turned her vision the right direction so she could see the light of the cross that shone bright. Through that light, she found her refuge and peace.

God is our refuge and strength, a very present help in trouble (Psalm 46:1).

When the answers seem scarce and the storm clouds immense, find comfort in knowing that through the Cross of Jesus Christ, you too can find comfort, peace, shelter and purpose. No storm will last forever and I assure you... God has not forgotten about you and yes, Jesus still saves.

Lord,

When the storms of life are raging, help me to find my refuge and peace in You. Please show me that You have not forgotten about me and allow me to see a glimpse of the sun shining above the clouds. May I feel the warmth of Your Son as You shine Your Light on me.

In Jesus' Name. Amen.

CHAPTER THIRTY-THREE

Something to Give

*"Every man according as he has
purposeth in his heart, so let him give;
not grudgingly, or of necessity:
for God loveth a cheerful giver."*
2 Corinthians 9:7

When we compare ourselves to others, we can become timid and unsure of ourselves. While we may not all possess the same types of resource, each one of us still has something significant to give...

The development of a new building had begun moving forward and a building campaign was being launched. I was trusting God with the details and remained steadily amazed as He daily seemed to be putting new pieces together that would make the vision a reality.

A lump formed in my throat when I answered the phone and the Chief Executive Officer (CEO) of Hills Pet Nutrition, Bob Wheeler, was on the other line. He was calling to invite me to a luncheon to share the current needs of the Mission with him, as well as CEOs and directors from other large companies in the area. While I was beginning to feel confident in the small presentations I gave in local churches, I had never before met with people of such caliber as Bob was describing. I was hesitant and nervous but swallowed hard and accepted the offer to attend.

When I arrived at Hills, I anxiously met with Bob and his secretary before the big meeting. Obviously aware of my extreme apprehension and fear, Bob broke the ice by making a joke and my tensions began to diminish. Though unaware of what would occur and lacking confidence in my own abilities, I silently thanked God for His hand in the work and entrusted the luncheon to Him.

Twenty-eight leaders filled the room for the luncheon that day. Having no fancy slides or other sophisticated props to present with, I nervously placed my makeshift drawing of what the Mission was endeavoring to do in front of the intimidating crowd. Shortly into my presentation, Bob quickly took over and challenged the group. The goal put forth was to raise a half-million dollars for the Mission and he began with a $50,000 pledge from Hills. I stood in amazement as others eagerly stepped up and offered their pledges. I went into the meeting with nothing more than some poster board and fear, and left with new allies and support that was beyond what I could have ever dreamt!

From that meeting on, Bob became a powerful ambassador for the Mission. He unreservedly made follow-up calls to each of the corporations represented in the meeting and continued to discover new innovative methods of sharing the needs and bringing the community together to usher in necessary support. One such way was through the development and coordination of what became known as the "Sleep-Out for the Homeless".

The Sleep-Out was a springboard activity intended to bring awareness of homelessness to leaders in the community. Two key leaders from the city were invited to join in a friendly competition of who could invite more participants to the event. As the word got out, 140 people signed up and participated in the affair which took place in the old Let's Help parking lot just off of Kansas Avenue.

March 15, 1990 was the day of the grand event. There was a myriad of presentations from current and former guests, as well as the opportunity for attendees to testify and participate in question and answers. After the program was complete, the attendees were each given a cardboard box to sleep in for the night. The goal was to raise the awareness of what many homeless individuals were exposed to on a nightly basis when the retreat of a shelter is not available.

The night was clear, crisp and the temperatures dropped to around thirty degrees. While all of the others did their best to find comfort and warmth from their makeshift shelters in the parking lot, there was one man I will never forget who refused to sleep inside of his box. Throughout the night, he laid shivering on the rough concrete with nothing but a coat, gloves, and a scarf to keep warm. His rugged appearance was one that made him look like he was truly homeless and, in spite of the cool air, he adamantly refused to accept a blanket or covering of any kind. When the morning arrived, he came into the dining hall of Let's Help and got a cup of coffee. As he sat down at a table he proceeded to write out a check in the amount of $25,000 for the Mission. He handed the check to one of the volunteers who then excitedly delivered it to me. As he walked out the door, I was able to catch him and engage in a conversation of thanks and introduction.

It turns out the mysterious man was actually Frank Sabatini, the owner of Capital City Bank. He told me that when he agreed to participate in the Sleep-Out he wanted to truly experience exactly what the individuals in the cold would experience, if there was no Topeka Rescue Mission to keep them sheltered and warm. Like Bob Wheeler, he has continued to support and advocate for the Mission ever since.

When the need for funds to build the new facility began, my mind often wondered how the money would actually be raised. While I was busy worrying, God was already touching the hearts of many to give every dollar needed to fund His new project. He knew exactly the way in which every need would be supplied and, by the time we moved into the new shelter, a total of 6,700 individuals and groups had donated to make it all possible. There were those who gave much and those who gave little. But it was through the generosity of each one that the new property was built and established debt-free.

In Matthew 25:14-30, Jesus tells a parable about a successful man who had distributed his talents to three of his servants. Each one received a different amount, some more and some less, but each one was examined based on what they had done with what was given to them.

Regardless of one's economic status in life, every one possesses something they can give. While monetary contributions are great and help our doors to remain open, those who do not have an abundance of financial resources are a blessing as well.

Freely you have received, freely give (Matthew 10:8).

Bob and Frank were two men who were blessed with successful businesses and prominent positions in life. They recognized the needs of the poor and opened their hands and lives to freely distribute what they had to give. While their images and positions in life seemed intimidating to me, God used these two leaders and many others like them to show me once again that it's not the external image a person portrays but the internal heart of a person that really makes a difference in this world.

We may look at the needs in this world and think we have nothing of worth to give. We hear of those who can give hundreds, thousands and more and think our little gifts don't mean a thing. Nothing can be further from the truth. No gift is insignificant when given in love.

While you might not have an overabundance of finances to give, God has still given you much you can share with those who are in need. He has lavished you with love and given you the ability to share it. May we never become so consumed with what we don't have that we lose sight of the abundance that we do. Give your time, give a smile, give your love. Freely you have received. You never know what a small token of love can do to bring life and healing to another person's heart.

What is it God has placed in you? If you're not sure, look to Him and search deep. There is abundance that lies within. You can be the one God uses to restore hope and bring love to a person who needs it the most.

Lord,

Help me to recognize the many blessings that You have given me and show me how I can use them to bless others. May my focus shift from the things I don't have to the abundance I do. Help me to freely give as I have so freely received.

In Jesus' Name. Amen.

CHAPTER THIRTY-FOUR

What Have I Done?

"Being confident of this very thing,
that He which hath begun a good
work in you will perform it
until the day of Jesus Christ."
Philippians 1:6

There are times when we believe God has given us direction in life; yet as we move forward, we experience nothing but crises and storms. We question where God is in the midst and wonder if we ever really heard Him at all. While it might not look like we expected, God does remain with us. This story is an account of just that...

It was May of 1991, and we had finally arrived at the place where the vision of creating a new state of the art facility for homeless individuals and families had become a reality. After receiving the $1.7 million to develop the building debt-free, we were ready to officially open the doors. The joy and excitement was contagious and we all stood in awe as we reflected on the miraculous journey that had brought us to this place.

The new building housed a shelter for men, a separate area for women and families, a new kitchen, and a dining room. Everything looked immaculate and was ready to receive the new lives that would soon occupy its space. There were just two major problems: we had no cook for the kitchen and no supervisor for the women and families.

My thoughts reflected back and my mind was soon consumed with the many words spoken by naysayers who said our plans would not succeed. Many said the task of creating a new homeless shelter could never be done but even if it was, that it would never survive because of the huge costs to maintain. As I stood before a kitchen with no cooks and a 67-bed shelter for families with no staff, I couldn't help but wonder if they had been right.

I had heard early on from other leaders that the sure sign of a successful rescue mission director was that he had placed at least five people between himself and his cooking of the evening meal. Here I was with *no one* between me and our meals. Surely I had failed.

It's interesting how we can trust God for part of the solution but then halfway through, fail to trust Him to finish the work He began. With the negative words that had been spoken ringing loud in my ears, I looked up to heaven and cried, "What have I done?!?!"

I glanced over at the local Let's Help facility and thought of their then director, Marge Roberts, with envy. She had done such a phenomenal job of recruiting volunteers for her organization while we had so few. Surely she had taken all of the willing hands from the community and there were none left to give.

I sulked in the grim reality that I had no money to hire staff and no ability to obtain volunteers. My only solution was to begin recruiting the homeless individuals staying at the Mission to help with the work.

For the next several months we followed suit with what had always been done historically. I directly supervised the individuals living at the Mission as they assisted in carrying out the daily functions of each operation. As time went on, I questioned God and asked why He had provided so abundantly for the construction of the shelter but was now seemingly abandoning us when it came to support for our daily needs.

The doubts of whether or not I had made a mistake in building the new facility continued to crowd my mind. In reality, I knew our old building had been falling down and we really had little choice. If we wanted to continue to provide shelter, a new facility was needed. But now there were so many needs and the provision just wasn't falling in place as I planned. My mind wandered back and forth as I tried to figure out where I had gone wrong.

One day as I was finishing my common prayer of, "God please provide," my eyes were suddenly opened to see the many ways in which He already had. Though it didn't look like I had envisioned, God was providing through many individuals with unique gifts and talents; those who lived at the Mission and appreciated the opportunity to serve while they were being served.

I was becoming enlightened but while doing so my faith continued to falter. If only God would send over some of the volunteers from Let's Help, or raise up a frontline cook, or send us a leader to oversee the women and families… then all of our needs would be met. The worries continued to come, but as I did my best to keep my focus on Him, God remained faithful and has never allowed our doors to close.

Indeed through the years, God has provided for every need. Whether it has been through homeless guests staying at the Mission, volunteers from the community, dedicated staff, or collaborations with professionals in the social service arena, God has created and called together a true army of compassion. Through banning together and remaining focused on the Lord, the Mission has remained standing and privileged to serve the many who come to us in need.

Have I overcome all of my fears and doubts? I would be lying if I said yes. There has been much I have learned about God's direction and provision since our new building was opened, but I am also cognizant in recognizing every step is unique and every day is one that brings both new challenges and new opportunities. Regardless of the challenges that come I know, in spite of my doubts and fear, God continues to remain faithful to supply and guide every step without fail. As long as I keep moving forward and trusting in Him, I know He will accomplish all He purposes to do.

Matthew 14:24-33 tells the story of a stormy sea and a loving Savior who walked upon the troubled waters. As He walked towards the disciples, they were fearful because they were seeing something different and something new they had never witnessed before. *Could Jesus really be here, in the midst of this storm?* Peter wanted to be sure so he tested Jesus and said, "Lord, if it's really You bid me to come." Jesus held out His hand and said to Peter, "Come."

Peter stepped out of the boat and, to his amazement, he too began walking on water in the midst of the storm. With his eyes fixed on Jesus, he walked steadily along. But the moment his gaze shifted to the winds roaring and the crashing waves around him, he began to fear and sink into the waters below.

Overwhelmed with fear, Peter cried out for help and even in his unbelief and doubt, Jesus lovingly reached out His hand and brought him safely out of the storm. It wasn't until the wind and waters were calmed and the disciples safe that they were able to say with awe, "Truly You are the Son of God" (Matthew 14:33).

As we go through life, we find those times when we become plagued with uncertainties and doubts. Though the Lord may have given us the directive and told us what to do, the storms raging around us cause us to lose focus and shift our gaze. When that occurs, we like Peter begin to fear and find ourselves sinking lower and lower into the dark sea below. However, it's when we cry out to the One who rules over the storms that we begin to see Him reach out His hand to pull us back to the place of safety and retreat.

Whatever storms are raging in your life, whatever doubts and uncertainties you face, know you're not alone in the tempest. The Lord is there waiting as He stretches forth His hand. It's up to you to trust Him enough to reach out yours and faithfully grab hold.

Lord,

At times I feel myself sinking and I recognize my doubts. Will You come and lift me out of the troubled waters and onto dry ground? Will You refocus my eyes to see nothing but You so that even in the midst of the storms I will not be fazed? Help me to reach hold of Your hand as You bid me to come. May I walk in the faith and assurance of knowing that which You have spoken, You will surely complete.

In Jesus' Name. Amen.

CHAPTER THIRTY-FIVE

Walking in His Steps

"...As I have loved you...
love one another."
John 13:34

Hundreds of dedicated staff and volunteers have served humbly and sacrificially at the Topeka Rescue Mission over the years. Each one is unique in their personalities and ministry, but each share the common trait of compassion and love towards those who are homeless and poor. While it would be impossible to pick just one who stands tallest amongst the rest, there is one whose exemplification of Christ I believe shines true as an illustration of all those who serve...

I met Donna Martin around 1991 when her husband, Bob, was serving on the Mission's Board of Directors. She came to me with a servant's heart and desire to assist as we moved from the old Mission facility to the new. Though she was in her retirement years, Donna had a great youthfulness about her and the strength to tackle more than most. Quickly Donna assumed a gamut of responsibilities. Most significant at the time was her oversight of the food service operations in the kitchen.

When we first moved into the new building there were no cooks in place. Our faithful cook of so many years had assumed the role of facilities manager and there was no one else to fill his shoes. Seeing the need, Donna eagerly stepped up. In no time she had cultivated a team of faithful guests to both cook and serve the meals.

The best way to describe Donna is that she loved God and feared no man. Her crew of cooks consisted of a former embezzler, a former heroin addict, a man who had eleven children from different women that he took no personal responsibility for, and another individual who had spent the majority of his life in prison for multiple crimes. Donna fearlessly took this motley crew and helped form them into some of the most obedient and diligent servants we had ever had. Donna always had the unique ability to take what seemed quite impossible and make it work.

One of my favorite memories of Donna is the birdcage she had mounted on the outside of her small office. Each of the cooks were assigned a stuffed animal and their names were pinned on each one of the animals' chests. Every morning, the men were to survey the birdcage first thing. If their animal was placed in the cage, they knew they were in trouble and needed to meet with Donna immediately. We all knew it was going to be a rough day when all of the animals were placed in the cage.

Donna didn't put up with guff from the guys. She ran the kitchen like a boot camp for military recruits and through it these roughneck guys began softening before our very eyes. We watched as each one slowly transformed into a willing servant who was used daily to feed hundreds.

One night around seven-thirty in the evening, I was at home attempting to fix my leaking faucet. It wasn't going very well and there was water spraying everywhere. In the middle of the chaos, my phone rang. It was Donna.

Without saying much else Donna ordered, "You need to get to the Mission right now." I told her the predicament I was in and asked if it could wait. She abruptly said, "No." She had fired all of the cooks and kicked them out of the

Mission. "All of them?" I asked, while also inquiring what happened. "Yes," she said as she proceeded to tell me how they had made an embarrassing scene during Chapel. While the service was going on, they were in the adjoining kitchen being rowdy and banging on pots. "They all know better," she said, "so I fired them and told them to leave."

I chuckled inside as I told her I wasn't able to make it down to the Mission but that she needed to go outside and immediately get the guys back. "Why would I do that?" she shockingly asked. "Because if you don't," I said, "you'll be cooking breakfast at five in the morning, I'll be making lunch and you'll be coming back to cook dinner!" Donna paused for a minute and said she would call me back. Just a few minutes later she called back to tell me she had brought back the guys. "But," she sternly warned, "they're all going to be in the birdcage in the morning!"

While it may sound like Donna was hard-hearted and rough, nothing could have been further from the truth. She loved the guys in the kitchen and they loved her.

Perhaps the true heart of Donna shone best through her relationship with Beth. Beth was a homeless woman who had come to us after suffering from Huntington's disease for several years. Once a registered nurse caring for people in need, she now found herself homeless and at the mercy of those around her. While all of us tried to do our best to minister to Beth, no one could reach her quite like Donna.

Beth spent her days constantly shaking uncontrollably. Her arms flailed, her feet shook, and her head twisted back and forth. Because of her unsteady hand, she could not wash herself well and the result was a persistent odor that streamed from her body. Her mouth often drooled and her speech was unintelligible. Few could understand her and even less tried.

Every month Beth received a disability check to help sustain her in life. Victimized time and again and unable to defend herself, the monthly theft that took place after she cashed her check left her homeless and wandering the streets. She began shoplifting to try and get by but even in those endeavors, she failed. Her shaking hands couldn't hold onto the products she was attempting to steal so she would instead be arrested and thrown back into the streets.

With nowhere else to go, Beth eventually found her way to us. She stayed with us on and off for years and embraced her new family, especially Donna.

Beth remained extremely challenged physically and unable to effectively care for herself. After numerous attempts, we finally found a more appropriate place for her to live. The plans were made and the day arrived when we would be transporting Beth to a new group home where she would receive full-time care and the support she needed.

Though Beth knew she needed the support, the thought of leaving her home at the Mission terrified her. Just hours before we were leaving to take her to her new home, she shook and cried uncontrollably; this time more from hysteria and fear than the effects of her disease. She was so distraught and her symptoms so severe she couldn't even sit in a chair without falling to the ground. I'll never forget the moment when Donna walked into the room and saw her.

Without hesitation, Donna ran to her side, got down on her knees and scooped Beth up in her arms. She poured out all of the love she possessed and hugged her tightly, wrapping her arms around her trembling body.

As Beth continued to travail, the mucus from her nose, the tears streaming from her eyes, and the uncontrollable saliva that flowed from her mouth began covering Donna. Donna didn't blink; she just continued to love.

The scene in front of me was amazing, like one I have never witnessed before. There before me I watched as a woman, who nobody wanted to touch, was embraced and consumed by another to such a degree that the love and compassion of Christ was all I could see.

Donna rocked Beth and held her close while gently assuring her everything was going to be okay and that she'd never be left alone. As Donna continued to embrace her tightly and pour out her love, Beth's entire demeanor began to change. What had been a body in horrid travail turned into one of peace and calm like never before. For the first time since I had known her, Beth's body quit convulsing and I watched as she melted in Donna's arms.

Before me I saw a vision of Jesus Christ. He had come up to a woman who was hurting so badly, put His arms around her and assured her it was going to be okay. Donna's were His arms now. As she held her close, the words of the Savior spoke to my heart, "Never will I leave you, never will I forsake you" (Hebrews 13:5).

Beth could be likened to a modern-day leper who led an extremely lonely and miserable existence here on earth. People were afraid of her, they scorned her, they rejected her and wouldn't go near. The Mission took her in but, without the Donna's inside, we are nothing more than a building. It is people like Donna who make us a home. We're not afraid of the tough guys, but we're also not afraid to throw our arms around the lepers and tell them it's going to be okay.

Countless times in scripture we witness Jesus embracing and touching the ones whom others wouldn't dare go near. He entered into the homes of the leper, He touched them, loved them and through His compassion made them whole (Mark 14:3, Mark 1:40-41). He wasn't afraid to reveal Himself to a murderer or commune with sinners (Acts 9:4, Mark 2:15). Regardless of the filthiest lives before Him, He embraced them and showed them His love. We too are called to walk as He walked (1 John 2:6). A quote from Teresa of Avila paints a picture for us.

Christ has no body but yours,
No hands, no feet on earth but yours,
Yours are the eyes with which He looks with compassion on
this world,
Yours are the feet which He walks to do good,
Yours are the hands, with which He blesses all the world.
Yours are the hands, yours are the feet, yours are the eyes,
you are His body.

Are our lives exemplifying the true body of Christ today? I witnessed Donna's life as she looked upon those most ignored. She walked towards them, held them and showed them great love. My prayer is that I would be able to serve with the same compassion, grace and love I have witnessed in her and so many others who have come through the doors of the Mission. Wherever we go and whatever we do, may we always be willing to lay down our lives to show forth His love.

Dear Lord,

Here I am… use me. Help me to look past the fears I may have of those who are different than me and help me to love. May I be Your hands, may I be Your feet, may I be Your eyes, may I be Your body. May I love as You love.

In Jesus' Name. Amen.

CHAPTER THIRTY-SIX

A Love Story

"And I will betroth thee unto Me
forever; yea, I will betroth thee unto
Me in righteousness, and in
judgment, and in lovingkindness,
and in mercies. I will even betroth
thee unto Me in faithfulness:
and thou shalt know the Lord."
Hosea 2:19

One of the major challenges we face on this earth is the cruel reality that people reject people. Some are rejected because of their beliefs or ethnicities; some simply because of the way they look. Tim and Peggy were two such people. While they spent the majority of their lives rejected and alone, in time they were able to receive a love far greater than any they had ever known...

Tim and Peggy came separately into the Mission when they were in their fifties. Both had spent the majority of their lives feeling unworthy and unloved.

There was nothing impressive about Tim. He had a slender build but the rest of his appearance was far from ordinary. His tattered clothes always sagged, causing the wrinkles to appear even more prominent and the mismatched colors more apparent. He suffered from severe eczema and as a result dry, crusted sores covered his face and arms. His greasy hair traveled in forty different directions and his glasses were broken so many times that even the duct tape holding them together was crooked and worn. His back was hunched and he walked with a limp.

Peggy's thin and frail body was accentuated by the unusual look of her facial features. Her nose was long and pointed. Her chin appeared so sharp it seemed to stand out like a mountain peak below her light, receding lips. The rest of her features were completely concave causing her eyes to sink deep into her pale, uneven skin. The hair atop her disproportioned face was damaged and brittle. Without knowing, it would be easy to mistake her for at least twenty years older than her actual age. Because of the judgmental nature of people, she could not find a job or friends and never found her place in life. Like Tim, through choices, rejections or a combination of both, she found herself with nowhere to turn. Rather than trying to survive on the streets, she opted for the security of shelter the Mission had to offer.

Since the inception, we've always tried our best to establish a place of acceptance for all. It doesn't matter what you look like, what you smell like, or what you have done. Because of the undeserved and unfailing love of a holy God, all are invited to come in. Tim and Peggy were two individuals who had gone through the rejections of life but despite their uncomely looks were welcomed in by a group of people who held onto the understanding that all are valuable in the sight of God.

As time progressed, Tim and Peggy separately began to find not only acceptance but also started experiencing a unique transformation in their lives. They began to recognize not everyone was out to harm them and that there were now people around them who would genuinely love them as well. One of the incredible fruits of that understanding was they began to realize, in spite of their outward appearances, they were in fact people of value. In turn, they were able to begin valuing themselves. As this occurred, the freedom to express the same to others came. For the first time in both of their lives they were beginning to feel secure enough in themselves to reach out and express the incredible God-given gift of love to others.

Over time, Tim and Peggy began to find and develop a different kind of love: the indescribable love God gives between a man and a woman. After a significant period of time working through their own personal issues and receiving foundational counsel, the two decided they wanted to become husband and wife.

Those of us who were there for the wedding had the privilege of witnessing what was likely the most incredible marriage ceremony there ever was. Tim, for probably the first time in his life, was wearing a neatly pressed tie with his oversized suit. His oily hair was neatly combed and he smiled from ear to ear as he took his place next to his best men, also friends and guests from the Mission.

The splendor that shone upon Peggy was one that to this day I still cannot quite describe. Wearing a dazzling white dress, she linked arms with one of the older men from the Mission who escorted her down the aisle. As she slowly strolled down the aisle, she looked more like an angel gliding on clouds than the woman I had previously known. They both looked absolutely stunning as they smiled and joined hands at the altar.

For the first time, tears flowed from my eyes at a wedding. I couldn't help but think we were no longer in a church, we were in heaven. As I gazed at the beauty before me, a brilliant light seemed to shine through the sanctuary. It was one of the most holy moments I can remember.

We left the church that day and Tim and Peggy went on to experience full contentment, acceptance and joy as husband and wife. Sadly, their journey was ended short when Tim contracted lung cancer. While Peggy faithfully stood by his side through it all, she was eventually left alone when he didn't survive the treatments. Thankfully, the new friends and family she had acquired at the Mission stood by her side, embraced and accepted her into their home. There she was taken care of for the remainder of her days. It wasn't too many years after Tim's death that she too passed away.

I conducted both funerals for Tim and Peggy and found myself shedding tears once again. While the message of rejection had rung loud throughout their lives, I was now able to see the message of redemption that rang even louder. God had redeemed the time for these two and took what seemed so unattractive to the world and made it excessively beautiful in His time.

As their walls of rejection were torn down and one of acceptance was built, Tim and Peggy were able to receive a short glimpse of what their eternal life of reception, love and beauty would be. Today I am convinced both are enjoying the fullness of life with the God who brought them together and showed them their worth.

In this life we may experience loneliness, rejection and low self-esteem. Tim and Peggy went through most of their lives experiencing devastating measures of all three. It was not until they were introduced to the true love of Jesus Christ they were able to discover their true beauty and the value and worth that was within. Suddenly, what the world had scorned and brushed aside was made glorious and beautiful, depicting one of the most amazing love stories of all… the story of Christ and His bride.

Even when we feel unlovely, unworthy and unclean, Jesus looks at us for who we really are and sees our beauty. While we may have betrayed Him in the past or done things that have tarnished our lives, through His immense love and forgiveness, we are washed clean and able to stand at the altar of His heart for eternity (1 John 1:9). As we do, the rejections we have experienced in this world begin to fade away as we recognize the One whose heart beats fully for us.

In the end we discover it is only His love and acceptance that really matters.

When Tim and Peggy began developing feelings for one another, they were like two teenagers in love. They spent nearly every waking moment together and it still was not enough to satisfy their desire to be with and know the other person more. Their love was what they thought of when they arose in the morning and laid down at night. Dreams of their wedding and the life they would spend together consumed their thoughts and brought joy to their hearts. Finally, the love and acceptance they had been deprived of for their entire lives was theirs. They became one and enjoyed the pleasures of a life filled with the richness of their love.

Even if you have never known such a love, the same can be yours through Jesus Christ. Coming to Him has never been just about finding a religion or going to church. It's about intimacy... spending time with the One who loves you more than any other ever could. When we allow the walls of rejection, abandonment and hurt to fall away from our lives, we are able to then receive the full and passionate love He possesses for each one of us. While it can be hard for our natural minds to comprehend, He loves each one of us as if there is only one of us to love. When we awake in the morning, we are on His mind. When we lay down to sleep at night, thoughts of us consume His heart (Psalm 40:17). His desire is for us to receive the fullness of love He has to give so that the rejections of man can harm us no more. When we are secure in His love, the acceptance from others no longer becomes our focus in life. Instead, He begins to consume our thoughts as our hearts begin to beat with an extreme passion for Him (Galatians 2:20).

Are you hungry for true love? Regardless of the love or lack thereof that you have experienced in life, the pure and zealous love you seek can be yours. Jesus doesn't see your spots or blemishes. Instead His love transforms you into a pure and spotless bride (Revelation 19:8). All you have to do is tell Him, "I do." He is passionately pursuing you just as Tim and Peggy pursued one another. As you join hands with Him and give Him your life, you are making an eternal vow and opening yourself up to receive a love truer than any other you have known. You will not only be able to receive His heart here on earth, but will one day enjoy the richness of eternal oneness with Him in the place He has prepared just for you (John 14:2).

You may have walked alone and been deprived of the love your heart has longed for in this world. Search no longer. Your true Spouse awaits. All you have to do is tell Him, "Yes" (Isaiah 54:5).

If you've already said yes to Jesus but the passion of your relationship has faded through the storms of life, He's beckoning you to return. Return to your first love, the first place of romance with Him when your heart was ablaze and your life consumed with His. He's wooing you back.

Receive His love. Join hands with Jesus and realize that you are rejected no more. Your greatest love story has not ended... it's only just begun.

Lord,

Thank You for Your love, for accepting me just as I am and welcoming me into Your arms. I say yes to You and with joy betroth myself to You. May my passion for You be stirred and my love rekindled as I eagerly await Your return.

In Your Name. Amen.

CHAPTER THIRTY-SEVEN

The Gift

*"For I know the thoughts that I think
towards you, saith the Lord, thoughts
of peace, and not evil, to give you
an expected end."*
Jeremiah 29:11

There are many people in this world who have tried to shut out the world around them. While their actions towards us may be unfavorable at times, it is when we continue to reach out in love that we are able to see the beginnings of change. While it seemed insignificant to me, God used the gift of a small toy to change the heart of one hardened child...

Sally's family was one that struggled greatly. While they never lived at the Mission, they were in need of tremendous support and, as my schedule allowed, I would visit them and do what I could to help. Each time I entered the home, I was greeted warmly by Sally's parents and her two older siblings. However, I could always count on a cold shoulder from Sally each time I arrived.

Sally was timid and hardened in her demeanor. When I looked at her, all I could see was a sadness and rigidity much deeper than any little girl of just four should possess. She would do her best to ignore me and nonverbally let me know I was not welcomed into her little world. If I walked into the same room where she sat, or attempted any type of conversation, Sally would immediately turn her head the other way and stubbornly refuse to acknowledge me in the slightest. My heart broke for this little girl and the pain she must have been holding deep within.

For three years, when Sally was between the ages of four and seven, I was a consistent presence in her family's life. Regardless of my attempts, she never once warmed up to me during this period.

After Sally turned seven, her appendix ruptured which led to her first surgery and hospital stay. While I knew I would not likely be received well by her, my heart beckoned me to visit. On my way to her room, I passed by the hospital gift shop and in the window spotted a sweet stuffed bunny rabbit with a red bow tied on one of his ears. I purchased the toy and then took the elevators up to where Sally helplessly laid. She was obviously experiencing a great deal of pain and trying to rest following the surgery she had experienced the day before.

As I walked in the room, I hid the gift behind my back. She responded just as I expected when she saw me by quickly turning her head the other way. Rather than giving up and walking away, I proceeded to call Sally's name a couple of times. Eventually, she reluctantly turned and looked at me with a scowl that seemed to question why I would be bothering her. As she watched suspiciously, I slowly pulled the bunny from behind my back and held it out towards her. She looked at me and then the furry bundle, not certain of how to respond. She did this a couple times before sheepishly and ashamedly looking into my eyes as if to ask, "Why would you bring this for me?" She stared at the bunny for a few moments before finally extending a hand to reach for it. For the first time in three years, I saw Sally smile. And as she held tight to that little bunny rabbit, she and I had our first conversation.

After Sally recovered and returned home, I went to her family's home to visit as usual. I was shocked and amazed when I walked through the door. This little girl who previously had gone out of her way to avoid me for as long as we had known each other, quickly ran up to me and gave me a huge hug.

Over the course of time, Sally and I became pretty good friends. As she grew, I was consistently invited to different activities and events she was participating in. Whenever she saw me in the community, regardless of who she was with, she would always come up and give me a warm, familiar hug.

Twenty years into our relationship, I received a Christmas card from Sally that included a picture of her new precious baby boy. The little girl I once knew is now married, has her own children, and has successfully completed college. While I can't take credit for any of her accomplishments, I can't help but wonder what her life and our relationship would have been like if I wouldn't have stopped at the gift shop to purchase that little bunny rabbit so many years ago.

It's amazing how the littlest of things can often bring someone happiness and hope. This little girl, so seemingly dejected and forlorn, acted as though there was nothing in this world that could ever brighten her days. While others offered her love, she rebutted in rejection. It wasn't until she received a stuffed little toy that I saw the hardness within her begin to melt. To me it was a simple bunny rabbit, but to Sally, it meant the world.

When people hurt us and chaos seems to surround us, it is easy to shut down and refuse to allow other people into our lives. Rather than risking the harm others may possibly bring, we put up a shield and don't allow hope to rise up for fear of being disappointed once again. Maybe it's people who have hurt us or hopes and aspirations we have had that never come to pass. Maybe it is dreams that are left unfilled or hearts which have been broken. When we go through these events long enough, the passions that once lived within us begin to die and we find ourselves cut off from joy and shut out from the world.

I don't know all of the circumstances that surrounded Sally, but I know they were severe enough to cause this young child to shut down and try hard to not allow anybody in. It took repetitive gestures of love and the receipt of a small gift before I witnessed her demeanor start to change and her youthfulness restored.

If there are people in your life who seem dejected and hard, don't allow their actions to cause you to give up on them. Inside may very well be a hurting child who is hiding in an attempt to protect themselves from the dangers they perceive of this world. Whatever you have to give to them in love is not going to be irrelevant. It might be a meal or financial aid but it might also be a kind word or a warm smile. No gift is insignificant when given in love. Each small act is able to perform a shift within a heart and bring forth a hope and change beyond what we can comprehend.

You may have gone through some tremendous disappointments or failures in life. You may have had a childlike faith long ago that has seemed to fade away over time, or you may have forced it away in attempts to protect your heart from further disappointment. Just as Sally finally let down her guard long enough to receive that small bunny rabbit, I pray that you too would begin to lay down your guard to receive the truth the Lord wants to give to you now.

He still has a plan for you and wants to offer you both a future and a hope (Jeremiah 29:11). The road up to this point may have been long and hard, but you have not yet come to the end. Dreams may not have come to pass the way you have long desired, but don't let that be a means for giving up on your future. There is so much of your life left to live. Don't waste it away by hiding behind a shield and not allowing anyone in.

Open up your heart to receive and don't be afraid to sow into the broken hearts of others as you do. Your one small gift just might change a life.

Dear Lord,

I want to live again and experience the joy that You have to give. Help me let go of past hurts from unfulfilled dreams and embrace the new dreams that You have for me to live. Help me also to see into the lives of others who are struggling who have built up walls around them. May I not be afraid to reach out and touch their lives with a token of hope. Open up their hearts to receive as I do.

In Jesus' Name. Amen.

CHAPTER THIRTY-EIGHT

One Man's Chapter

*"... I am God, and there is none like
Me, declaring the end from
the beginning...."*
Isaiah 46:9-10

*When we find ourselves in the middle of devastating
circumstances, we may think our lives are over or will never
improve. However, if we keep putting one foot in front of the other
we can eventually recognize that the challenges we face are not the
end, but instead just small chapters in our book of life. When one
businessman became homeless for the first time, he was able to
receive hope and strength from the knowledge of just that...*

Over the years I have been asked by numerous people
to "describe homeless people" to them. In reality, that is
impossible to do other than to say they are people just like
you and me. Each road which leads a person to
homelessness is quite different and unique. I have
encountered those who have known nothing but poverty
throughout their entire lives while others have grown up in
wealth. There are some who have never made it past the
third grade, while others have completed college and gone
on to attain their doctorates. Many have had a hard time
maintaining jobs while others have been the owners of
successful businesses. There are those who have never
owned a car, and those who have owned car dealerships.

While each person becomes homeless for different reasons, each one is a person just the same...

Phil was one of the Mission's largest supporters. He held events for the ministry and helped us to raise tens of thousands of dollars over time. He was a successful business man who owned and managed three large car dealerships throughout the country. While he was not a Christian, he supported our humanitarian efforts and always did what he could to help the Mission financially.

One Christmas Eve morning, I received a call from Phil. He told me he was in Kansas City, heading to Topeka. He had become homeless and needed a place to stay. I had known Phil for years and experienced, through his support of the Mission, his great generosity and wealth. I thought this was a joke and told him, "Yeah right." However, after a pause on his end followed by a serious response, I knew this was no joke. He said he would fill me in on the details as soon as he arrived.

When Phil pulled up in front of the Mission, I expected to see him in one of his fancy dealership cars. Instead, he pulled up in a tiny used car that was barely running. I was thoroughly confused.

He came in from the cold and sat down inside my office. He shared how his success had taken him far and how he had done quite well until just two years prior. That was when the heavy drinking which led to experimentation with cocaine began. Before he knew it, the addiction was beyond his control and he could not escape from its grips. His entire world began falling apart. His wife divorced him and his children wanted nothing to do with him. He made numerous unwise financial decisions, lost his businesses, and now was sinking in debt with nowhere to go and no friends left to turn to.

The man, who once helped to keep the Mission's doors open, was now walking through them in need of the refuge they had to provide.

I told him he was welcomed as he hung his head in shame. The journey would be long, but I encouraged him to hold on and see what God was going to do. Not interested in hearing any talk of the Cross, he skeptically nodded and walked out of the room.

At that time, the number of guests who stayed with us was much smaller. A generous donor always paid for us to take the guests out to eat on Christmas Eve. We would bus everyone down to what used to be Doug's Diner and enjoy a nice meal. It allowed the guests a special treat while staff and volunteers prepared the Mission's building and dining area for the festivities which would take place on Christmas Day.

The diner was fairly small for our large group and everyone was squeezed in at least six to a booth. As I walked through the packed aisles I realized there was hardly any room left to sit. My eyes canvassed the room and fell upon Phil. He looked depressed, nervous and out of place as he stared down at his plate and slowly fiddled with his food. It was Christmas Eve and he was homeless for the first time in his life.

Next to Phil on both sides in the tiny booth sat two other men who were homeless and distraught. Sadly, they were unable to converse because of the mental illness that had taken over their minds. They were both actively hallucinating and having conversations with themselves, unaware of anyone else in the room. The man directly across from him was also quite sick and caught up in the identical state. Phil was now sharing his holiday meal with people who just months before he would have ignored or quickly brushed past. He now realized he had something very in common with them.

Phil's face was downcast as I approached and he was trying his best to ignore the realities of what was going on all around. I approached him and offered a word of encouragement. "One day when you get through all of this, you will probably write a book… and this will just be another one of your chapters." Though he showed little emotion at the time, he told me later that those simple words had given him a glimmer of hope. Through the meal he had been envisioning his life ending as one of the guys who sat around him, but the words made him think there was a possibility this was not going to be the end after all.

The next four months at the Mission were not easy for Phil. He opened himself up and began confronting the realities of his past. He recognized the ways he had been dishonest and used people for years, later deceiving himself and struggling with the addiction to a substance that had tried to take over his life. He had begun entertaining the thought of God, but still had no grasp of the full reality of who He wanted to be in his life. While the healing had begun, he had significant ground yet to gain.

As Phil's strength and stamina continued to return, he decided he would leave the Mission and try making it on his own. I recognized the struggles still present and was fearful it would only be a matter of time before Phil became homeless and in need once again.

It was about a year later before I heard from Phil. He called me from Kansas City and I was greeted by the sounds of crying through the phone. He had returned to the grips of addiction and, while drunk and high on cocaine, had crashed head-on into a semi-truck on Interstate 70. Thankfully, the driver of the truck had not been seriously hurt but Phil was in Kansas University Medical Center receiving treatment for two broken legs and a gamut of internal injuries. His life had gone even further downhill through the previous year but he was now at the end of himself and asking for prayer.

I did what I could to encourage him and prayed with Phil over the phone. He was in the hospital for several weeks and then returned to the small and meager apartment in Kansas City where he had been living.

Over the next three years, Phil did his best to rebuild his life and we kept in close touch. When the phone calls stopped, I once again became concerned. After a few months of not hearing from him, I finally received a call from California. He had begun reestablishing his life there, had found a small apartment, and was working as a car salesman. He told me he was calling to share something beautiful, yet bizarre, that he was sure I'd understand.

He had walked out of his apartment one day and looked down on the floor of the foyer in front of his door. There, before him, lay a Bible. He had never owned one before and never read through its pages. Out of curiosity, he leaned over to pick it up and then looked around. There was no one in sight. He took the Bible inside and curiously opened its cover. Written inside was the name of a woman and a phone number. Puzzled, he set it aside.

For days he looked at the Bible and pondered the name written inside. Finally, he mustered up the courage to make contact. He told the woman how he had found the gift and wondered if she could offer any explanation. She had given away countless old Bibles over the years and said someone had probably just dropped one that had been given a long time ago. While she couldn't offer much help in solving the mystery of how it had appeared at his door, she did extend an invitation for him to attend a Bible study the following night. Though he was still struggling with addiction, he decided to attend.

When Phil introduced himself and began sharing his story, the woman was amazed. She too was from Topeka and then mentioned my name. Apparently she had been involved in ministry in Topeka but the Lord had moved her to California to further share the Gospel. She told Phil it was not a coincidence he had walked out of his apartment and looked down to see the Good News.

Phil paused before continuing to relay the story to me. He then declared he had given his life to Jesus Christ and finally realized what it was I had been trying to share with him all along. Now, through the orchestration of two lives from Topeka that met up in California, he could finally see how God had been pursuing him and trying to get his attention all along.

To this day, Phil and I continue to talk. He lives in Alabama now and is once again financially stable and sober. Through his experiences in life, he has become a new man and is now able to help homeless individuals in a way that he never would have been able to before. While he was once able to give solely from his pocketbook, he's now able to give through compassion and love, sharing also of the eternal shelter and home that can be received through the One that gave him so much.

Phil started off wealthy and proud. Through a series of circumstances, he became homeless and humble. Over time, he was able to rise back up out of the ashes. While his riches may not have been what they were before, the wealth he gained was far more valuable than that which any money could provide.

Jesus tells us to not store up treasures in this world where moth and rust can destroy, but to instead focus on our eternal riches in heaven which can never be destroyed

(Matthew 6:19-20). Through homelessness and poverty, Phil finally understood these words. For years he had been focused on pursuing wealth and extravagance in life, only to have it taken away. When the depths of his wealth ceased, he believed his life had come to an end.

The economic uncertainties that many people face can be challenging and overwhelming. When circumstances change, people who were once comfortable and sure can become apprehensive and fearful, wondering what will happen to them when their money dries up. None of us knows what tomorrow holds or what our financial situation will look like in the future. But if we hold onto God and focus squarely on Him, we will recognize a new perspective beginning to develop within us.

Songwriter Helen H. Lemmel writes:

> *O soul, are you weary and troubled?*
> *No light in the darkness you see?*
> *There's a light for a look at the Savior,*
> *And life more abundant and free!*
>
> *His Word shall not fail you, He promised;*
> *Believe Him, and all will be well:*
> *Then go to a world that is dying,*
> *His perfect salvation to tell!*
>
> *Turn your eyes upon Jesus,*
> *Look full in His wonderful face,*
> *And the things of earth will grow strangely dim,*
> *In the light of His glory and grace.*

Phil had been a man of wealth who became weary and troubled when his possessions began to fade away. As he sat in the booth on Christmas Eve, sandwiched between two homeless men who were severely mentally ill, he saw no light in the darkness he faced. He tried all he knew to overcome, but none of his efforts brought lasting results. It wasn't until he turned his eyes upon Jesus that he was able to begin seeing the true Light that shone bright even in his darkest of nights. His Word did not fail him and Phil began to see that all of God's promises were true. He then, filled with hope, returned to the world around him that was dying and told of His glorious Light.

The situations you are faced with right now and the uncertainties in the future before you may be devastating and bleak. Even if you see no light in sight, know that Jesus holds the key and this is not the end of your book; it's only one of the chapters. You can be assured if you are walking with Jesus, regardless of the hardships you may endure right now, you will be victorious in the end (2 Corinthians 2:14). Let go of your worries about treasures in this earth and place your future and all it entails into the hands of our ultimate Provider and Lord. He knows what is best for you and He will ultimately supply for your every need.

Lord,

Help me to hold my material treasures with an open hand and grab hold of the eternal treasures I have in You. In the seasons of life when there are financial unrest and uncertainties, I know I can depend on You. Help me to willingly release the things I do not need and trust You to provide the things I do.

In Jesus' Name. Amen.

CHAPTER THIRTY-NINE

Searching for Love

*"There is no fear in love; but perfect
love casteth out fear: because fear hath
torment. He that feareth is not
made perfect in love.*
1 John 4:18

*Abuse can take on many different forms in people's lives.
For those who survive it, their hearts can become hardened and
their perception of love forever skewed. Tonia endured more than
most. While she was at her lowest point of despair, she was
introduced to a pure love that forever changed her life and finally
brought healing to her heart...*

Tonia was an emancipated juvenile when she came to
the Mission at the age of fifteen. Filled with defiance and
rage, she was no longer under the jurisdiction of her parents
and already had two young children of her own. For three
years she had tried to make it independently as a single
mom, but was now reaching out for help.

Over the course of the next fifteen years, Tonia
bounced in and out of the Mission. She would get her feet
firmly planted but then quickly fall backwards. Not
knowing her story, it would be easy to cast judgment and
find blame. After years of seeing her struggles, I knew a
different story.

It was a cold and wet February during Tonia's
twentieth year, and she was staying with us once again.
After she had been at the Mission for a few days, I heard that
Tonia actually had a secure place of her own. It was a

Section 8 apartment where she had been living and all of her belongings still remained safely inside. Because of the stipulations attached to the housing voucher she had obtained, I knew failure to maintain her home would lead to the loss of her certificate and the inability to obtain affordable housing for the next several years.

I called Tonia into my office and shared with her that I had become aware of the fact she was not really homeless and could no longer stay with us as a result. The shelter was already full and providing a room for her and her children was taking away from the potential needs of others who were coming through our doors. Tonia became agitated and responded by obstinately telling me she was not going back to her apartment. I pressed her for a reason why and explained the grave consequences that would occur concerning her housing if she didn't follow through. Regardless of my attempts, Tonia wouldn't budge. She continued to tell me she wouldn't return but wouldn't give me any reasoning why. From what I could see, Tonia was just reverting back to her childish ways for no reason other than immaturity and pride.

I continued several times to press Tonia for a reason behind her unwillingness to return to her apartment. Each time I was met with crossed arms, rolled eyes and the same smug but firm response, "Because I don't want to." While I had no intention of really throwing her or her children out on the streets, I told her she could stay the night but the following day she would have to either return to her apartment or find somewhere else to go. I was bluffing in hope that she would see the severity of her situation and take responsibility for her family. Regardless of my best attempts, Tonia still wouldn't budge. While I couldn't understand why, she would have rather been with her small children on the streets in the cold and snow than to return to her apartment. When she left my office, there remained no answers in place. I felt like all of my bullets had been fired and no ammunition remained.

The next morning I received a phone call from a case worker who had known Tonia since she was a young child and through the years had developed a very intimate relationship with her. She told me she had heard of Tonia's refusal to return to her apartment and the new predicament she was facing at the Mission. She asked if I knew why Tonia was refusing to return. It was then I found out the reasons behind this young woman's fears and the torments she had faced for the majority of her life.

Tonia had been abandoned by her parents at a very young age. With no other family in place, she ended up being raised predominately by her grandmother. Unfortunately, her grandmother owned an adult entertainment bookshop and it was there Tonia spent most of her days growing up. While most girls her age were playing with dolls and other children in the neighborhood, she spent most of her time forced into a back room. She was exposed to sights most adults don't see and was used over and over again by customers seeking to fulfill their own lustful desires. As I listened, my heart broke and I began to see the reasons behind the layers of hardening, defiance and aggression that had developed in Tonia's short life.

After telling me Tonia's childhood history, the case worker continued to share of the present situation she was in. Just before her return to the Mission, the man who lived above Tonia had forced himself into her apartment and violently raped her. She was terrified to return to her home as a result. I hung up the phone startled by the reality of the depths of Tonia's suffering.

I shared the details I had just learned with a female staff member and asked for a meeting between her, me and

Tonia. This time as I looked at her, it was through a new set of lenses. As I shared with Tonia the information I had learned, she sat with her eyes gazed at the floor seemingly detached from the conversation that was taking place. With a father's compassion, I asked why she hadn't just shared with me. With her eyes still glued to the floor she answered softly, "I was just too embarrassed." My heart sunk as I listened and she continued to share how ashamed she was of who she had been. She told me the reason why she hadn't wanted me to know was because she viewed me as a father figure and friend. She thought if I really knew of her past, I would no longer love her.

The words hit me like a ton of bricks. I was the one who was ashamed. *How could I have not been more intuitive and prayerful when she displayed such stubbornness about her unwillingness to leave? How could I miss something as devastating as this?* I became determined to never miss such an incident again.

Tonia continued to come back and forth to the Mission for many more years. She would get the help she needed, leave and become involved in the wrong relationships, become abused, and return to us for help once again.

On one of her returns, Tonia came to me more broken than ever before. By this time, she had given birth to three children. In an attempt to escape the suffering in her life, she had begun using drugs and neglecting her duties as a mother. As a result, the court system made the determination to remove all of her children permanently from her care. She was told she was not permitted to have any contact with them until their eighteenth birthdays. She went on to angrily share how the judge had ridiculed her for her extremely poor parenting and told her she would never amount to anything.

As Tonia relayed the details of what had just happened, the tears streamed down her face and she confessed she didn't want to live anymore. She paused only momentarily to look into my eyes and tell me in a very hostile manner, "And don't you tell me about a loving God." I knew I had to be delicate with the words I chose and found myself asking her, "How would you like to prove that judge wrong?" She was perplexed by my question, so I repeated it. I asked how she would like to actually become someone... someone who would make both her and her children proud so that on the day they met again she would have the opportunity to be the mom they always wanted her to be. She sniffled and looked at me with disbelief as she asked, "How is that possible?" I explained to her that it wasn't, but together with God and her willingness, all things would be.

I told Tonia I truly believed that with God's help she could become a woman of character. She got a mischievous look in her eyes and with somewhat of a defiant look told me, "I'd really like to prove that judge wrong." As I told her of the woman I believed she could become, tears flowed down her face as she bowed her head and humbly said, "Please show me how."

I connected Tonia to a female staff member and together they began working on a new character quality each week. For the next several months we began to see remarkable changes in the way Tonia looked and conducted herself with the unfolding maturity that was beginning to develop in her life. After several months of her diligent efforts, something else happened that took me off guard. Tonia came into my office one afternoon and said, "You know what? I think I am becoming a woman of character." She then went on with a smile, "And I think I am ready to hear about that God-thing now."

Tonia accepted Jesus Christ as her personal Savior, started attending our chapel services, became involved in a local inner-city church and came to the full understanding that Jesus loved her more than anyone else possibly could. Her troubles didn't all go away at once and she did continue to be tempted with wrong relationships, hopelessness and drugs, but through the process of consistency on God's part and the love from those who reached out to her, she began growing up and truly moving forward in life. She went back to school and eventually became certified in the medical community.

Tonia hasn't been back to the Mission for years, other than to share her testimony of how the love of God and the love of others had brought hope into her hopeless life.

Not long ago I received a call from Tonia. Her oldest child had just turned eighteen and wanted to come stay with her. She was nervous about her abilities and timidly asked, "Do you think I am ready?" I smiled on the other end of the receiver and said, "You bet I do, Tonia... you bet."

Countless numbers of individuals are victimized through rape, molestation or other sexual assault every day. Often the horrific crimes go unreported and the victim is left feeling shamed and alone. Tonia experienced so much of that trauma during her life that it caused her decision making abilities to be impaired and her life permanently altered. Her interpretations of love became skewed and she went through life striving to be accepted and looking for ways to mask all of her pain.

When Tonia first heard about the love of God, she wanted no part. To her, Jesus represented yet another man who would use and abandon her when she needed Him the most. When she began to open her heart to the purity of His love, she recognized that the gift He had to give was greater than any precept of love she had ever previously conceived.

There is nothing in this world that can take away the scars left from wounds inflicted upon us in our lives. The trauma runs deep and can cause us to believe horrible thoughts about ourselves that are by no means true. Jesus is the only answer and the One who can truly allow our wounded hearts to heal.

If you're one that needs healing in this area, recognize now that the actions performed against you were never your fault. Release unto Jesus the memories and the shame, guilt and condemnation that have terrorized your soul and tormented your heart. As you do, His peace will soon enter and the agonies from trauma will cease.

There is no fear in love; but perfect love casts out all fear… *(1 John 4:18).*

The love our Lord has to give is not like that of this world. It is pure, patient and kind. It will heal your wounds and never leave you abandoned. It won't bring you harm, but only hope and peace. Where others have failed you, His love will not. It's the answer you seek and the healing that you've sought.

Don't be afraid to receive His love and the healing it brings. With outstretched arms, it awaits you today.

Dear Lord,

Take away the trauma that surrounds the memories of my past. Take away the pain, the shame, the guilt and condemnation I have allowed to build up over time. I need Your healing touch and I willingly receive of Your love. Help me to trust in the purity You have to give.

In Jesus' Name. Amen.

CHAPTER FORTY

Should We Let Him Die?

*"As we have therefore opportunity, let
us do good unto all men..."*
Galatians 6:9

Failures and challenges may have come our way but I've learned if we hold onto them, we become paralyzed and unable to fully embrace the possibilities of today. For three years I experienced rejection and disappointment as I tried to help a man in need. But through perseverance and faith, the tides finally turned...

Rosario showed up on our doorstep looking extremely ill. He spoke no English but we could tell by his appearance that he needed significant medical treatment right away. When we got him to the hospital, we found he was experiencing kidney failure. He was homeless, living in the country illegally, and had no friends or family nearby. We made the routine calls to law enforcement and immigration services but, because of his severe medical condition, no one was eager to intervene. Rosario was discharged from the hospital and, with nowhere else to go, returned to the Topeka Rescue Mission.

Rosario was a tiny man, no more than five feet tall. He was only in his thirties; however, his dark weathered face looked much older as a result of the many years of hard labor spent in the blazing sun. As his health deteriorated, his bones became weak and broke frequently causing at least one body part to be in a cast at any given time. Because he was an illegal immigrant, there were no appropriate jobs available and no government assistance could be received. We did our best to help him relocate back to Mexico, but to no avail. Despite his grim circumstances, he was as kind and pleasant as could be. He loved to joke and loved when we served Mexican food. He often humorously complained our food was not spicy enough for him.

Numerous attempts at working with the United States and Mexican governments to get Rosario back to his small hometown in Mexico had repetitively failed. It wasn't until two years into his residency at the Mission we were able to make plans in a positive direction. An airline ticket was purchased that would fly him from Kansas City to San Diego. There, Mexican officials would pick him up and transport him back to his home. I had grown to love Rosario but his health had continued to decline and I was thankful he would be able to spend his last days with his family.

I was helping Rosario get ready to board the plane when my phone rang. It was an official from the Mexican government touching base and asking if I could guarantee that Rosario would get in the car with them to go across the border once the plane landed. Rosario was attached to the Mission and a little fearful of returning home. However, with all of the efforts that had occurred, I was confident he would follow through with the plans. I told the official that while I could not give an absolute guarantee, I was certain he would get in their car. Abruptly my hopes were shattered. The official told me that without my guarantee, they would no longer arrange to pick him up and advised me not to put Rosario on the plane. He hung up the phone and that was the end. I could not believe that after two years of unsuccessful attempts of reuniting this man with his family and then coming so close, we had failed again. My faith and energy were depleted as Rosario and I drove back to Topeka in silence.

The only way Rosario had remained alive up to this point was through the free dialysis services which were generously provided to him from a local clinic that had heard of his story and compassionately offered their support. I was serving on a medical ethics committee at the time and had brought up Rosario's situation as a point of discussion in one of our meetings. I was horrified at the response. After much discussion and debate, the consensus was that the treatments should stop. While the result would be Rosario's death, they reasoned he was using resources intended for Americans and could give nothing in return. Rather than continue in that vein, the majority agreed that he should be left to die. To say I was troubled is an understatement. I was confused and my heart crushed. *Why was it that so few could see the worth of this man's life?*

Another year passed and Rosario became sicker with each passing day. We continued to provide him shelter and the dialysis clinic went against the advice from medical professionals by continuing to provide the necessary treatments. It was only a result of God's hand of compassion and the services provided that he remained alive.

It was three years into his stay at the Mission before we were finally able to again make connections with his family in Mexico. This time, now weak and dying, Rosario was more eager and ready to go home. I contacted the Mexican government and gave them the guarantee. Seeing the physical state he was in and knowing his life would be ending soon, they agreed to help him get back to his home.

We drove Rosario to the airport again and this time our plans succeeded. He got on the plane, landed in

California, and then rode with Mexican officials who took him back to his home. He was greeted with warmth and love from a family who cared. Rosario died in their presence just two weeks later. I was saddened to hear of his death, but grateful to know he had taken his last breaths in the comforts of his home instead of the confines of a homeless shelter in a land that was foreign.

The Mission is a last resort for just about everybody who walks through our doors in need. On the surface it may just appear to be a place where one can receive a bed, find something to eat and obtain some new clothes. Underlying all of the services are people like Rosario who have come to us with unique stories that are desperate, often hopeless and complex. We believe the compassion of Christ demands that we not turn our backs on a single one. While their needs may be emotionally, physically and spiritually complex, the Lord still calls us to love.

There have been people and circumstances in my life I have been tempted to give up on. Situations have seemed as though they were engrafted in stone and there was nothing I could do to chip away at the challenge at hand. Like with Rosario, I had put forth my best efforts for years and still my attempts failed.

Have you ever been there? Has there been a relationship or circumstance so challenging that you found it difficult to believe it could ever change? Philippians 3:13-14 holds a key: *Forget about the past and look forward to what lies ahead. Press on to reach the end of the race for there awaits a heavenly prize.*

Disappointments can weigh us down and paralyze us from ever trying to move forward again. When I was working with Rosario it seemed like every day there was a new disappointment or roadblock placed in my way. I could have chosen to dwell on the past failures but, if I would have, I would have never had the strength to press forward into what laid ahead. Every day I had to make a choice. I could focus on what had gone wrong and the failed attempts I had made the day before, or I could seek the Lord for a new strategy and put forth my best effort once again. Though the road was challenging and long, in three years my efforts eventually paid off. While it may not seem like a big deal in light of the multitudes who are suffering in this world, one life that God placed before me was changed. His life was prolonged and he was able to die in the arms of a loving family, versus the pain and anguish of a premature death on the streets.

Regardless of who crosses our paths, how difficult they are, where they come from or where they've been, Christ calls us to love. We may yearn to reach the multitudes but we must start with the ones who are in front of us right now. Maybe there is a relationship in your life that has proven a struggle for years. God tells us in His Word, "love never fails" (1 Corinthians 13:8). I urge you, regardless of the lack of results you may have seen over the years, don't give up. Keep pressing forward and continue to love.

Lord,

In all of the challenges, battles and trials I face, help me to never lose hope. Because You never fail and have never given up on me, help me to extend that same grace to others I might be tempted to forsake. Help me to turn my back on the past and embrace the new possibilities of the future.

In Jesus' Name. Amen.

CHAPTER FORTY-ONE

The Look

*"...for when I am weak,
then I am strong."*
2 Corinthians 12:10

When the answers seem scarce and my abilities inadequate, I have found peace in knowing that the outcomes of the challenges which surround me are not up to me. God doesn't expect me to fix every problem; He expects me to love. As I focus on being obedient in that, He can be trusted with the results...

It was a dismal autumn afternoon and the air outside was damp and cold. Driving back to the Mission my eyes caught a glimpse of a strange sight on the side of the road. There was an older woman, obviously tired and in distress, sitting under the tree atop the wet fallen leaves. She was wearing a dirty, ragged nightgown and her head was bobbing back and forth. You could tell she was doing her best to sit up but, in spite of her best efforts, she kept toppling down upon the cold ground and wet leaves below.

I drove around the block to see how I could help and realized the woman under the tree was a former guest of the Mission. Julie had suffered for as long as I had known her from chronic mental illness and alcohol abuse. This day she was extremely intoxicated. As she struggled under the tree, she had lost control of her bodily functions and was sitting in her filth as a result. Seeing the state she was in, I knew she needed immediate medical attention. I called for an ambulance and Julie was quickly taken to the hospital. I couldn't help but wonder if I would ever see her alive again.

After receiving hospitalized treatment for a few days, Julie was discharged to the streets. Realizing she had nowhere else to go, she quickly ended up back at the Mission. After she had been with us for a few days, she contacted me. Her physical state was still not the greatest so she asked if I could meet with her. While I had no significant words of hope or inspiration to offer, I still went. Our words were few when I did. She was broken and tattered and her eyes told the devastating story of a long and hard life.

Julie was with us for a couple of months and struggled through her program. Eventually, she completed her goals and found an apartment in the community once again. I was aware when she left of how her past always seemed to haunt her and lure her back to the familiar place of abuse and addiction. I feared the pattern would continue and that the next time I saw her would be either back at our doorstep or dead in a morgue.

Many years went by and I never heard any news of Julie; until one day when I received an unexpected call. She was on the other line and wanted to set up a meeting. I expected the worse and braced myself for the devastation I thought for sure I would encounter.

When Julie arrived at the Mission for our meeting, she was not the same person I remembered. The woman I expected to see near death and in a state of brokenness and despair was instead full of life and vitality like I could have never envisioned. Had I seen her on the street, I am not sure I would have recognized her. Her demeanor was altogether altered. She was vibrant and healthy and even appeared to have a sparkle in her eyes as she greeted me, looking at least ten years younger than her near sixty years.

We sat down in my office and she asked if I could remember the last time we had met. I recalled the brief encounter at the Mission so many years before. While I didn't recollect the exact amount of time that had passed, she informed me it had been ten years, citing the exact day, month and year of our last meeting. I could hardly believe it. She smiled as she humbly told me she had been sober for the entire decade that had passed.

As she reflected back, she asked if I could recall the conversation we had on the day we visited last. I apologized and shook my head no, while she did the same. She said she couldn't remember anything we had talked about either but what had stayed with her for years was the look that was on my face. I was perplexed. Julie had changed so much for the better. She was sober and now sitting in my office asking about a conversation neither of us could remember. *What was the purpose?*

She interrupted my thoughts and continued, "It was your look!" She couldn't describe it but recounted the day she was lying in her bed ready to give up on life. She was more hopeless than she had ever been and didn't have the strength to go on. Somehow, unbeknownst to me, she said I had given her a look that told her everything was going to be okay. "Ever since that day," she continued, "I've never had a craving for alcohol."

I was amazed at her testimony but knew there wasn't really anything on my own accord I had done. Julie looked at me with full sincerity and told me she was there to thank me for what I had done that day. While I tried to persuade her to instead give thanks to God and the others who had faithfully stood beside her, she politely agreed but persisted in her stance. She said she had to thank me for the look that was on my face that day. To her, that one look I had been completely unaware of changed her life and made all of the difference in the world. She had since become sober, reunited with family, and accepted Jesus Christ as her Lord and Savior.

Julie then got a very serious expression on her face and began to lean forward in her chair. With more genuineness than I can describe, she confessed she was still smoking. "Could you give me the look again?" she asked. While I knew she was extremely serious, I chuckled as I told her I couldn't remember what it was like the first time. "But if I did, I'd sure be making a lot of money with this look!" We both laughed and the Lord's joy filled the room until we said our goodbyes.

As I drove home that night, I was reflecting on the day and asked God what the meeting with Julie was all about. Immediately, He spoke to my heart and gave me one of the most profound spiritual experiences of my life. He said it was about something He had been trying to tell me for a long time. It wasn't up to me to solve all the problems of the people He had put into my care. It wasn't up to me to bring in all of the provision of money, food and shelter. All He asked of me was that I remain faithful to what I was called to do and, in return, He would use whatever means He felt best to provide for and heal those who were broken; including a simple look on my face of which I might not even be aware.

I recognized fully now that it was never about my abilities, it was about my obedience. It's about showing up for the assignments the Lord places before us, even if we don't feel we have anything to give when we arrive.

True, the needs around us can be great and our abilities lacking but, even when we don't have the answers, we can still love. Rather than ignore or hide from the areas where we don't know what to do, we can stop and love the one who is placed before us. Doing so can bring forth far more change than our striving for solutions could ever accomplish.

I went to Julie humbly with the awareness that I had no tangible solutions for the brokenness she faced. While I was responsible for providing her shelter, clothing and food, she needed something more. She needed to know she was loved. While I may not have eloquently shared that truth with my words, God used my willingness to look into her eyes and take the time just for her to dramatically change her life. His ability to speak to her through a look on my face was not a result of me, but of God using my emptiness and recognition that, in and of myself, I had nothing to give.

From the God's Word Bible translation, the words of Jesus are shared in a phenomenal way: *Blessed are those who recognize they are spiritually helpless. The kingdom of heaven belongs to them (Matthew 5:3).* We might be reluctant to go forward to the places God is directing because of our fears of failure when we arrive; but, in reality, it is through our weakness that God can use us the most. When we lay aside our abilities and acknowledge we are bankrupt within ourselves, He is able to take control of our lives and most effectively use us for His purposes.

Knowing God wants to demonstrate His love through us, and that He then takes full responsibility for the results, has given me immeasurable peace throughout the years. When we step forward in faith, regardless of what we do or do not have to offer, He is in control of the results; not us. During times when the challenges and responsibilities have been great in my life, I have found comfort in remembering that all the Lord asks me to do is to reach out in love. When I do that, He takes care of the rest.

The same is true for you. As you draw closer to Him, He will reveal Himself through you in times when you are not even aware. You are a conduit of His love and a carrier of His hope to the people around you. Find peace in knowing that as you move forward in faithfulness and love, He can be trusted with the results.

Dear Lord,

I thank You that I do not have to rely on my own strength to make it through the challenges of life. Thank You that as I love You with a whole heart, I can receive of the peace that comes from knowing and trusting in You. Use the unseen through me to bring forth change into the lives of others.

In Jesus' Name. Amen.

CHAPTER FORTY-TWO

The Impact and Sacrifice of One

"...for I am not come to call the
righteous, but sinners to repentance."
Matthew 9:13

It wasn't until I was invited to perform the most unusual of funerals that I began to fully realize the immense love the Lord holds for the lost. For the first time in my life, I experienced an overwhelming glimpse into the depths of His heart and the compassion it holds. While the events leading up to the funeral were tragic, the life that came forth as a result could not be compared...

I received a call one evening from a funeral home here in Topeka. The director asked if I heard about the recent homicides which occurred in one of the local strip clubs. I had read about it in the newspaper and was familiar with the story. A belligerent man had gone into the club and fired a semi-automatic machine gun. It was a gruesome scene as three individuals were murdered and several others were hurt.

The director asked if I had known one of the employees who was killed. While I didn't recognize his name, I realized I did know some of his family members. Apparently they had called the funeral home and asked if I could do his service.

I immediately thought there was no way this was an engagement I could take. There was no inkling of desire within me to perform such a service, especially for someone I didn't know. Rather than instantly turning him down, I asked if I could call him back with an answer once I was sure. The director agreed and I hung up the phone.

My mind was buzzing with uncertainties. *This wasn't really something the Lord wanted me to do, was it?* I went before the Lord to seek His heart. As I prayed, I sensed very strongly He was telling me that this was a commitment I was to accept. I did my best to rationalize with the Lord the reasons why I didn't want to but, even so, I continued to feel it was an assignment He wanted me to take. I called the director back and let him know I would conduct the service.

I was apprehensive about the funeral and really didn't know what I was going to say or do. I had never been involved with such a circumstance but found comfort in believing, as his family did, that the gathering would be small and the service likely short. Rather than trying to prepare something in advance, I decided I would wait and gather some thoughts together right before the service once I arrived.

The day of the funeral came and, as I attempted to find a spot in the parking lot, I was amazed. It was forty-five minutes before the service was to begin and already there was no place to park. I rationalized there must have been an earlier service for somebody else that just hadn't finished yet.

I parked across the street and walked towards the parking lot, thinking I had plenty of time to prepare. I felt scared and apprehensive so I prayed, "Lord, I need your wisdom." The second I finished that prayer and stepped into the parking lot, a remarkable thing happened. All of a sudden, I felt power and a surge of energy running through me like I had only felt a few times before. I had a strong sense of confidence that was coming from beyond myself and I knew it was God. It wasn't until the service began, that I would understand why.

I found out earlier, by speaking with the family, that the man whose funeral I was to conduct had died in a heroic attempt to save others. He watched the scene unfolding and, as others were getting shot, he jumped out in front of the gun to save the lives he could. After receiving eight bullets, his life was lost so that others could be saved.

As I walked through the doors, the place was packed. People were already standing in the lobby because there was no more room to squeeze in. All of the strip clubs in the area had heard of this man's brave efforts and come to show their support. I was told by the funeral home's staff to brace myself for what I would see when I stepped into the room.

I entered the front of the room and looked out. I was stunned to see over 300 people packed into a room equipped for about a third of that. There were people packed into the room, the halls and the lobby... and more were still coming in.

Scanning the room I could see the majority of people in attendance were young women who were in the business and dressed like they were ready for work. Others were well-dressed business men, the owners of the clubs, and the large husky bouncers who worked at the doors. I gulped as I wondered what I would say. While I was still feeling the surging power pulsating through me, I also had fears and uncertainties of how to proceed.

I sat down in a chair that was right next to the podium as the music played. I knew at its conclusion I would need to stand for my remarks. I had received a history on the man from his family and knew the story of his heroism but, other than that, I had nothing to share.

I said a silent prayer and asked God to help me understand how He felt about the people who were before me. Immediately I began to sob. Tears poured from my eyes and down my face as I looked out at the women in their scanty attire, the bouncers with faces of iron, and the prosperous owners of these establishments. The tears became so strong that people began to stop what they were doing to look at me with curiosity wondering what was going on.

It wasn't just sadness I was feeling. It was overwhelming compassion and love. As I continued to cry, I asked the Lord if this was my answer. *Was this how He felt?*

I couldn't quit crying as hard as I tried. I finally told the Lord I understood and begged for the emotions to stop. As soon as I did, the tears ceased. I wiped my face and recovered. The music was over and I stood up to speak.

I went through the man's history and spoke of the heroic efforts which took his life that fatal night. I knew the man had not been walking with God but did my best to remain as encouraging to the group as possible.

Once finished with the information I had obtained, I came to a crossroads. Should I stop there and end the service, or keep going with a spiritual message? I paused as I said a silent prayer and heard the response from God, "Be bold." I chose the latter and went forward.

I shared with the crowd that even though the man was a hero, he had led a life which wasn't pleasing to God. I boldly called his lifestyle, sin. As soon as those words left my mouth, some very irritated looks began shooting my way. I ignored them and went forward as the call to be bold continued ringing in my spirit.

I told the crowd God had created each one of us for His purposes and it wasn't that He didn't want us to enjoy life or have fun, but that there were certain things He knew would bring us harm. I then delved into the message of sin and the consequences of immorality.

By this time I was getting even more angry looks and jeers from the audience. People were looking at each other in disbelief, not really believing I had the nerve to say the words which were coming from my mouth. There was a great restlessness in the room as I proceeded to address the people before me and the lives I knew they were currently caught up in.

Grateful for the power and understanding of God's immense love He had given me through my tears just moments before, I continued. I explained that even though this man hadn't walked with God, the example of how his life ended was the illustration of God's Son. I shared of how He willingly died for us in order that we might be forgiven and saved. I told them compassionately God was not a kill-joy; He was the personification of love. "He loved the man who lies before us," I shared, "and He loves you too. That's why He doesn't want you to get hurt, get diseases, or miss why you're here on this earth."

I had turned the corner to help them understand God loved them and had a greater plan for their lives. As I did I realized I was sent to this group, not to judge and condemn, but to share love and truth. The longer I spoke, the more the former hardness that was directed my way began to melt. Before I knew it, an audience of tears was beginning to flow. The service ended with many lives touched and transformed by the power of a loving God.

I rode in the hearse to the gravesite. As we drove, the driver looked in his rearview mirror and exclaimed in amazement that we had one of the largest processions in their history following behind. Nearly 200 cars were making their way to the cemetery.

The sun had been shining but it was a cold, bitter morning. When we pulled up to the graveside, thick dark clouds began to roll in. As cars pulled up, many poured out wearing high heels and little clothing, almost entirely unprotected from the cold. We gathered under the tent as the cold whipping snow blew, causing the tent to flap violently and fresh flakes to swirl all around us.

I began sharing more about God's love and purposes, the forgiveness available through Jesus Christ, and the hope of a new life. As I closed, I asked for everyone who was in agreement to bow their heads and join me in prayer. As I looked around, nearly every head was reverently bowed. As the prayer ended and I breathed, "Amen," a resounding echo bellowed through the crowd. The once hostile faces were now looking at me with solidarity and peace having received the good news of Jesus Christ and the hope of a new life.

The service ended and a line quickly formed. One by one, women came up to me with make-up and tears flowing from their eyes. Each one thanked me for sharing, for being kind, and for giving them hope.

I rode back to the funeral home in a limousine with owners of two strip club establishments and a lawyer. It was an uncomfortable car ride but God's Spirit continued to flow.

Within hours, I received a call from one of the owners I had ridden with in the car. He shared with me that, after today, he was deciding to close his business. They still had a bunch of steaks in their kitchen and wondered if they could be donated to the Mission. I breathed a sigh of joy and unbelief as I humbly accepted his donation.

I had read in the Bible many times before about the ways in which God loves the sinner. Jesus had dined with them and many followed everywhere He went. He told us it was never the healthy who needed a doctor, but the sick (Matthew 9:12). Now, I had experienced a larger glimpse of His heart and realized how incredibly true was His love for the wayward. While I could have stood up and condemned, God showed me the better way as He revealed we are to have compassion for everyone, regardless of what they might struggle with in life. While we aren't to condone the sin, we are to be sure the truth of our speech towards it is always tempered with love.

Before Jesus was crucified, He dined with His followers. When the meal was over, He got up and wrapped a towel around His waist. Filling a basin with water, He went to His disciples and began washing their feet. At that time in history, the majority of travel was done by walking. Because of the places they had been, their feet were dirty, calloused and tired. Out of servitude, love and compassion, Jesus knelt down and began washing each one clean. While they didn't understand at first, He told them the washing was necessary in order to fully follow Him (John 13:1-20).

Each one of us has a past. Some are filled with a filth and residue that has built up in our lives. Just like the disciples' feet, we become worn, calloused and soiled. Regardless of how dark our past might be or where we have walked, Jesus wants to reach down and, with the same compassion He displayed to His early followers, wash us clean. There is no life so tarnished that it cannot be made pure by Him. It's part of embracing Him and the new life He has for us to live. It's necessary in order for us to go forward; otherwise, we will stay stuck in our past.

It's never too late for you or anyone else who might cross your path. May you receive the cleansing He has to offer and walk forward in the freedom and life He has to give.

Dear Lord,

I place my brokenness and my life into Your hands. I confess my sins and ask that You would fully cleanse me and show me Your way. Thank You for washing me and setting my feet on the right path once again. With the same love and compassion You give to me, may I offer the same to those around me who are bound in destruction and lost.

In Jesus' Name. Amen.

CHAPTER FORTY-THREE

Miracle in Topeka, Kansas

*"For the vision is yet for an appointed
time, but at the end it shall speak,
and not lie: though it tarry,
wait for it; because it will surely
come, it will not tarry.*
Habakkuk 2:3

*Have you ever become so excited about an endeavor and
begun moving forward with zeal, only to quickly hit a brick wall
which prevented you from going any further? I truly thought I had
received a God-inspired solution to a major challenge being faced.
When no one else around me seemed to agree, I learned an
invaluable lesson in surrendering my plans and trusting God's
timing above my own...*

In the latter part of 1996, it was apparent the picture
of homelessness was beginning to change dramatically both
nationally and locally. While it had been predominantly men
who were experiencing homelessness, the shift was now
turning towards an exponential growth in the numbers of
women, families and children facing the same. The
wonderful Mission building established in 1991 was no
longer adequate to care for the numbers of women and
children we were seeing and who were predicted to be
headed our way. The question was coming to us from
numerous individuals and agencies partners, "What can you
do to assist?"

By mid-January of 1997, I believed God had given me
the concept of what the Topeka Rescue Mission could do to

address this issue by creating another shelter. Excited with the new ideas I believed had come from the Lord, I came prepared to the monthly Board meeting with drawings, statistics and great enthusiasm. I energetically presented my findings and vision for the creation of this new shelter to the Board members, fully convinced they would share my eagerness and zeal. As my presentation concluded, I was surprised to be met with the exact opposite. I could hardly believe my ears. There was not one person in favor of my well-articulated idea. I was dumbfounded. I tried different methods of explanation to try and conjure their thinking but to no avail. I walked out of the building that night wondering how I could have missed the boat so entirely. *Why was it I was so excited and passionate about this plan, had all of the evidence to support it, and yet no one was in agreement?* It wasn't until three years later I received my answer.

As the next six months passed, I couldn't let go of the vision I believed had been placed upon me. I struggled with God and internally struggled with the Board of Directors who, in my opinion, were not doing their jobs. However, my heart eventually became convicted that I was wrong in regards to my negative attitude towards the men and women who I believed God had placed in leadership at the Mission. The conviction of how wrong I had been became so strong that I believed I was to go to them the night of the next board meeting and confess.

I humbly and boldly shared with the Board members that June evening. I expressed how disappointed and angry I had been at their decision to turn down my proposal but I also told them how wrong I had been. I asked each one for their forgiveness and promised to back away from my advocacy of the vision... but I also encouraged them to pray that if the plans had truly come from the Lord, He would speak to their hearts and make it abundantly clear to us all.

After listening to my heart, they were surprised. They had no idea I had been harboring negative feelings for so long. Momentarily, I thought maybe I shouldn't have said anything but the reminder of God's conviction quickly returned. The burden I had been carrying for over six months had vanished and only the peace of God remained. The need for shelter was still there; however, it was as if the responsibility of building one was no longer resting on my shoulders. I felt a lightening in my spirit and a relief to my soul. I knew by releasing my plans and placing them into the hands of the Lord and those He had appointed above me, the proper order was being reestablished.

In the following months I went ahead and continued to develop the plan I believed was given to me from God. The difference now was that the relief from the burden remained and I no longer felt as though it was my responsibility to bring it to pass. As I fine-tuned the vision, I was reminded of a story from George Muller, a famous man of faith. In every challenge he faced, George trusted God fully. I always had the desire to walk in the same type of faith as he. He said one time that the first step to answered prayer is to be able to eliminate any personal ambition to the request put before the Lord. Even though I still had a passion for the vision, my personal ambition was finally surrendered to God.

One year later, on June 8th of 1998, I sat in the Board meeting once again. This time the Board members approached me and unanimously said they believed it was time. The vision that had been rejected eighteen months prior was now burning in their hearts as it had in mine so many months before. The timing was right and we were all ready to move forward in the plans God had laid. We decided we would wait until July 24th to make our plans public. As we concluded the meeting that night we collectively prayed, "Lord, if this is of You, we will do our very best to be Your hands and Your feet to carry out the work to create it... please show us a sign of confirmation that we have correctly heard."

After our Board meeting, my instinct was to break out files from our former building campaign and begin to develop a similar strategy. However, as hard as I tried, I kept sensing the Lord was telling me there would be no campaign. I was confused. *How could we raise the $2.2 million necessary for the project apart from a building campaign?* When the Lord continued to tell me, "No," I rationalized the timing must still not be right. I went to three separate prayer warriors with the dilemma and asked them to pray. Each one came back and said they believed I had heard from God. We were to build the building but there would be no formalized campaign.

It was the day after the Board meeting when I received a call from Steve Johnson, a construction manager who had been involved in our first building development. Steve was just coming back to Topeka and calling to see if the Mission had any special projects we needed help with. My curiosity was peaked and I shared a piece of the decision that had been made the night before. He chuckled and said he now knew why he had been awake since two o'clock in the morning with nothing but the Mission on his mind. By the end of the phone call, free construction management services valuing near $100,000 were in place.

Two days later another good friend of mine placed an unplanned call to me as well, Jim Browning with Capitol Concrete. He had donated concrete blocks for the first shelter and was calling to tell me they had some extra concrete blocks they would like to donate. He wondered if the Mission had a current need. I explained to him the potential plans to build an additional shelter for women and families and asked how many blocks they had. Two hours later I received a call back from Jim telling me they would have all of the blocks for us free of charge. I smiled in awe as I remembered the prayer we had prayed just three days prior, "Lord, could You show us a sign?" Little did I know this was just the beginning!

By Friday of that week, I received a call about a man who had recently passed away. He had spent most of his life working at a gas station in North Topeka and had no family around. After a life of hard work, he left the Mission his annuity worth $300,000. The excitement of what God was orchestrating was continuing to build.

The next week Doris Foster, our faithful Business Administrator, came into my office with a check in her hand for $117,000 from the estate of a person we had never known. I laughed when she excitedly asked how this could be happening; I knew it was God. It was only a few days later before she returned with two more checks, one for $50,000 and the other for $75,000. At the same time I received a call from a man who wanted to make a special donation in the amount of $100,000 in honor of his parents.

The next week I received a call from an attorney asking if I could remember a certain man I had visited once in a nursing home. The man had been very lonely with no family or friends. He had lived in a trailer and his only possessions were a bed, chair, television and vehicle. Apparently the gentleman had designated the Mission as his beneficiary. The attorney was calling to inform me that a check for $250,000 was on its way! We stood in continued amazement as special gifts from estates and other unsolicited donations infiltrated our mailbox.

On July 24th, just 46 days after we had prayed, we were able to confidently announce the plans to build an additional shelter that would house women, families and children. What we were able to announce even more enthusiastically was that God had already provided $1.1 million towards the campaign! Everybody in the room was amazed, including me. All we asked for was a simple sign but God came through in ways far beyond what we could have asked or imagined.

After the announcement was made, there were several interviews with the media. One reporter from a television station said to me, "Barry, you call this a miracle. Do you really believe it's a miracle?" I laughed and asked her what she would call it instead. She had no response other than a smile. That night the leading story from her station was "Miracle in Topeka, Kansas."

Without a formal building campaign, the additional $1.1 million was quickly raised and the Hope Center for Women and Families was opened on April 1, 2000. God knew I wouldn't have the time to coordinate or oversee a formal campaign, so He took the reins and did it for us.

There were many times I reflected back on the poor decision I believed the Board members had made and my months of frustrations which ensued as a result. My ambition to get something done was greater than my determination to fall into alignment with God's timing. The majority of the funds that came in to support the building endeavors came from estates. God knew the precise moment the good-hearted people who chose to leave the Mission endowments would part from this earth. Had I pressed forward and continued in what I thought was best, rather than handing it back over to the Lord and those in leadership above me, the dollars God had orchestrated would have never been there and this miraculous story would have never been told.

This experience not only led to the creation of an incredible shelter for women, families and children; but it has also served as a testimony to the incredible unfailing love and superior plans God has for us. In spite of our perceived understandings, impatience and ignorance at times, God is still able to continually use us for His greater glory and purpose.

There may be dreams, aspirations and visions you have longed for and wondered if they would ever come to pass. Know that if God placed it there, there is no obstacle too great or attack too fierce to prevent it from coming forth. God calls us to wait patiently on Him, even when we don't fully understand. As we do, we will be able to one day look back in awe at the beauty revealed as His great plan in perfect timing unfolds.

As Jesus prayed in the Garden, He dreaded the long and tragic road He knew was before Him. In essence, He asked God to take it away or make the road easier. But in the end He surrendered and said, "Not My will, but Yours be done." He was in so much anguish concerning the road that lay ahead that He sweat droplets of blood. It wasn't until He surrendered fully to the will of the Father, that He was able to arise and move forward in what the Lord had for Him to do. (Matthew 26:36-46, Luke 22:39-44)

I had toiled over the vision I had received concerning the Hope Center. I was confident I had heard from God, yet everyone He had placed in leadership above me was rejecting my plan. At first I became angry and bitter, thinking ill of the leadership above me and proudly thinking I knew better than they. But, as I continued on that wrong path of bitterness and judgment, God opened my eyes to see the big picture.

It was His timing that needed orchestrated in order for the vision to come to pass, not mine. Many times we will receive a word from the Lord and get excited for it to come to pass. We may receive a dream or vision we truly believe is coming from Him, only to be discouraged when no part of it seems to materialize.

1 Corinthians 13:9 says, "We know in part and we prophesy in part." We may get a small glimpse of the vision God has prepared for the future, but we have to recognize it's only a fraction of His larger plan. If it doesn't come together as quickly as we would like, we mustn't give up or think we didn't really hear from God. We must wait for it because, if He spoke it, it will surely come to pass (Habakkuk 2:3).

Regardless of the disappointments you have faced in your past, it's time to pick your dreams back up and press forward with God. Just because they haven't come to pass, doesn't mean they were not from Him. Surrender them and your ideas of how they will be fulfilled over to God. Giving them back to Him does not mean you are quitting or giving up; it means you are relinquishing control and allowing Him to work on His timetable instead of trying to force Him into your own. Have faith in His unfailing purposes and allow Him to rekindle the visions within you once again.

Lord,

Forgive me for giving up hope when things in my life have not come together in the timing or the ways I had planned. Thank You that You make all things beautiful in their time. I pick back up the dreams and visions You have placed within me. I give them to You and wait for Your purposes and timing to align.

In Jesus' Name. Amen.

CHAPTER FORTY-FOUR

Daddy, Make Me a Promise

"Thou hast turned for me my
mourning into dancing: Thou hast
put off my sackcloth, and girded me
with gladness; to the end that my
glory may sing praise to Thee, and
not be silent, O Lord my God, I will
give thanks unto Thee forever."
Psalm 30:11-12

I have met several people throughout my life who have seemed to experience more than their fair share of tragedy. But even through their pain, there are lessons to be learned. Jack's life is one such example...

Jack spent several years at Ohio State University, working towards a degree in mechanical engineering before joining the Navy. He spent the next ten years enjoying a successful Naval career. Over time, Jack met the love of his life, married, and soon the two were eagerly expecting the arrival of their new twin girls.

The first in a series of tragedies occurred on a day which should have been filled with joy. Their first child was delivered stillborn, while the second survived.

Jack and his wife were grateful for their new daughter but were still deeply mourning the loss of their first. In an attempt to regroup, they decided to take an evening away. Their one-week-old daughter, Emily, was safe at home with a babysitter as the couple headed out. On their way to the hotel, the couple came to a four-way stop. As they did, a drunk driver hazardously sped through, violently striking Jack's car. His wife was killed instantly; Jack survived.

The next 220 days were spent in the intensive care unit as Jack received treatment for a broken neck, back, two broken legs, and severe head trauma. His body was severely mangled and it would be months before he could walk again. Thoughts of Emily were the only thing that kept breath in his body.

Years passed and the joy of Emily's life warmed Jack's broken heart. He watched as she grew from an infant to toddler and captured his love. At the precious age of three, Jack received tragic news. His little girl was diagnosed with leukemia and only had a few months to live.

As days turned to months, disease ravished Emily's small petite frame. While she laid on her deathbed, she feebly looked up to her adoring father with one last request. "Daddy," she said in her sweetest voice, "I want you to make me a promise." Jack listened intently as tears filled his eyes. "I want you to stay happy until you see me in heaven." He smiled as he embraced her tight in his arms. "I promise," he said, not knowing just how hard that promise would be.

Emily joined her mother and sister in heaven and Jack did his best to move forward the best he knew how. Over time, the weight of his tragedies overwhelmed him. Not knowing how else to cope, he turned to alcohol to numb the fierce pain. A deepening of depression ensued and admission to the state hospital soon followed. It was there he received the acute help he needed to deal with his suffering.

After a short stay, Jack was discharged and looking for work. He was hired as a project engineer with a mechanical engineering firm and assigned the task of designing a cooling system for a new homeless shelter being built. Little did he know the shelter, for which he now worked, would one day become his new home.

Shortly after his project was complete, Jack suffered a severe stroke. The effects left him compromised and unable to work. With the sudden loss of income and the continuing pressure of bills, Jack became homeless and arrived back at the Topeka Rescue Mission; this time for help.

Jack lived at the Mission and eventually began working at the front desk. As his body recovered and his fortitude returned, Jack moved out; but, within a year, another tragedy struck when he suffered a massive heart attack. The familiar pattern returned as his job and possessions were lost and he became homeless once more.

When Jack returned to the Mission he was greeted with the compassion and love needed to begin healing from his wounds. "It is through that," he shares, "I learned to appreciate God and His plans for my life."

It's been twenty years since his first heartbreak occurred and his countenance is now one of joy and vitality. Jack was able to forgive the man who took his wife's life and lives his days holding fast to the promise he made to his daughter so many years ago.

Jack is one of the most likeable people I've ever met. He always has a smile on his face and is eager to serve. He has become well-known and respected in various sectors of our community; never failing to extend a hand to help or to share his appreciation towards each person he meets.

When I reflect on Jack's life, I think of a similar man named Job. He too was one who lost everything. His misfortunes were great and there were days when he longed to die to escape from the pain. Yet, in the midst of it all, he remained faithful to God. In the end, his life was restored and his captivity vanquished (Job 1:1-42:17).

As I look at these lives, I sit back and wonder. *How is it someone can go through all of the loss and adversity these men did, yet continue to walk forward with a smile? Could I do the same?* Though my disappointments may seem tremendous at times, they pale in comparison to the lives of these admirable men. I shake my head as I realize, I have no right to complain. If Jack can continue to walk forward with a smile, then I should have no problem at all.

It's been a humbling privilege to walk with the Jack's of this world. So many times, through just watching their lives, they have helped to put things in perspective of what really matters most. It is through them I truly have been able to see the light in the midst of darkness.

If you ask Jack how he does it, he'll tell you it's simple. "I was shown the love of Christ by those who follow Him... I'm looking forward to the day when I am reunited with Emily and can say, 'Daddy kept his promise. I stayed happy... for you.'"

Whatever your losses, whatever the pain, God can reach into even the darkest of situations and shed forth His light. If you've felt you would never breathe again because of the pain in your heart, please know there is hope. What God has done for one, He can do for you. May you receive His strength, His joy and His hope. My prayer is that you will make the decision to keep standing today.

Dear Lord,

I know in my mind there is always hope in You. May that reality seep into my heart. Would You reach in to my hurt, my tragedies and my pain and let Your healing balm bring peace? Turn my mourning to dancing, my sorrow to joy and may my life praise You once again.

In Jesus' Name. Amen.

CHAPTER FORTY-FIVE

The Darkest of Nights

"There is a way that seemeth right
unto a man, but the end thereof
are the ways of death."
Proverbs 16:25

When presented with a difficult challenge, I tried to come
up with a solution on my own. It was only through the great
remorse and many tears that followed I was able to see the errors of
my ways. The night became one of my darkest but, through it, God
was able to teach me an invaluable lesson about always entrusting
my dilemmas to Him...

Within months of opening the new Hope Center for
Women and Families, nearly every one of the 150 beds were
filled. The Mission had practically doubled in size in just a
few weeks and the environment was rapidly changing. With
the increase of needs and surplus of women and families, it
was obvious we were not properly staffed to effectively
handle the large number of individuals now streaming
through our doors. The staff we did have were visibly
exhausted, worn, and at risk for burning out quickly.

As the numbers continued to rise, we were faced with
some very difficult decisions. I was anxious and torn. I
didn't want to start turning away the many in need, but I
also didn't want to continually overstretch our staff and risk
their health and well-being due to the exhaustion they faced.
After serious analyzation and contemplation, I came up with

a plan. From now on, our priority would be to serve those who were from the Topeka and Shawnee County area. If we reached a maximum number of guests at the Hope Center, we would begin turning away people from outside of our community and reserve the remaining beds for those who were from our immediate area. When I presented my plan to the staff there was a sigh of relief, which caused me to breathe one as well. We were all impressed with the great strategy on paper, until the next day when the hard reality of what it really meant confronted us at the door.

I was sitting in the Board meeting on that hot, August night when our discussion was interrupted by a knock on the door. A staff member from the Hope Center reluctantly motioned for me to come outside. A couple from a local church was waiting in the lobby. With them was a single woman who had become homeless and stranded in Topeka. In an attempt to enforce the new policy, staff had tried to turn them away. However, the couple was not pleased and requested to speak with the main person in charge.

I walked through the hall and was greeted by a young professional looking couple who, out of compassion and concern, had brought to us a homeless woman in need. They explained her predicament and I was challenged with one of my own. I looked around into the eyes of those who were eagerly waiting my response, each one possessing a viewpoint and opinion of their own. The staff were eager to see if our day-old policy would really be enforced. The couple wondered with anticipation if we would offer support, and the hopeless woman in need just stood apathetically waiting to see if she would receive some form of shelter and relief.

The pressure was on. How could I say no to this woman in need but, then again, how could I say yes with an already overburdened staff and full house?

I looked at the couple and attempted to explain once again the reason behind the policy in place. They looked at me with sheer disbelief as I stood firm on my explanation and decision that had been made. Their faces showed great frustration at their inability to understand why an exception could not be made just this one time. I tried to be compassionate, but maintained my ground. I secretly hoped as they listened that they would take the next step by offering the woman a room in a motel or possibly aid from the church. Instead, they walked away in anger and left the woman at our door.

I was disappointed, but felt there was nothing more I could do. I turned to the woman before me and with quiet sincerity apologized that we didn't have a place for her to stay. She looked at me with a blank stare, then turned and walked away.

After a minute or two, I decided to follow out the door. I watched as she walked down the street with her head hung low beneath a darkening sky. As I did, I experienced the emptiest feeling I have ever had while working at the Mission.

The couple had seen a stranger in need alongside of the road. Like good Samaritans, they had brought her to the inn expecting us to give care in her time of need. Rather than take her in, I had told them there was no room left. It was my responsibility to know what to do when the inn was full and now I was responsible for turning this one away. I stood in the street and watched with numbness as the stranger in need walked across the railroad tracks, just north of our facility, and vanished into the dark night.

I went home that night and, after an exhausting day, finally got to sleep around midnight. By three o'clock I was wide awake as the vision of the woman walking off into the darkness consumed my mind. As I stared at the ceiling, I sensed in my spirit I was to get up and go to the living room. I went in, turned on the light, and immediately my eyes landed upon the Bible that lay next to the couch. I knew God was telling me to pick it up. I obeyed as He ushered me to open it. As I randomly did, the words I read pierced my heart: *Do not oppress the widow or the fatherless, the alien or the poor (Zechariah 7:10, NIV)*. The heavy conviction of what I had done wrong consumed me and I felt a knot form deep within.

I sat still for a moment and tried to take it in. In exasperation I finally cried out to the Lord, "What was I supposed to have done?!" I proceeded to blame Him for allowing me to be placed inside of a catch twenty-two where any decision I made would have been harmful for someone. If I chose to let the woman stay and no longer enforced the policy, I risked someone else from the local community coming and having no space. I also risked the staff burning out and having no one to care for the guests who were in our care. I argued with the Lord, but His only response was silence.

After ending my rant and sitting in stillness for a while, I finally bowed my head and humbly asked the question, "God, what did I do wrong?" No sooner had I breathed those words when I sensed the Lord speak to my heart in response, "You never asked Me about it." I realized at that moment I had gotten so caught up in the problem and so burdened by trying to become a solution finder that I had failed to stop and ask God what He wanted me to do.

I was ashamed of my actions and horrified by what I had done. Great anguish consumed me and heavy tears began to fall from my eyes. I knelt on the floor and spent the next hour repenting and crying out to God, asking Him to forgive me and save the one I had turned away.

The dark night had ended and the sun finally rose. When I arrived at the Mission, I quickly pulled the staff together for an emergency meeting concerning the policy that had been put in place just two days before. I explained what I had done and shared of my intense reprimand from God just hours before. As a result, I let them know the policy was no longer in force. Instead, we would be enforcing an ever greater policy: to consult our Lord and Savior every step of the way. Though the dilemmas were still before us, we knew the One who was sending people to us would somehow provide and show us the way. I knew from that point on God would never abandon us to make the critical decisions on our own.

We follow the latter policy still to this day. With sincerity and faith, we regularly ask the Lord to send us the people we are to care for and ask that He would provide alternative options for the others. We then humbly rely upon Him to help us to care for those He has placed in our hands.

Jesus shared a story about a man who had been traveling from Jerusalem to Jericho. He was attacked and then left stranded and wounded with nowhere to go. A priest and then a Levite walked by but, rather than attending to his needs, they quickly passed by. Finally, a Samaritan passed by and had compassion on the man. He bandaged his wounds and took him to the inn for refuge. The innkeeper received the man and agreed to look after him and meet his needs for shelter and care. (Luke 10:30-37).

The couple who came to the Mission found a similar woman who had become stranded while en route from one place to the next. She was scared and alone. While others passed by her, this couple had compassion and brought her to us for help. Jesus gave us the example of the Samaritan and told us to "go and do likewise" (Luke 10:37). This couple had followed through with His direction but sadly the inn, through whose refuge and shelter they sought, told them they were full. As a result, the woman was dejected once again and left stranded with nowhere to go.

My heart still breaks when I think back to that day. There were countless times I prayed for God to reach down and touch the one who was turned away and bring her into a place of safety from life's storms. I don't know what happened to her, but I do know God used her life to forever impact mine.

When I knelt on the floor on that darkest of nights, I promised the Lord I would never again turn anyone away because of space unless there were absolutely no options left; but, even then I would do my best to come up with an alternative. At the time of this writing it has been eleven years since that promise was made. In that time, I have been able to keep my word and God has been faithful to always make room in our inn for those in need. While we've come within two cots of needing to turn people away, the door has never been closed again on anyone who was hurting or in need as a result of space.

I thought I had come up with a plan, but later recognized that without God's insight, all of my plans are but dust that will quickly scatter into the wind.

When we are faced with challenging decisions, it is easy to fall back on the rationalization of what makes sense in the natural and quickly make a choice. However, it is only when we seek the Lord and allow Him to guide the way that we will be able to find peace and rest in the assurance that we made the right choice.

God calls us to act as the Samaritan and love our neighbors as ourselves (Mark 12:31). If there is a decision that you have to make, seek God first and listen for the counsel He has to give. If there's an option that is going to bring harm upon a neighbor who He's placed in your path, you can most likely be assured it's the other path He's calling you to choose. If it's not so cut and dry, He still holds the key. Go before the Lord and share your dilemmas with Him; then wait on His response. If it is silence you hear, examine your heart and see if there are any preconceived notions or plans you hold that may be blocking your ears from hearing His response. He wants you to hear but sometimes it takes surrendering our plans before we can clearly hear His.

Dear Lord,

You know the decisions I have to make and the way I think I should go. Right now, I surrender my plans and ask You to reveal Your way to me. If it is different from what I believed, I accept and surrender to You. Thank You for making my path clear and allowing me to hear from You.

In Jesus' Name. Amen.

CHAPTER FORTY-SIX

The Long Bus Ride

*"It is of the Lord's mercies that we are
not consumed, because His
compassions fail not.
They are new every morning:
great is Thy faithfulness."*
Lamentations 3:22-23

Jennifer's life had spiraled out of control. Rather than looking at herself, she continually blamed everyone else for the problems she faced. It wasn't until everyone turned their backs on her that she realized the change needed to come from within. As she moved beyond her circumstances and allowed her challenges to propel her into her future, she left a tremendous imprint on my heart and forever touched my life...

Jennifer showed up at the Topeka Rescue Mission's Hope Center late one Friday evening. She was accompanied by her two young sons and was pregnant with her third. More than hopelessness and despair, this young mother was filled with anger. She was appalled at the idea of staying at a homeless shelter and resented the fact she was there.

Jennifer had been raised in a Christian home. Both her mother and father were active in their local church but during Jennifer's teen years, marriage difficulties developed. During her senior year in high school, the couple divorced. The blow of the impact led Jennifer down an intense path of bitterness and rebellion. She quickly became heavily involved in alcohol, drugs and partying. As a result, she became a young mother of two children by different men with a third one on the way by yet another father.

Jennifer had been accustomed to a middle class lifestyle and was extremely judgmental towards the guests who were in need of the Mission's services. She openly thought she was better than the rest. However, her family no longer knew how to cope with her anger and rebellion so she found herself with no other options. She was now in her early twenties and facing the shocking reality of the many bridges she had burnt in life.

In earlier years when relationships were severed, Jennifer always found it very easy to find a new man who would take her in. However, on a night of heavy partying, Jennifer was in a serious car accident. She ended up going through the windshield of the car she was riding in and a substantial scar was left on her beautiful face. Using her beauty to secure a new place to live was no longer as simple as it once was. Now there was nowhere for her to turn except a homeless shelter.

In previous relationships, Jennifer was always accustomed to getting her own way. Because of this, she immediately made it her business to tell the staff of the Mission what they needed to do for her and how they needed to run the shelter. According to Jennifer, rules did not apply to her because she thought she was above them. She not only challenged the rules with anger but would also refuse to follow curfews and take care of the basic housekeeping issues of the room she was given at the Hope Center. She was so defiant she wouldn't even make her bed when it was requested of her.

Many people have a difficult time when they first enter the Mission for shelter. Often there is a great level of shock and disappointment and they are overwhelmed at the fact that they became homeless. However, after a period of time, many of these individuals begin to realize the Mission is a refuge for them in their time of need and they become grateful for the love, support and safety they receive. Jennifer was not one who had yet arrived at that place. Instead, she chose to blame everyone around her for the problems she faced. The staff often suffered the brunt of her outbursts. Frequently she would tell them it was their fault she was still there and that they needed to do a better job to get her out.

The future possibilities for housing and income for Jennifer were pretty bleak, so she ended up signing up for government assistance. In order for her to receive that support, she was required to attend classes through Social Rehabilitation Services (SRS). Out of pride and arrogance, she would ignore the numerous appeals from SRS and instead throw the reminders into the trash.

One day I received a telephone call from a caseworker with SRS notifying me of the situation. He told me Jennifer had violated the procedures so many times that if she missed her next required meeting she would have no further opportunity to receive government benefits and would be cutoff for life. I brought Jennifer into my office and explained the seriousness of the situation and importance of her attendance at the next meeting. We devised a plan and even scheduled transportation for her. She said she understood the severity and agreed to go to the appointment.

When the meeting day arrived, Jennifer was nowhere to be found. Our fears became reality later that week when Jennifer came into my office with a letter from the State of Kansas indicating she had violated procedures too many times and now would no longer be eligible for financial aid. A sinking feeling came over me as I realized, not only did

Jennifer not have options, but the Mission was very limited on options as well. I had no idea what we were going to do.

Jennifer sat before me, filled with anger and crying profusely. She looked at me through sobs and asked for a solution. Instead of reminding her of her failures and pointing out her contribution to the position she was now in, I answered her plainly, "You're going to get a job." Jennifer looked at me in shock as the excuses began. I calmly told her she was not able to stay at the Mission forever and in order to move out she would need income. Since the government, her friends and family would no longer support her, it was her responsibility to now earn finances through employment. I wasn't surprised when Jennifer wadded up the letter from the State, threw it on the floor, and stormed out of my office, slamming the door on her way out.

I notified the staff at the Hope Center that Jennifer was on her way back. Since it was Friday, we arranged for additional staff support. She was extremely despondent, hopeless and desperate. There was a potential danger of Jennifer bringing harm to herself or her children so we wanted to ensure that did not occur. None of us rested well that weekend because of the concerns surrounding what Jennifer might do. We watched her and her children very closely, and prayed a lot.

When Monday morning finally rolled around, I was surprised that I had not received a call from someone saying something very awful had happened. I was even more surprised when one of the staff members contacted me to give a report about how things went. She informed me a miracle had happened that very morning. I could hardly believe my ears... Jennifer had made her bed!

While it may not seem like a miracle to most, to us it truly was. After three months of struggling, this was the first time we had seen any hint of cooperation from Jennifer.

Later that day, she came to me very broken but open to discussing options. I shared with her how we cared about her and her children but that we couldn't allow her to permanently reside with us. Her only option at this point was employment. She despondently agreed to make the effort.

Within thirty days, she was offered a position in a nursing home as an aide. She had never worked in that area before but was now beginning to find skills and interests that she didn't know she had. As she persevered, the staff at the nursing home gave her great encouragement and the residents were appreciative of her great compassion and care.

Jennifer was on her way to experiencing a level of responsibility she had never known before. The staff at the Mission would consistently comment on the wonderful job she was doing at maintaining her children, her personal hygiene and her room. Her demeanor was rapidly changing from one of anger, bitterness and combativeness to kindness, gentleness and cooperation. The small miracle of making her bed turned into a large unfolding miracle in Jennifer's life.

After about two months of working at the nursing home, Jennifer, now seven months pregnant, came to see me. She sincerely told me how appreciative she was of all we had done for her and how much she was enjoying caring for others. As she continued, she told me that in spite of how well things were going she, like many other guests of the Mission, really needed a vehicle. It is easy for most of us who have vehicles to take for granted the ease to which we are able to get around our community. For most who are homeless however, they are dependent upon either walking, riding a bike, or using public transportation.

I knew Jennifer had been using a bus to get to her job and questioned if that was not working well for her. She replied with gratefulness and said it was, but that it would be much easier if she had her own car. When I asked her why, she went on to share her daily schedule which still brings tears to my eyes.

Every morning Jennifer would wake up around five-thirty in the morning to get herself ready and then prepare her two boys for daycare. She would bathe them, dress them and then walk with them across the street for breakfast. From there, she would walk to the bus stop with her boys to wait for the bus which would take them to her three-year-old son's daycare. She would check him in and then take her four-year-old back to the bus stop to wait for the second bus to take him to his daycare. They would then walk from the bus stop to the daycare and get checked in. She then returned back to the bus stop to wait for the bus that would drop her off near her job. She would walk to the nursing home and just barely make it there in time to begin her eight-hour shift. When she finished her work day, she would walk back to the bus stop and go through the lengthy routine all over again. When the three finally got back to the Mission, they were able to eat a late dinner before collapsing in their beds only to repeat the same routine the next day. She told me how much she loved her job, her children and the Rescue Mission. She also told me she had been saving money and asked, "Will you please help me find a cheap car? It would sure help us so much."

Listening to the daily schedule of this young mother, now well into her third pregnancy, completely wore me out. I told her I realized she was a woman with more strength and ability than I had imagined. I also shared honestly that I was not sure I could do as well with the same set of circumstances. I promised her I would do everything I could to help find her a car.

I shared Jennifer's story later that day with staff at the Mission and others in the community. I relayed all of the steps she daily had to take to get her children and herself to daycare, work and back to the Mission. Everyone I shared it with was overwhelmed. We've heard the phrase that we should not judge a person until we have walked in their shoes. This situation was an eye-opener to me and many others about the challenges numerous people who are homeless, impoverished and broken face every day.

After some time, we were able to find the car which made Jennifer's working experience while staying at the Mission much easier. Her new found success in life, the opportunities before her, and the strength she discovered within were evidences that family and positive friends in her life eventually began to notice. She began going back to church with her mother and became a role model for other individuals coming into the Mission who found themselves in the similar place of bitterness and despair.

Jennifer had to take a break from work to have her third child. However, it wasn't long before she settled back into her new found passion through employment. Today, Jennifer is a very successful mother of three, productively working in a local care facility, and is happily married to a very supportive husband. While her life was one that came to us heading in total destruction, now her days are spent helping others find their way out of the dark path that she once was walking. God took what was once chaos and challenge and turned it into something that produced passion and purpose.

The first eight chapters of the Book of Acts give us an interesting glimpse into the ways in which God will use difficult situations to relocate us into the place He desires us to be. Before Jesus ascended into heaven He charged His followers to stay where they were for a little while but, when the Holy Spirit came upon them, they were to move and begin testifying of the Gospel in other places.

The Holy Spirit came as promised but after He did, the followers remained in the same place. Rather than going as Jesus had directed, they began establishing themselves in their current place in life. Eventually, many began suffering persecution from a man named Saul. He arrested and tormented believers, even having some put to death.

He made havoc... therefore they that were scattered abroad went everywhere preaching the Word (Acts 8:3-4). It wasn't until they experienced suffering from intense persecution at the hands of Saul that they moved forward into the fullness of the plans the Lord had intended for their lives.

Jennifer came to the Mission damaged and broken. It seemed with each passing day something new would go wrong in her life. She wasn't making an effort to do anything different though and remained complacent in the place she was. It took a permanent rejection from the State of Kansas to cause her to move forward in life and to pursue what God had originally intended for her. As she stepped out of her comfort zone and began the new adventure forward in life, she discovered talents and passions she had not known existed. While the suffering she endured at the time was not pleasant, it caused her to become the new woman she is today.

When persecutions and attacks seem to come at you from every direction, use them as a reminder to slow down and examine your life. Are you where God has purposed you to be, doing what He has designed you to do? Are you using the passions and gifts He has placed inside of you? If not, it's possible that He is allowing the persecution from the Saul's of this world to open your eyes and move you forward towards the real place that you are supposed to be.

Don't be afraid to move forward even when it looks impossible. If God has directed, He will supply the strength you need to follow through.

Lord,

Direct my path. Show me the purpose in the persecutions I face and reveal Your plans if they are different from my own. Remove the fear within me that would try to keep me from moving forward in where it is You are leading me to go. Show me the way, I ask.

In Jesus' Name. Amen.

CHAPTER FORTY-SEVEN

Listening to the Still Small Voice

"...and after the fire a
still small voice."
1 Kings 19:12

If you have ever felt like completely giving up, or doubted if anyone really cared, God has something very important He wants you to hear...

I had just finished giving a presentation on behalf of the Mission to a Vacation Bible School taking place in a small community church just west of Topeka. I still had some extra time before my next meeting, so I decided to enjoy the scenery and take the back roads back into town.

I drove through the winding Flint Hills, appreciating God's captivating landscape. As I traveled, the name of an elderly man who lived nearby suddenly popped into my mind. As I reminisced on the work we had done together helping others in the past, I heard the soft prompting, "Go visit him." I quickly tried to dismiss the thought. It had been close to a year since I had talked to Roy and I had never felt comfortable making unannounced visits to people's homes.

The further I drove on my scenic route, the more the thought returned and began consuming my mind. While I had not had a signal on my cellphone for most of the drive, I bartered with God and told Him I would go to Roy's house only if I could call and ask his permission first. I looked down at my phone and at the bend in the road up ahead. I decided to cast my fleece before the Lord (Judges 6:37-40). "If there is a full signal on my phone when I go around this corner, then I will make the call."

I rounded the bend and looked down. My eyes broadened as I looked at my phone... five bars, a full strength signal.

I called Roy, shared with him that I was in the area, and asked if I could drop by for a quick visit. There was a long uncomfortable pause before Roy finally said it would be okay.

I pulled up the long drive, not knowing what to expect. Roy greeted me at the car and welcomed me into his home. I sat down on the couch, but didn't really know what else to do. I knew I was supposed to be there but I hadn't a clue the reason why.

There was an awkward silence as I pondered what to say. Finally, Roy interrupted my searching thoughts by asking about the Mission. Small talk then followed as we conversed about ministry and family. Within thirty minutes our conversation had ended.

I was feeling a bit of emptiness inside as I wondered why I had felt so strongly to come to this man's house when I really had nothing to say. I stood up, shook Roy's hand as I told him how nice it had been to see him, and walked towards the door. As I opened it to leave, Roy stopped me and said, "Before you go, I have to tell you something."

I turned to listen as Roy shared how things had been pretty rough in his life lately. Things had gotten so dark and painful that he had made a commitment within himself that very morning.

As he walked out to the mailbox earlier that day, Roy had a conversation with God. Empty, he told the Lord he didn't want to live anymore. He said that unless God showed him a sign, he was never picking up the mail again. Roy had determined to end his life.

Roy began crying as he shared his petition to God just hours before. "Will You please send someone by to come see me today? I know how impossible that is because nobody ever comes to visit, but if You do this, then I will know You are still there."

Tears streamed down Roy's face as he looked up at me and softly said, "Thank you for listening to God... *you saved my life.*"

I wept as I told Roy what I had experienced as I drove in my car. Truly, this had been God's orchestration. The realization of how serious this visit was, and could have been if I would have failed to answer the Lord's leading, hit me like a flood. This man's life would have been lost.

Years have passed since my drive through the Flint Hills and Roy is now full of life and doing extremely well. He and his family are consistent volunteers and supporters of the Mission. The darkness and suffering he once experienced have been used as an incredible tool to help many others who are facing similar situations in their own lives. When he and his family serve meals and listen to those who are in need, Roy understands the darkness and is now able to not only lend a listening ear, but to also share his testimony of hope and knowledge of a God who still hears our prayers.

Elijah was a man of influence and power when it came to declaring the word of the Lord. He had seen and experienced the mighty hand of God countless times in his life. In spite of his close walk, negative words were spoken in his ear which caused him to become fearful for his life. Rather than continuing to trust in the promises of God, Elijah chose to run away. After vanishing into wilderness, he sat down under a tree and petitioned the Lord to take his life. In his mind, there was no reason to keep living. Life had just become too hard.

As Elijah continued to drown in his sorrow, he hid in a dark cave where the Lord met him and ushered him out and up to the top of the mountain. Suddenly, there came a great and mighty wind so strong that it broke the rocks to pieces. But God was not in the wind. Once the winds ceased, an earthquake followed. The ground shook and the mountains trembled, but once again God was not in the mighty shaking. As the quaking earth calmed below Elijah's feet, a blazing fire erupted before him. Yet once again, in the fire the Lord was not found. It wasn't until the flames passed away and the earth stood still that Elijah was able to hear the faint whisper of God's still small voice directing his path. It was then that he was able to flee from his dark cave and experience life again (1 Kings 19:1-12).

Life can be hard. There are things that occur which make some days more difficult to go on than the next. Weights pile down on us, people hurt us and the darkness seems to overwhelm our lives. We may find ourselves hiding in the cave of sorrow and despair ready to take our own lives and walk away from it all.

Regardless of how dark your circumstances may seem, tomorrow is a new day. The problems you face are temporary and will not last forever. Give God a chance to work on your behalf. Don't give up. There is hope that lies ahead, just around the bend.

Both Roy and Elijah believed that God had forsaken them and they could no longer go on. The truth was that God was still with them and loved them very much. Because of the value of their lives, He used a still small voice to speak to them and show them His love. Let this be the still small voice that you hear from God speaking directly to you today:

> *You are not alone. You've not been abandoned or forsaken and you do have the strength to move on. The challenges you've faced have been hard, but they will not last forever and you will make it through. If only you could see what lies just ahead around this temporary bend in the road that you face. It won't last forever. While it might not feel like it right now, your life is a gift to this world and there are more people who love you than you could possibly know. You do make a difference. Don't ever give up.*

Is there something now that the Lord wants to speak to another through you? Be sensitive to His still small voice and don't hesitate if He asks you to go. There are countless people who are hurting and desperately grasping for just a glimmer of hope. You may be the one who the Lord uses to save someone's life. But sadly, tomorrow may be too late.

If you are the one who is struggling, please don't give up on yourself or the future that God has planned for your life. It might not make sense right now and your troubles may seem as though they will last forever, but they will not. I pray for the sweet peace and comfort of God to come and reveal the light that exists in your current darkness. Give it a chance to shine through and please, don't walk away from this life. You are much too significant and your value too great.

Lord,

Some days I just want to walk away from it all. You know my heart and You know the strength I need to daily survive. Be my supply. Allow me to receive the refuge, life and peace that only You can give. Show me others around me who need to receive the same in their lives. May Your light shine brightly and fill us with hope.

In Jesus' Name. Amen.

CHAPTER FORTY-EIGHT

Becoming Barry

*"I will praise thee; for I am fearfully
and wonderfully made..."*
Psalm 139:14

*For years during my Christian walk, I had been tempted to
pattern my faith off of what I had seen displayed in others. When
my views were challenged, the Lord began to show me who I really
was. Rather than continuing to try and have the faith of somebody
else, the Lord used this circumstance to help mold me into the
person He created me to be...*

The year of 2003 was one of financial free-fall for the
Mission. Throughout the year, we watched as funds
depleted and new donations to match the ever-present needs
were obscure. For the first time in seventeen years, the Board
began looking at me with great concern asking what *I* was
going to do.

For nearly two decades I had been walking by faith
trusting God with all of the details, especially when it came
to finance. People in the community had come to know my
many stories of faith and the miraculous ways God had
provided. The problem now was that the stories weren't
coming, and neither was the provision.

There was a woman named Jill who had made
considerably sized donations to the Mission in the past.
Though I had never met or spoken with her, she was very

respected and well-known in the community. She called me during this time to share that she was going to be making a donation of five thousand dollars to the Mission. After thanking her for her generosity, she asked me how everything was.

I was honest with Jill and shared that things were a bit difficult at the moment because the funding was not coming in as it used to. Without pausing, she asked the direct question, "Well, who are you telling about it?" Up to this point, I had never spoken to this woman or known anything of her walk spiritually. Regardless, I proceeded to tell her my stance on asking people for money. "Walk by faith and trust God with the details," I explained to her. She listened and then politely told me she thought that was nice. "But," she said, "you still need to tell people what you need."

When I hung up the phone I was troubled. For years I had gone about fundraising by what I deemed "the Muller way." George Muller was a man of God who worked with thousands of English orphans in the 1800's. Every step of the way, he walked by faith and never breathed a word of his needs to anyone but God. God honored his faith and daily provided in miraculous ways. I admired George and always longed to have a ministry that mirrored the miraculous provision of his.

Now I was confused. I had always been excited about what I thought I knew, but now was challenged by a well-respected woman with resources who was suggesting something new.

Right there in my office, I got down on my knees and with my face in my hands, humbly asked God what He wanted me to do. I confessed I was totally at a loss. I had thought my faith endeavors were honoring and pointing people directly to Him. *If that was the case, what was I missing? What had gone wrong that the provision had suddenly ceased?*

I paused in my prayer and heard the gentle rebuke, "Even in this good thing, you are a man of pride. You are using My blessings and the way I have set this up and you have become very prideful with it. I'm not going to let that happen."

I went home that night and contemplated the time on my knees, wondering if I had really heard from God. I examined what I knew of the Bible, George Muller, and myself. So many times in my past I had petitioned God to make me "just like George." As I pondered over it all, I cynically asked God if He remembered those prayers. As I questioned, He spoke. "I made George like George and I've made you like you. I'm not going to do it like I did it with George. I'm going to do it the way I've designed for you." I didn't know how to respond. I realized now that I had capitalized on the blessings of the Lord and allowed pride from past successes to lead me astray.

I continued before the Lord concerning our present needs and took Jill's advice. I mentioned our needs in the upcoming newsletter and saw, through the compassionate hearts of many, God once again provide. While it wasn't something George might have done, it was a stepping stone that God led me to cross. As I did, I learned to become more comfortable in the person God designed me to be. I also learned the importance of always remaining humble and flexible before the Lord and what He wants me to do, not what I think is best.

Sometimes we find people in life who seem to have it all together. We see the testimonies and radiance that seems to follow them and we want to pattern our lives after theirs. The Lord has shown me that He has created each one of us uniquely in His image to be the person He has designed us to be.

I will praise you for I am fearfully and wonderfully made… In this scripture from Psalm 139:14, the Hebrew meaning of the word "wonderfully" means unique, set apart, uniquely marvelous. Out of billions of people alive on this earth, there is only one you. You were uniquely and marvelously made! Don't waste your time trying to be someone else when God has created you to be you. You are the only one who can fulfill the unique purpose that He's placed within.

If you're not sure of that purpose, go to the Source. Just as the potter knows the clay he is molding and what it will one day become, so our Father in heaven knows us. It is only through looking at Him and not man, that we will truly become the people we were created to be.

While I will always admire George, I'm still learning every day to just be Barry. May you come to see the beauty in yourself and know the reason for which you were formed. I know, beyond a shadow of a doubt, the purpose is great.

Dear Lord,

May I never esteem any man higher than I esteem You. While I recognize there are those You have placed in my path for me to learn from, may I never strive to fit into the pattern of who You have created them to be. May I find comfort in being me and will You each day reveal more and more of who that person really was meant to be.

In Jesus' Name. Amen.

CHAPTER FORTY-NINE

The Fish with a Coin

"But my God shall supply all your
need according to His riches
in glory by Christ Jesus."
Philippians 4:19

I've realized in life that a lot of my thoughts have been wasted by worry. I wonder how, why, when and then spend sleepless nights trying to figure everything out. This is never God's intent for our lives. It is when we come to Him as our provider and trust Him fully that we are able to experience every need being met...

Serving as both a dedicated volunteer and faithful donor for a number of years, Grace was a familiar face around the Mission. She was a kind and giving woman who spent all of her free time knitting hats, gloves, and scarves for those who were in need. At times, she would go to the grocery store with what little money she had and load up the back of her old rickety Chevy with freshly purchased food for the Mission. For many years she even provided all of the brisket needed to feed nearly 700 people on Christmas Day. She was filled to the brim with compassion and love for the Lord, and all those He placed in her path.

Cash flow at the Mission was sparse during this time. The needs were continuing but in this season the donations were low. It was during a Board meeting one Monday night when we discovered that exactly $27,000 was needed in order to meet financial obligations due later that week. As we discussed the current needs before us, I felt extremely impressed that this was a concern we were to present to the Lord and nobody else. The Board was in agreement so we bowed our heads and prayed for a miracle.

Within two days, $7,000 of the money needed had already arrived. While we were encouraged by this victory, a small level of concern was beginning to mount as our deadline was arriving in just two more short days.

On Thursday morning, I walked into my office and immediately saw a sealed envelope. As I opened it, I was elated to find a check in the amount of $20,000. My excitement turned to confusion, however, when I saw the check was from Grace. Even though she had always been generous in bringing us finances, food, and warm scarves, it was my understanding that she lived on a fixed income and I knew the old car she drove was barely operational.

God taught me very early on that I was to never use any hint of manipulation to try and get money. My concern was that in attempts to softly influence her, someone had talked to Grace about our need and, due to her generosity and compassion, she was making an unwise donation.

I called Grace immediately and left a message on her answering machine asking her to please call or come see me right away. The day passed and I got no response. Now I was in a real dilemma. We received the check for $20,000 we had prayed for, but I was not sure if we should cash it.

On Friday morning, while I was still struggling with what I should do, Grace walked through my door. I had never been happier to see her. She sat down in a chair across from my desk and politely listened as I thanked her for all of the generosity she had shared with the Mission for so many years.

I then held up the check and said, "Thank you, but I'm not sure I can take this." She looked at me with perplexity and asked, "Why in the world not?" I shared with her the understanding I had of the limited resources she lived on and told her honestly I didn't feel she could afford the gift she had so abundantly given. I mentioned the condition of the vehicle she drove and suggested she instead consider using the money to purchase herself a new car.

A scowl began producing on Grace's face as she slowly leaned forward and grabbed hold of the front of my desk. "There is nothing wrong with my car," Grace spoke sternly. She softened a bit as she leaned back but she spoke very seriously as she said, "Apparently you don't understand. That's not my money, that's God's money... and He told me to give it to you."

I thanked Grace again but asked her to please tell me who it was on the Board who had shared with her our need. She shook her head and told me it was none of them. "A staff member?" I asked. She too denied such a claim. "Well did someone tell you about our need?" "Yes," was her response, "and I already told you who... it was God." She said the day prior He had told her to give, and so she unreservedly did. She had the money for several years always knowing He would one day tell her what to do with it and when.

I listened, but I also gave one last attempt to try and clarify by giving her the opportunity to at least take a portion of the money back to buy a new car. She shook her head as she looked at me and said, "Barry, you still don't get it, do you?" She told me how she had gone without a car for fifteen years so if hers died tomorrow, it would not be a loss. She said the money was God's and that, whether I accepted it or not, it was for the Rescue Mission. "Now," she asked with her eyebrows raised, "is there somebody else I need to speak to?"

All of a sudden it occurred to me that before me sat an amazing woman whom I had known for a long time, but who I didn't really know. I sat back and asked her, "Grace, will you please tell me your story?"

For the next hour I was mesmerized by the story of a woman who had been totally sold out to the service of the Lord. She shared how she and her husband had moved from city to city throughout their lives before he passed away to simply do one thing: faithfully pray over the city where God had told them to go. Each town they arrived in, they would look for work in order to pay the bills; but, their primary focus was prayer. The last place they had been assigned was Topeka, Kansas. While he laid on his deathbed, her husband told her she was to stay in Topeka and hold onto the savings she would obtain. He shared that God would let her know who the resources were for and when.

Grace said there had been days in between jobs when they didn't know where the food or the rent was coming from, and that there were many times when they lived on as little as three dollars a week. During that time, God would always faithfully provide and there were countless times when she would go the mailbox and find a dollar bill inside or a check from someone they had never met. At other times they would have good paying jobs but it had always been about doing what God wanted them to do, where He wanted them to do it. "This $20,000," she said, "is just part of what we've always done."

I sat and listened to Grace in total silence. I felt so incredibly blessed to be in the presence of such a faithful servant of the Lord. I was reminded of the story in the Bible about the widow's mite and what Jesus had to say about her compared to many of the others who gave. Truly through her sacrifice, she gave more than any other possibly could (Mark 12:41-44).

Grace left that day and the answer to our prayer concerning our financial deadline was received. While it was God who had answered our prayer, it was also as a result of the faithfulness of one who listened to His voice and followed His direction that our bills were paid. It is experiences like this, so unique, rich and miraculous, which makes the work of ministering to the poor, impoverished and homeless even more rewarding.

While in his home one day, Peter heard a knock on the door. It was the tax collectors who were looking for money. Peter, presumably having no money to give, turned to Jesus whose response was a strange one, "Go to the sea, cast a hook, and take up the fish that first comes up; and when you have opened his mouth, you will find a piece of money: take that and give unto them for me and you" (Matthew 17:24-27). There is no account of Peter arguing with the Lord. From what we can tell, he simply did as he was told and the need was met.

We live in an age where financial responsibilities seem to fly at us in every direction. It may be money for taxes, mortgage payments, utilities or rent; student loans, hospital bills, past debts or credit cards; groceries and clothes, bus fare or gasoline. The list can go on and on.

The Mission had quite a list during the time when we needed $27,000 in just a few days. Rather than run to anyone else, we followed the actions of Peter and turned to Jesus first. As we sought Him, we trusted Him as the source of our provision.

I didn't know two days before our deadline that God had whispered to one woman's heart to give what she had to fill our immediate need. While I was apprehensive and concerned wondering how the money would come, God already knew and had orchestrated the answer on our behalf. The money had already been placed in her hands for our time of need, just as the coin had been placed in the mouth of the fish for another need God knew of in advance.

Scripture tells us God knows what we stand in need of before we even ask and promises that according to His riches, He will supply (Matthew 6:8, Philippians 4:19). Many of us spend sleepless nights worrying about how the bills will get paid or how the refrigerator will get filled. Do we believe God is able to supply in even what seems like an impossible situation?

Our Lord longs to hear from us, provide for us and amaze us with His love. There are times when all He is waiting for is you and me to ask with faith in knowing He will provide. As impossible as it may have seemed for Peter to find a coin in the mouth of the first fish he caught, the finances materialized and the need he faced was met. As you turn your needs over to Him, may you see Him provide for you in ways that are beyond your realm of comprehension. You never know what He is already orchestrating or whose ear He has already whispered in on your behalf.

Dear Lord,

You see the needs before me and the deadline for each one. I trust in Your provision and know that while this may be impossible to me, it is not too hard for You. Thank You for working behind the scenes in ways I cannot see and for providing for my every need. Release a miracle in this area, I ask.

In Jesus' Name. Amen.

CHAPTER FIFTY

Thank You for Keeping Me

*"Render therefore to all their dues...
honour to whom honour."*
Romans 13:7

We never know for sure how today's actions will influence tomorrow. Sometimes it's not until years later that the impacts of our decisions are fully understood...

Over the years I have had numerous opportunities to speak to students ranging from elementary school to college. Many times I have been approached afterwards by a student expressing how the services at the Mission had blessed their family. Sometimes that blessing came through their experience as a volunteer or when a family member needed support. Other times the connection is even more direct.

I was being interviewed one morning for a television program through one of the local high schools. As I looked out into the audience of students and faculty, my eyes were drawn to a young man whose eyes were keenly fixed. The intensity of his gaze let me know he was holding onto every word. His eyes filled with tears as I continued to speak. There was nothing very personal about what I was sharing, but this eighteen-year-old boy was obviously touched as he wiped his tear-stained face with the back of his hand.

The room began to clear as I prepared to leave but the young man stayed behind, evidently waiting for the appropriate time to approach me in private. When the last person left, he walked forward and bravely shared.

When he was just a baby, he and his mother became homeless. His biological father had disappeared; his mother had no money and knew very few people in Topeka. Hopeless, with nowhere else to turn, they moved into the Mission. For the first time in his life, while listening to me speak, this young man began to realize what it must have been like for his mom. She had told him over the years it was because of God and those who served at the Mission that she had survived the experience. It was only now that he caught a glimpse of what she had meant.

As the young man continued, he shared of friends he knew who had gone through similar situations. The difference with them was that their mothers had walked away and given them up. With an expression of gratitude and awe he faintly said, "But my mom kept me." The tears were now streaming down his face as he looked up and with all sincerity said, "Thank you for helping my mom."

In time, his mom got back on her feet and did what she could to give him the best life possible. His face lit up as he spoke of the amazing man she married who had become his new dad and of his two younger siblings. He was now making plans for college and was excited about his future. Before saying goodbye, he shared with a smile, "It wasn't until today that I realized how much my mother has done for me... and I can't wait to tell her tonight when I see her."

Seeing the gratitude of this young man's heart reminded me of my own mother. My biological dad was killed in an airplane crash in Germany while my mom was pregnant with me. He was in the Army and as two planes collided, he plummeted to his death. I knew some of the story but never asked questions. Since it happened before I was born, I never gave it much thought.

At age thirty-five, I was married with two small daughters and my mother was living in Alaska. Rather than haul everything with her, we were keeping some of her items in our basement for storage.

While fiddling around the basement one day, I came across an old box of her memorabilia I decided to peruse. As I opened the box and began rummaging around, I came across an old newspaper clipping from the Topeka Capital-Journal. The large picture on the front captured my eye; in it stood three smiling women. They were in the New York City harbor as they stood on a ship, waving cheerfully as it slowly pulled away. I smiled as I read the article about the young ladies who were eagerly leaving the United States to join their husbands in Germany. My heart filled with pride as I thought of my mom.

I finished the article and put it aside. Directly underneath was another clipping with an entirely different feel. "Three Went, One Came Back Alone," the headlines read. My heart sank as I realized the article was about my mom and the devastating tragedy that had taken the life of my dad. She was now coming back to Topeka, twenty-one years old, pregnant and alone. Then reality hit me... the child in her womb had been me.

Feeling sorry for her, some soldiers had snuck her onto a huge cargo plane so she wouldn't have to endure the two-week trek home by ship. For hours, she bounced in the air suffering from the effects of her pregnancy, motion sickness and sorrow.

When Mom did arrive back in town, she had nowhere to turn. The survivor's benefits from the military had not yet kicked in and she had no income. Had her parents not still been alive and in town, she too would have been homeless.

While I read the article, my heart was gripped for the first time with the realization of the sacrifice of my mother and what she had done for me. She could have easily given me away or attempted to seek an abortion. Instead, out of her love and sacrifice, she held on and gave birth to her son.

I trembled with great emotion, heaviness and gratefulness in my heart as I picked up the phone and called Alaska. "Mom?" I said as she picked up the phone. She responded but I couldn't speak. I had a lump in my throat the size of a watermelon and no words could escape. She asked if I was okay. When I couldn't respond she asked if Tami was okay... and then about the kids... and then once again, she asked about me. I still couldn't speak. Finally, through the cracking of a tearful voice, I whispered, "Yes... I just want you to know how much I love you."

I explained to my mom what had occurred and how I had read the newspaper articles from so long ago. I told her I never realized the extent of all she had endured and done just for me. "Thank you for keeping me," I breathed.

Still trembling I spoke and continued to share and thank her for the many ways she had been such an amazing mom.

The young man I met at the high school knew, but hadn't realized, the sacrifices that had been made just for him. When I looked at my mom, I now realized the same. The loss, the fear, and the pain these two women had to endure just to keep their boys, is still more than I can hardly comprehend.

Jesus had a mom. She carried Him in her womb, nursed Him, nurtured Him and stood by His side. The difference between this child and others was that He was born to die. I can only imagine the pain she felt as she walked through her life. The rejection she endured as her pregnancy was scoffed, the sorrow she felt knowing one day she would have to release her firstborn from her care, and the unexplainable pain she experienced as she watched Him die in anguish before her very eyes. As Jesus sacrificed His life, she sacrificed her son… all so that you and I might live.

Are we really aware of the many sacrifices that have been made for us?

There were days for these mothers when they must have wondered if they could really go on; if their sacrifices were really worth the effort. But through their love and in spite of the hardships that came their way, they pressed on and continued to care for the children God had placed in their hands. Through Christ, each one of us can find the strength to do the same. You do have the strength to carry on.

I thank God that He sent His Son, that through Jesus I would have eternal life. And I thank my mom that she endured through the pain and trials that I might experience life in this world.

Who is it that you have to be thankful for today? It's never too late to say "thank you," and give honor where honor is due. May you never forget the multitude of sacrifices that have been made, just so that you could live.

Lord,

My heart cries out in gratitude to You. Thank You for the abundant sacrifice You gave that I might live. Give me an understanding and revelation of others who have sacrificed, allowing me to be alive this day. May I reverently go to them with my thanks and appreciation and may their lives be blessed for their giving.

In Jesus' Name. Amen.

CHAPTER FIFTY-ONE

Pray God Will Kill Me

*"And the second is like, namely this,
Thou shalt love thy neighbor as
thyself. There is none other
commandment greater than these."*
Mark 12:31

*I'm not sure I understood what it meant to really "love my
neighbor as myself," until I met Lucy. Through her struggles, fears
and generosity, my eyes were opened in a new way to the
significant ways in which multitudes in our nation are challenged;
but also, how each one of us plays an important role in helping to
bring forth assistance and change...*

I hadn't yet met Lucy when she first called me on the
phone. She had a donation for the Mission and wondered if
we could schedule a time to meet. Her voice on the phone
was articulate and clear. When I met her in person, I realized
her challenges in life didn't quite match her speech.

Lucy had struggled with autism for most of her life.
Because of the magnification of the sounds she heard, she
wore large headphones to cover her ears in an attempt to
block out some of the noise. I realized I had frequently seen
her walking through town wearing her headphones and
carrying several plastic grocery sacks. I always wondered if
she might have been homeless.

When she came to visit, nothing could have prepared
me for what would take place. It was a heartbreaking and

gut-wrenching situation. Through it, my eyes were opened in a new light to the ways people suffer when our systems, so carefully put into place, fail.

When Lucy walked into my office, she stuck out her hand and greeted me with a firm handshake and a smile. She sat down and immediately began sharing how much she appreciated all the Mission did for people in need. She had been saving money for quite some time and pulled out a shoebox filled with coins she wanted to give. While she had never been homeless before, she knew people who had and saw the difficulties they faced. Though she didn't have much, she wanted to give what she could to hopefully help make life easier for some of them.

As Lucy sat her coins down on my desk, she opened up to the real reason why she wanted to meet me in person. She was seeking prayer. I smiled and told her she didn't have to give a donation to receive prayer; I would be happy to pray for her regardless. Something shifted and suddenly her very eloquent, clear demeanor began to rapidly change. Her speech became hurried and stressed, and a new level of intensity filled her voice.

Lucy was an intelligent woman and had read about the potential shifts to funding structures for persons who were disabled in our state and nation. In doing so, she heard of the possibility that funding would be so dramatically cut that she would no longer receive her disability check. Because of her illness, she could not handle the external stimuli that came with full-time work and was never successful in maintaining employment as a result. She knew if her disability income ceased, she would not be able to maintain her housing and that she too would become homeless. The thought terrified her.

Lucy explained to me the way in which even the smallest noise could cause her to unravel. While others might not even pay attention to the quiet noises they are exposed to throughout the day, Lucy's senses would not permit her to tune them out. Crowds of people were intolerable for her and the sound of a crying baby would cause her to snap. Even the sound of clanging silverware and dishes was too much for her to tolerate.

She knew the Mission was a safe place; but, she also knew that because of all of the people, crying babies, clinking silverware and other noises, she would never be able to receive our services. Not because she didn't want to, but because she knew it would be too much to bear. She believed the stress from the environment would literally cause her to die.

With determination in her face, Lucy took a deep breath and asked if I would do her a favor. Confidently and desperately she asked, "If they defund the monies that help me to live in my apartment... will you pray that God will kill me?" I stared in shock at her request. She was serious. I was taken aback by the depth of her words and the sincerity in her eyes. I had never been asked anything like that before and didn't know how to respond. I could sense the anxiety she was experiencing and the fear that was overwhelming her. I knew what she was talking about was a reality and that, as a result, it really was quite possible that her ability to sustain herself could cease. If our state and nation did not consider the ramifications of the political policy and legislative changes that were being passed, this disabled, fifty-year old woman would, in fact, become homeless until her death on the streets.

I compassionately looked at Lucy and told her I could not pray for the Lord to kill her. Her face became red and her voice began to rise in anger as tears flowed from her eyes. "You have to pray that God will kill me!" she cried. "I cannot be in your shelter and I will not survive the streets...

I will die a slow... painful... death." Lucy begged in desperation and anguish, "Please, PLEASE promise me you will talk to God and ask Him to kill me!"

I didn't know what to do. I had encountered human suffering and tragedy for many years but never like this. This woman was being consumed by a legitimate fear that I could not alleviate. I was speechless, heart-broken and stunned. I had no solutions to pull from, no platitudes to share, and no realistic comfort to give. Her fears were a reality and I realized they spoke on behalf of the potential millions in our country facing similar plights.

Lucy was determined and I could tell she was not going to leave my office until I prayed. I was stuck. I couldn't do what she was asking, but I knew there was no other way she was going to leave. I watched as she shook and trembled before me. Her weeping was uncontrollable and I knew I had to do something. I reached out and gently touched her hand. "Let's pray," I offered. She nodded and sniffled, then slowly bowed her head.

I didn't pray for the Lord to kill Lucy that day, but I did ask Him to comfort her with His promise to watch over her and never leave or forsake her. I don't recall what else I prayed, but I know the peace of God transcended upon us both in that room. Finally, Lucy's crying ceased and she was able to rest in the calm of His presence. While the reality of her circumstances remained, she was able to walk out of my office with a new assurance of God's love for her and His presence in her life.

Lucy and I still remain in contact to this day. She lives in one of the most meager and basic housing accommodations that exists in our community. She has not lost her housing or become homeless, but the risk still remains. To supplement the small income she still receives from disability, she daily puts on her headphones, takes her plastic bags and picks up the cans she finds along the street. She takes whatever part-time work she can find, as long as she can handle the stimulus it produces. Every chance she gets, Lucy still continues to share what she can with others who have less than her. While she may be one of the most challenged people I have ever met, she is also one of the nicest, compassionate and most giving people I have ever known.

I received a letter from Lucy the other day. In it, she again expressed her appreciation for the Mission and included a donation inside. Once again, she was also asking for prayer. She was feeling void of purpose and said, "I just want my life to count for something... I want to be able to put a smile on somebody's face."

Even though I saw the light that shone from Lucy everywhere she went, her vision was clouded from being able to see it. She was searching for value in her life and didn't think she had ever really helped anyone. In reality, she had helped me and many others through the steady life she lived and the generosity of her love she always freely gave.

To me, Lucy's life depicts a determination, perseverance and faith that is rare in this world today. In spite of the hardships she endures, she never forgets about those who are struggling more. She lives her life to give and, though she doesn't always realize it, she puts a smile on the faces of many she meets.

It is people like Lucy who help me in so many ways to keep moving forward. I see how she struggles to survive, yet her strongest desire is to do whatever she can to help someone else. When I look at Lucy, who wants to give of her life and meager resources to help make someone else smile, I look at my own life and wonder: *What more can I do with the many gifts I've been given that she has not? Am I fully living my life for the sake of others?*

Throughout scripture we are told to open our hands and care for the poor. In Deuteronomy we are shown the outcome of blessing the poor: *If there is a poor man among your brothers in any of the towns of the land… do not be hardhearted or tightfisted toward [him]. Rather be openhanded and freely lend him whatever he needs. Give generously to him and do so without a grudging heart; then because of this the Lord your God will bless you in all your work and in everything you put your hand to (Deuteronomy 15: 7-10, NIV).*

Can we truthfully say we are living out this scripture today?

How easy it is to sit back in the comfort of our homes, offices and churches, and fail to consider people like Lucy. For years, I have watched as policy decisions concerning those living in poverty have been made as an afterthought. Many times, it has seemed as though the disadvantaged were being treated as an unnecessary burden that we just don't know how to get rid of. When money and budgets are tight, their services are almost always the first to get cut.

What if Lucy came to your office, your church, or your doorstep?

What if she begged you through tears and desperation to pray she would die, instead of enduring a life of homelessness should her ability to financially care for herself be removed?

How would you respond?

There is a level of desperation and suffering in our world that is growing daily. There are millions of Lucy's who are living in fear. They have lived their lives without the physical or mental ability to function fully on their own in society and they are reaching out for help. If that help is lessened or denied, they will be showing up on all of our doorsteps, either pleading for some glimmer of hope for their lives or desperately looking for a way to escape from their pain. These problems have increased in our nation to the point where turning our heads and looking the other way is not possible. The problem is great; but there is a solution, and each one of us can play a part.

The Bible tells us the greatest commandment is to love the Lord with all of our heart, soul and mind. The second is to love our neighbors as ourselves. Of all the commandments, Jesus tells us these are the greatest (Mark 12:30-31).

Lucy had never experienced homelessness, but she did what little she could to help those who did. She related to the devastation she would feel if she became homeless. Rather than sitting idly by and doing nothing, she did what she could to try and make a difference in the lives of her neighbors who were struggling with less than her.

We are all called to do the same. It's not just the government's responsibility and it is not just the church's either. The American government is "we the people." In my opinion, this means there is no separation of church and state. Instead, we the people are to come together to address the challenges that many experience in this life. We may have two different approaches, but we must work together for the good of our brothers and sisters who are desperately searching for help.

There are some people in our nation who are on assistance programs and are capable of being weaned off. There are others who are abusing the system and not really in need of the services it provides. We cannot, however, penalize all for the insincerity of some. There are still many like Lucy who would literally die if their support was discontinued. *How will we as a nation and as individuals respond?*

Whether you are a policymaker, preacher, housewife or anyone in between, there are resources and abilities which only you possess. Each one of us, through our actions, has the ability to change a life... for better, or for worse. Our nation and the people who dwell within are collectively our responsibility.

Regardless of what our own personal struggles may be, we still have all received the command to love and care for each other in the ways we would want for ourselves. Lucy struggled immensely, yet I'm not sure I've ever met another who has grasped this truth so fully.

If we want to see change come forth, we as a nation must embrace the commands of our Lord to care for those in need. To those of you who have already done this, know that your efforts have made a difference.

Each one of us is responsible and none are exempt. Rather than turning our heads, may the first step to change begin with you and me today.

Lord,

Help me to see the needs of those who surround me. Forgive me for the times when I have been so consumed with my own struggles that I have lost sight of others who were more desperate around me. Thank You for providing for me, for challenging me, and for showing me how I can make a difference in the lives of the many who suffer in this world.

In Jesus' Name. Amen.

CHAPTER FIFTY-TWO

Mending a Broken Heart

*"For whether we live, we live unto the
Lord; and whether we die, we die unto
the Lord: whether we live therefore,
or die, we are the Lord's."*
Romans 14:8

*When the pain in our lives becomes overwhelming, it's not
difficult to lose sight of God. Doc is one who knew pain beyond
most. Yet his life is a true testimony and reminder that, regardless
of how intense our struggles become, there is always hope when we
are walking with Christ...*

Doc spent over ten years of his life homeless on the
streets. Over time his heart became extremely hard. He was
suspicious of everyone, had a strong addiction to alcohol,
and did not have any interest in God.

Day after day the hardships grew, causing his
appearance to be weathered, his mind troubled, and his
body extremely worn. When he finally reached his breaking
point, he knew it was time for a change. Though his
expectations were low, he came to the Mission searching for
help. At the age of sixty-two, Doc joined our long-term
recovery program. It was there that the shift began. Not only
did he find a new home through the Servants In Training
(S.I.T.) program, but also a new family and new life.

We watched as Doc's heart towards both God and
people began to slowly soften. With suspicion and

apprehension, he couldn't help but examine the lives of those around him who seemed so in love with God. As they freely shared their love with him, his attitude began to shift and the hardness that had calloused his heart for so long began to heal.

In time, Doc handed his life over to the Lord and began to embrace and fall in love with the Savior he now served. By the conclusion of his year in the program, he was truly a new man. The Lord had not only transformed his heart, but also transformed his mind and given him a new chance at life.

Just prior to his graduation from the S.I.T. program, Doc was offered a full-time position at the Mission's Distribution Center (DC) as the Receiving and Shipping Coordinator. His strong work ethic and amiable nature were evident and we were blessed to receive him onto the team. He was responsible for the oversight of all the material donations that came in and were then distributed through the DC. He also began managing the Mission's large recycling operation and indirectly mentored many of the guests and volunteers who gave their time at the DC to serve. He quickly became a great role model and encourager for those who worked at his side. Because of his background and experiences, it was easy for him to relate to others who were struggling in life. When someone came to the doors of the warehouse in desperate need, it was his genuine empathy that allowed him to reach out with an even greater level of compassion to meet their needs.

Two years went by quickly and Doc continued to excel in life. He was living on his own in the community, continuing to grow in his walk with the Lord, and doing a phenomenal job in his role at the DC. His heart towards people was expanding with each passing day and he always had a word of encouragement or smile to share. Doc's warm countenance and witty sense of humor won the hearts of many. He was loved by all who crossed his path.

Over time, Doc began developing health problems. It began with a sore throat that plagued him for weeks. He tried his best to ignore it but, when his voice started to become hoarse, he finally conceded to see a doctor. Immediately, he was referred to a throat specialist who shared the dreaded news... Doc was suffering from a severe case of throat cancer.

Rather than beginning with just one type of treatment, the recommendation was to aggressively attack the cancer with both radiation and chemotherapy. While others around him became fearful and discouraged at the news, Doc remained light and positive, often being the one to bring a smile to their faces. His concern from the very start was not of himself, but for others. Instead of receiving sympathy, he wanted to continue to live his life as an encouragement to others and as a testimony of Jesus.

Doc's treatments began and produced more pain than can adequately be described. Numerous other physical complications also came forth. Yet, in spite of the many challenges he faced, Doc continued to amaze us all. Even when coworkers and friends encouraged him to slow down, he consistently pushed forward and never wavered in his desire to give his all.

I had an office at the DC and was working late one evening after everyone else had gone. Aside from the jarring of passing trains and the lights on in my office and hall, the warehouse was quiet and dark. Consumed in my work, I was surprised to hear the door unlock and see Doc walk down the hall. Before checking on the receiving area to make sure everything was in place for the next morning, he stuck his head in my office to say hello. It was then a conversation took place that will forever remain embedded in my heart.

When Doc walked into the warehouse that night he was experiencing an even higher level of excruciating pain than usual. In order for the long-term treatments to begin, all of his teeth had to be extracted due to the high risk of treatment related complications if they remained. It was just hours before he came to the DC that night that the procedure had taken place.

I hadn't much opportunity to talk with Doc before this night, but knew of his struggles. I asked him the current status of his health and shared how very sorry I was to hear of his pain. His response to my words left me startled and taken back. I listened intently to some of the most profound and heart-piercing statements I've ever heard someone say.

Standing in my office with a body ravished with pain, Doc raised his eyebrows, nodded his head and admitted that he was hurting. "But," he went on to say, "You can take a pill to make this pain better." He gave a slight smile as he continued, "There's a pain that you can't take a pill for that is much worse than this... that's the pain of a broken heart."

His words gripped me. I could only imagine the intensity of the physical pain he was experiencing as he spoke. I looked at the man who stood before me. Though his body and face were worn, the sparkle in his eyes spoke deeply to my soul and the emotion from his words hit me like a cannonball. I began to feel unsteady and actually had to take two steps back to grab hold of the wall because of the impact of the truth I felt.

I swallowed hard as Doc began to share and allow me the privilege of seeing a glimpse into his heart.

His heart had been broken many years ago. A relationship that had become his life went the wrong direction and left him wounded and alone. The brokenness was so deep that he lost all ambition and hope for life. As a result, he became homeless and found his solace in the streets for over a decade.

Tears filled his eyes as he cleared his raw, dry throat and then continued to say, "That's the kind of pain you can't take a pill for. You can drink it or drug it, but it never gets better." Tears were now in my eyes as I felt the sincerity and truth in the words he shared.

While his words were simple, they radiated a truth I had seen so evident in countless people's lives. Before my eyes flashed images of thousands of individuals I had worked with in my life. I thought about how many times we put so much effort into examining and attempting to fix the external challenges that people face. We offer programs and refer to other services, but all too often we miss and overlook the greatest pain of all... the pain within their broken hearts; the root cause behind why their lives began spiraling downward in the first place.

Doc told me that when he found the Mission, he began to see his heart heal. Choking back tears, he shared about the love he had found from so many. The names of many staff members and volunteers he had encountered and worked with over the years flowed from his lips. He said their love healed what he never believed could be; and, because of their love and the love of God, he could face whatever was before him with confidence. He had already experienced the worst of pain and knew now if God could heal that kind of pain, "whether I live or die, I will be healed from all pain in the future."

I fought back the tears that filled my eyes but inside I wanted to weep like a child. There was so much brokenness and hardship this man had experienced in his life, but yet he remained confident in God and displayed a faith rarely seen in this world today. I was speechless and in awe.

I watched as Doc walked out of my office and back through the warehouse to work on his task. Still choking back tears, the Holy Spirit spoke to my heart. He showed me that the words spoken were everything He had been trying to teach me, all wrapped into one. Once again, I was reminded of the clear reason why God had placed me at the Mission over twenty-five years ago. It wasn't just about providing food and shelter, it was about helping people receive the love of Jesus Christ so they could find healing for their broken hearts and receive a new chance and hope for their lives.

Doc lived many years of his life hopeless, broken and bitter. He distrusted people and had no belief in God. It wasn't until he was able to see the love of Christ manifested through man, that he was drawn to the Lord and willing to surrender his life. As he did, not only was his life changed but the lives of countless others who he influenced as well.

Doc slipped into eternity while this story was being written. The days leading up to his death were filled with some of the most profound demonstrations of love I have ever encountered. His desire was to live until Christmas, his favorite holiday. Sadly, we knew apart from a miracle this would not occur. On his 65th birthday, instead of just a celebration of life, the DC was decorated for Christmas and joy was exchanged as many came to share their greetings and love. It was later that day, while enjoying fellowship with a brother he had not seen in years, that Doc began having difficulty breathing and was admitted into hospice care. During his four day stay, there was not a single moment when he was there alone. Not only was the sweet Presence of God in his room, floods of people came through his door to pray, fellowship and share of their appreciation and love for the man God had used to touch their lives. This man, once so broken, angry and alone was now restored in spirit, joyful and surrounded by more friends than most people have the privilege of experiencing in a lifetime. Even when fading in and out of consciousness, Doc had a smile to share, an innocent joke to tell, or the faint whisper of "Jesus" on his lips. In time, the healing he was confident of came forth as he peacefully entered into eternal rest with his Savior.

The service held afterwards at the Mission to celebrate his life was one I will always remember. Scores of people filled the large dining hall with tears of both sorrow and joy that his pain was now complete. Many shared of the extraordinary ways their lives had been changed as a result of this one man. The life that was once wary of both man and God was transformed to lead many unto salvation and bring others a new hope. Doc left a legacy through his life and I'm not sure that anyone who had the privilege of knowing him will ever forget his warm smile or familiar embrace.

Everyone I have ever met has experienced some type of heartbreak at least once in their lives. Whether it has come from the loss of a loved one, a relationship that has been severed, or some other tragic occurrence that cannot be removed, scars build up from the trauma and are often left as permanent damage to our hearts. While our physical bodies can experience suffering, what often hurts greater is the pain on the inside that no one sees and many rarely try to understand.

Jesus sees into our hearts and cares about the invisible pains that lie deep within. That is why He chose to become like us so that He could suffer with us. *All because He never intended for us to walk alone.* The pain you have carried, the burdens you have worn, Jesus came so that you would have to hold onto them no longer.

He heals the brokenhearted and binds up their wounds (Psalm 147:3).

When the relationship ended that had broken his heart, Doc thought his life had ended as well. And, for ten years, he lived that way. It was the love of people around him that God used to pierce his heart and show him there was still life left in his being. But, in order to receive of it, he had to lay his life down for a new one... a new life through Jesus Christ. He invited Him into his heart and let the Holy Spirit do the rest. As a result, healing from his deep wounds began to come forth and the promise of hope for the future grabbed hold of his heart. It was then he knew with confidence that he could look at his future and know that, whether he lived or died, he was going to be okay. As he prepared to enter into eternity, peace was upon him and confidence in the Savior's arms that would greet him, radiated from his being. He knew that "to live is Christ and to die is gain" (Philippians 1:21) as he looked with anticipation upon the new journey before him. Those of us who knew him could hear the words of the Father as that journey began, "Well done, My good and faithful servant" (Matthew 25:23).

Doc was an ordinary man who God was able to use in extraordinary ways to touch the lives of others around him. All because he simply embraced the Savior he found and chose to hold onto His promises above the trials he faced. He knew with all confidence that his circumstances would not last forever and, regardless of the outcome, God was still worthy to be praised. It was because of his unwavering faith that multitudes of lives have been touched and transformed for the glory of Christ. While a miraculous healing in Doc's body would have been phenomenal and preferred by us all, I am confident that through his death many have received life. He would be humbly honored to know if even one was changed as a result of his walk.

Regardless of what you are facing, what pain consumes you or what trials surround you, God is with you. He is ready to release His peace and hope if only, like Doc, you would look with confidence to Him and trust Him no matter how horrible your circumstances seem. Your pain may be great and overwhelming at this moment in time, but I promise if you put your trust in Him, the anguish will not consume you forever.

Christ came to give you life, heal your wounds and fill you with love. Let Him take the heaviness, pain, loneliness and fear and replace it with the hope for all your tomorrows. Don't go another minute without receiving His life and all that He has for you. His love is eternal and His healing complete.

Lord,

I hand my life, my sorrows, my pain and my tragedies over to You. I ask You, Jesus, to come dwell in my heart and replace my life with Yours. Take my pain, take my past and give me the hope of tomorrow so that I too may look forward with the confidence that comes only from You.

In Your Name. Amen.

It's Never Too Late

*"But these are written, that ye might
believe that Jesus is the Christ,
the Son of God;
and that believing ye might have life
through His Name."*
John 20:31

*For the past 52 chapters, it is my hope that the ultimate
message has been clear: Jesus loves you and you are never alone...*

Over twenty-five years of experiences at the Topeka
Rescue Mission have shaped me into the man I am today. I
have met countless individuals who have struggled through
life wondering if their circumstances could ever change. I
have seen hopelessness, despair and heartache beyond
measure. Even in my own life during this time I have
experienced crises of faith, hopelessness and doubts.

In all that I have experienced and through all I have
seen, I remain confident of one thing: *Never do we go through
any season of our lives alone.* Even in the moments when we
have given up on God, He has and never will give up on us.

I started off in my Christian walk wondering if God
really moved in the world today and if I would ever really
experience His Presence for myself. As I set out to seek God,
He revealed Himself through the lives of the people I've met
and the trials and circumstances I've faced.

While my faith still falters from time to time and my walk is not yet perfected, I daily press on towards the prize that awaits me... an eternal rest with my Savior, Jesus Christ. He is my hope. He is the reason why I get out of bed every morning and have the strength to face each day. On my own, I can do nothing.

If you have read through these pages and felt the Lord stirring in your heart but not yet fully embraced all He has in store for you, it is never too late for you to experience the hope that Christ has for you today. Regardless of who you are, there is a loving God who is knocking on the door of your heart and gently asking to come in. While the challenges in life may not cease completely once He does, you will have the assurance of knowing that you will no longer have to walk through any of them alone.

The Old Testament of the Bible is filled with laws, practices and rituals devised to address the sins we have all been guilty of. The whole purpose of God sending His Son, Jesus, into the world was to break the power of those laws of sin and death (Romans 8:2). When Jesus died on the cross, it was so you and I would never again have to perform religious acts to try and get to God. We can go to Him directly at any time, in any place, and during any circumstance. Jesus made the way. He paid the price. He died so that we could finally live. And He left His sweet Holy Spirit to help us along the way (John 14:16). All we have to do to receive Him is believe, accept Him, and walk forward with Him.

If you've never fully given your life to the Lord, it's not too late. There's nothing you have done that would make Him desire you less. You are His creation, His masterpiece, His love. Receive the gift of life and hope as you go through this journey called life. It's simple... Jesus just wants *you*. As you earnestly pray one final prayer before closing the cover of this book, I pray that the fullness of God will invade and begin transforming your life. I pray that He will reveal a love to you so amazing, a peace so consuming, and a hope so surpassing that you will never be the same again. May His richest blessings be upon you as you embrace your new life in Him.

Lord,

I confess that I have sinned and fallen short of Your plans for my life. I ask that You would come and cleanse my past, forgive my sins and allow me to start life anew. Jesus, I believe that You have come to give me the abundant life that can only come from You. I confess that You are Lord and invite You into my heart to forever dwell. I lay down my life and humbly place it in Your hands. Mold me, God, into the person You have created me to be. I vow to live all my days for You as best as I know how.

In Jesus' Name. Amen.

Barry F. Feaker

Barry has served the homeless and community as the Executive Director at the Topeka Rescue Mission for over twenty-six years. Prior to his service at the Mission, he spent ten years working in the field of mental health. For most of his life, he has desired to draw closer in his relationship with God by walking alongside those who suffer. Frequently his eyes have been opened to see and experience God, while helping those who are in the midst of depression, hunger, homelessness, mental illness, addiction, anger, and hopelessness. It has been through this that he has come to recognize that even in the darkness of suffering, a light still shines.

Barry has spent his entire life in Kansas, residing for the majority of the time in Topeka. He and his wife, Tami, have two grown daughters, Rebecca and Elizabeth, a son-in-law, Mark, and a grandson, Jacob Franklin.

Though still moving forward by faith, Barry's prayer is for the lives he comes in contact with to be changed and hope to be restored through the unfailing love of Jesus Christ. He knows it is only through Him that all things truly are possible.

Tami R. Feaker

"I have shewed you all things,
how that so laboring ye ought to
support the weak,
and to remember the words of the
Lord Jesus, how He said,
It is more blessed to give
than to receive."
Acts 20:35

Tami has played an instrumental role in each of the stories written in this book and has been vital in helping to shape the ministry of the Topeka Rescue Mission into what it is today. For over twenty-six years, she has served as a Volunteer for the Mission and throughout her life has helped individuals who have experienced rejection, suffering and discouragement.

She and Barry have been married for thirty-five years. While serving her family and providing Home Education programs for their daughters, Rebecca and Elizabeth, she worked behind the scenes to assist Barry with research, resources and a myriad of details.

During her high school years, she knew she needed to encourage others and find a vocation to help those in need. Through this book, her desire is that those who read and hear these stories would experience the hope and the light that comes from the love of Jesus Christ for them.

Jessica S. Hosman

"But none of these things move me,
neither count I my life dear unto
myself, so that I might finish my
course with joy, and the ministry,
which I have received of the
Lord Jesus, to testify the gospel
of the grace of God."
Acts 20:24

Jessica currently serves at the Topeka Rescue Mission as Director of Special Projects. One of her intense passions is to bring hope and life through Jesus Christ to all who cross her path. Her prayer is that the stories found in this book, and her prayerful development of the applications and prayers written, will be used to draw each person who reads them into deeper intimacy and fellowship with Him.

A missionary at heart, Jessica has served internationally in South Africa and Mozambique. Her residency in the United States has included ministry to homeless individuals through street outreach and service at homeless shelters in both Pennsylvania and Kansas. She and her husband, Justyn, have a son, Zechariah John. Through him she has not only found much joy, but also the new exciting mission field of motherhood. In addition, she has a step-daughter, Isabella Faith, who is a blessing in her life.

Jessica lives daily to draw closer to the Lord. She recognizes Him as her everything and notes that in all things, it is to Jesus Christ to whom all honor is due.

The Topeka Rescue Mission is a non-denominational Christian organization that was founded in 1953 to help individuals and families who are homeless and/or in need. They provide shelter, meals, clothing and other needed items, programs, and services, to homeless men, women and families. Additionally, food and other necessities are provided to those who are in need.

For detailed information about the services provided, to make a donation, or to sign up for the monthly newsletter please visit the Mission online at www.trmonline.org or contact them directly using the information below.

"Faith with its Sleeves Rolled Up"

Topeka Rescue Mission
PO Box 8350, 600 N. Kansas Avenue
Topeka, KS 66608
Phone: 785-354-1744
Email: trm@trmonline.org
Website: www.trmonline.org

All proceeds from the sale of this book directly support the Mission.

Subject Index

Acceptance / Accepting Others

Chapter Ten – Learning to Skate 57

Chapter Thirty-One – Kitty – An Unlikely Messenger 177

Chapter Thirty-Five – Walking in His Steps 201

Chapter Thirty-Six – A Love Story 207

Chapter Forty – Should We Let Him Die? 235

Chapter Forty-Two – The Impact and Sacrifice of One 247

Chapter Forty-Eight – Becoming Barry 291

Confusion

Chapter Five – The Best Christmas 23

Chapter Thirteen – Eggs, Milk and Butter 73

Chapter Nineteen – Desperation 109

Chapter Twenty-One – The Lure of Compromise 123

Chapter Twenty-Seven – Acquiring the Impossible 155

Chapter Thirty-Four – What Have I Done? 183

Chapter Forty-One – The Look 241

Chapter Forty-Three – Miracle in Topeka, Kansas 255

Chapter Forty-Eight – Becoming Barry 291

Subject Index - Continued

Contentment

Chapter Two – The Scary Guy with the Big Heart 7

Chapter Ten – Learning to Skate 57

Chapter Fifteen – Homeless in Chicago 81

Chapter Forty-Eight – Becoming Barry 291

Chronic Challenges

Chapter Seven – The 600-Year-Old Man 33

Chapter Eleven – When I'm Tempted to Run 63

Chapter Eighteen – One Vet's Story 103

Chapter Thirty – Finding Rest 171

Depression

Chapter Five – The Best Christmas 23

Chapter Forty-Seven – Listening to Still Small Voice 285

Chapter Fifty-Two – Mending a Broken Heart 315

Enduring Challenges

Chapter Six – Cooking with Umbrellas 29

Chapter Nineteen – Desperation 109

Fear

Chapter Seventeen – The Intruder 97

Chapter Nineteen – Desperation 109

Subject Index - Continued

Fear (continued)

Chapter Twenty – The Freezer 119

Chapter Twenty-Two – The Man with the Gun 127

Chapter Twenty-Six – Standing in the Midst of Falling.....151

Chapter Twenty-Seven – Acquiring the Impossible 155

Chapter Thirty-Two – Hope in the Storm 183

Chapter Thirty-Four – What Have I Done? 195

Chapter Thirty-Nine – Searching for Love 227

Chapter Forty-Nine – The Fish with a Coin 295

Chapter Fifty-One – Pray God Will Kill Me 307

Financial Uncertainty

Chapter Five – The Best Christmas 23

Chapter Twelve – Ground Beef 69

Chapter Thirteen – Eggs, Milk and Butter 73

Chapter Twenty-Six – Standing in the Midst of Falling.....151

Chapter Twenty-Seven – Acquiring the Impossible 155

Chapter Thirty-One – Kitty – An Unlikely Messenger 177

Chapter Thirty-Three – Something to Give 189

Chapter Thirty-Eight – One Man's Chapter 219

Chapter Forty-Three – Miracle in Topeka, Kansas 255

Subject Index - Continued

Financial Uncertainty (continued)

Chapter Forty-Nine – The Fish with a Coin 295

Chapter Fifty-One – Pray God Will Kill Me 307

Finding Purpose

Introduction – Finding Purpose............................... x

Chapter Eleven – When I'm Tempted to Run 63

Chapter Thirty-Three – Something to Give 189

Chapter Thirty-Five – Walking in His Steps 201

Chapter Thirty-Seven – The Gift 213

Chapter Thirty-Eight – One Man's Chapter 219

Chapter Forty-Six – The Long Bus Ride 275

Chapter Forty-Eight – Becoming Barry 291

Chapter Fifty-One – Pray God Will Kill Me 307

Forgiveness

Chapter Twenty-Two – The Man with the Gun 127

Chapter Twenty-Four – The Kiss 139

Healing from the Past

Chapter Nine – Beauty and the Beast 49

Chapter Eighteen – One Vet's Story 103

Chapter Nineteen – Desperation 109

Subject Index - Continued

Healing from the Past (continued)

Chapter Twenty-Two – The Man with the Gun 127

Chapter Thirty-One – Kitty – An Unlikely Messenger 177

Chapter Thirty-Eight – One Man's Chapter 219

Chapter Thirty-Nine – Searching for Love 227

Chapter Forty-Two – The Impact and Sacrifice of One 247

Chapter Forty-Five – The Darkest of Nights 267

Chapter Fifty-Two – Mending a Broken Heart 315

Healing of the Heart

Chapter One – A Drunk in the Street 1

Chapter Eleven – When I'm Tempted to Run 63

Chapter Sixteen – The Worst Disease 89

Chapter Eighteen – One Vet's Story 103

Chapter Thirty-One – Kitty – An Unlikely Messenger 177

Chapter Thirty-Six – A Love Story 207

Chapter Thirty-Seven – The Gift 213

Chapter Thirty-Nine – Searching for Love 227

Chapter Forty-Four – Daddy, Make Me a Promise 263

Chapter Fifty-Two – Mending a Broken Heart 315

Subject Index – Continued

Hearing God's Voice

Chapter Fourteen – Shredded Lettuce 77

Chapter Twenty-One – The Lure of Compromise 123

Chapter Forty-One – The Look 241

Chapter Forty-Five – The Darkest of Nights 267

Chapter Forty-Seven – Listening to Still Small Voice 285

Joy

Chapter Two – The Scary Guy with the Big Heart 7

Chapter Fifteen – Homeless in Chicago 81

Chapter Forty-Four – Daddy, Make Me a Promise 263

Judgments

Chapter One – A Drunk in the Street 1

Chapter Eight – Learning to Love 43

Chapter Twenty-Three – From Awkward to Amazing........133

Chapter Thirty-One – Kitty – An Unlikely Messenger 177

Chapter Thirty-Three – Something to Give 189

Chapter Forty-Two – The Impact and Sacrifice of One 247

Loneliness

Chapter Fifteen – Homeless in Chicago 81

Chapter Sixteen – The Worst Disease 89

Subject Index – Continued

Loneliness (continued)

Chapter Forty-Seven – Listening to Still Small Voice 285

Chapter Fifty-Two – Mending a Broken Heart 315

Loss

Chapter Seventeen – The Intruder 97

Chapter Forty-Four – Daddy, Make Me a Promise 263

Chapter Fifty-Two – Mending a Broken Heart 315

Loving Others

Chapter Eight – Learning to Love 43

Chapter Nine – Beauty and the Beast 49

Chapter Sixteen – The Worst Disease 89

Chapter Twenty-Five – Laying Down their Lives 145

Chapter Thirty-Five – Walking in His Steps 201

Chapter Forty – Should We Let Him Die? 235

Chapter Forty-One – The Look 241

Chapter Forty-Two – The Impact and Sacrifice of One 247

Chapter Forty-Five – The Darkest of Nights 267

Chapter Fifty-One – Pray God Will Kill Me 307

Subject Index – Continued

Offenses

Chapter Twenty-Two – The Man with the Gun 127

Chapter Twenty-Four – The Kiss 139

Overcoming Obstacles

Introduction – Finding Purpose x

Chapter Four – The Beginnings of Rescue 19

Chapter Six – Cooking with Umbrellas 29

Chapter Seven – The 600-Year-Old Man 33

Chapter Nine – Beauty and the Beast 49

Chapter Ten – Learning to Skate 57

Chapter Eleven – When I'm Tempted to Run 63

Chapter Sixteen – The Worst Disease 89

Chapter Eighteen – One Vet's Story 103

Chapter Twenty-Seven – Acquiring the Impossible 155

Chapter Twenty-Nine – Underground Fuel Tanks 167

Chapter Thirty – Finding Rest 171

Chapter Thirty-Two – Hope in the Storm 183

Chapter Thirty-Four – What Have I Done? 195

Chapter Thirty-Five – Walking in His Steps 201

Chapter Thirty-Eight – One Man's Chapter 219

Subject Index – Continued

Overcoming Obstacles (continued)

Chapter Forty – Should We Let Him Die? 235

Chapter Forty-Four – Daddy, Make Me a Promise 263

Chapter Forty-Five – The Darkest of Nights 267

Chapter Forty-Six – The Long Bus Ride 275

Chapter Fifty – Thank You for Keeping Me 301

Chapter Fifty-One – Pray God Will Kill Me 307

Patience

Chapter Four – The Beginnings of Rescue 19

Chapter Thirty – Finding Rest 171

Chapter Forty – Should We Let Him Die? 235

Chapter Forty-Three – Miracle in Topeka, Kansas 255

Chapter Forty-Five – The Darkest of Nights 267

Peace

Chapter Thirty-Two – Hope in the Storm 183

Chapter Thirty-Seven – The Gift 213

Chapter Thirty-Eight – One Man's Chapter 219

Chapter Thirty-Nine – Searching for Love 227

Subject Index – Continued

Perseverance

Chapter Four – The Beginnings of Rescue 19

Chapter Five – The Best Christmas 23

Chapter Six – Cooking with Umbrellas 29

Chapter Seven – The 600-Year-Old Man 33

Chapter Nine – Beauty and the Beast 49

Chapter Eleven – When I'm Tempted to Run 63

Chapter Fourteen – Shredded Lettuce 77

Chapter Sixteen – The Worst Disease 89

Chapter Twenty-Six – Standing in the Midst of Falling.....151

Chapter Twenty-Eight – The Praying Man 161

Chapter Thirty – Finding Rest 171

Chapter Thirty-Seven – The Gift 213

Chapter Thirty-Eight – One Man's Chapter 219

Chapter Forty – Should We Let Him Die? 235

Chapter Forty-Three – Miracle in Topeka, Kansas 255

Chapter Forty-Six – The Long Bus Ride 275

Chapter Fifty – Thank You for Keeping Me 301

Subject Index – Continued

Rejection

Chapter Eighteen – One Vet's Story 103

Chapter Twenty-Three – From Awkward to Amazing.......133

Chapter Thirty-Six – A Love Story 207

Chapter Thirty-Nine – Searching for Love 227

Chapter Forty – Should We Let Him Die? 235

Chapter Forty-Three – Miracle in Topeka, Kansas 255

Searching for Love

Chapter Nine – Beauty and the Beast 49

Chapter Thirty-Six – A Love Story 207

Chapter Thirty-Nine – Searching for Love 227

Chapter Fifty-Two – Mending a Broken Heart 315

Serving Others

Chapter Two – The Scary Guy with the Big Heart 7

Chapter Ten – Learning to Skate 57

Chapter Twenty-Five – Laying Down their Lives 145

Chapter Thirty-Three – Something to Give 189

Chapter Thirty-Five – Walking in His Steps 201

Chapter Fifty-One – Pray God Will Kill Me 307

Subject Index - Continued

Strength

Chapter Twenty-Six – Standing in the Midst of Falling.....151

Chapter Twenty-Seven – Acquiring the Impossible 155

Chapter Thirty – Finding Rest 171

Chapter Thirty-Eight – One Man's Chapter 219

Chapter Forty-One – The Look 241

Suffering

Chapter Ten – Learning to Skate 57

Chapter Seventeen – The Intruder 97

Chapter Thirty-Nine – Searching for Love 227

Tragedy / Trauma

Chapter Seventeen – The Intruder 97

Chapter Thirty-Nine – Searching for Love 227

Chapter Forty-Four – Daddy, Make Me a Promise 263

Trusting God

Chapter Three – An Angelic Encounter? 13

Chapter Five – The Best Christmas 23

Chapter Eleven – When I'm Tempted to Run 63

Chapter Twelve – Ground Beef 69

Chapter Seventeen – The Intruder 97

Subject Index – Continued

Trusting God (continued)

Chapter Twenty-One – The Lure of Compromise 123

Chapter Twenty-Eight – The Praying Man 161

Chapter Twenty-Nine – Underground Fuel Tanks 167

Chapter Forty-One – The Look 241

Chapter Forty-Three – Miracle in Topeka, Kansas 255

Chapter Forty-Five – The Darkest of Nights 267

Chapter Forty-Nine – The Fish with a Coin 295

Trusting God with a Loved One

Chapter Nine – Beauty and the Beast 49

Chapter Fourteen – Shredded Lettuce 77

Chapter Sixteen – The Worst Disease 89

Chapter Thirty-Seven – The Gift 213

Chapter Forty – Should We Let Him Die? 235

Unbelief

Chapter Three – An Angelic Encounter? 13

Chapter Twenty-Six – Standing in the Midst of Falling.....151

Chapter Thirty-Four – What Have I Done? 195

Subject Index ~ Continued

Uncertainty

Chapter Thirteen – Eggs, Milk and Butter 73

Chapter Nineteen – Desperation 109

Chapter Twenty-One – The Lure of Compromise 123

Chapter Twenty-Seven – Acquiring the Impossible 155

Chapter Twenty-Nine – Underground Fuel Tanks 167

Chapter Thirty-Four – What Have I Done? 195

Chapter Forty – Should We Let Him Die? 235

Chapter Forty-One – The Look 241

Chapter Forty-Three – Miracle in Topeka, Kansas 255

Chapter Forty-Eight – Becoming Barry 291

Walking by Faith

Chapter Three – An Angelic Encounter? 13

Chapter Five – The Best Christmas 23

Chapter Eleven – When I'm Tempted to Run 63

Chapter Twelve – Ground Beef 69

Chapter Twenty – The Freezer 119

Chapter Twenty-Nine – Underground Fuel Tanks 167

Subject Index – Continued

Weariness

Introduction – Finding Purpose x

Chapter Eleven – When I'm Tempted to Run 63

Chapter Thirty – Finding Rest 171

Worry

Chapter Three – An Angelic Encounter? 13

Chapter Twelve – Ground Beef 69

Chapter Thirteen – Eggs, Milk and Butter 73

Chapter Twenty-Six – Standing in the Midst of Falling 151

Chapter Twenty-Seven – Acquiring the Impossible 155

Chapter Thirty-One – Kitty – An Unlikely Messenger 177

Chapter Forty-Nine – The Fish with a Coin 295

*If this book has been used to touch
your life in any way,
we'd love to hear from you!
Please contact us at
alightshines@trmonline.org.*